Practical Python Design Patterns

Pythonic Solutions to Common Problems

Wessel Badenhorst

Apress®

Practical Python Design Patterns: Pythonic Solutions to Common Problems

Wessel Badenhorst
Durbanville, Eastern Cape, South Africa

ISBN-13 (pbk): 978-1-4842-2679-7 ISBN-13 (electronic): 978-1-4842-2680-3
https://doi.org/10.1007/978-1-4842-2680-3

Library of Congress Control Number: 2017957538

Cover image by Shutterstock (www.shutterstock.com)

Managing Director: Welmoed Spahr
Editorial Director: Todd Green
Acquisitions Editor: Steve Anglin
Development Editor: Matthew Moodie
Technical Reviewer: Michael Thomas
Coordinating Editor: Mark Powers
Copy Editor: April Rondeau

Distributed to the book trade worldwide by Springer Science+Business Media New York, 233 Spring Street, 6th Floor, New York, NY 10013. Phone 1-800-SPRINGER, fax (201) 348-4505, e-mail orders-ny@springer-sbm.com, or visit www.springeronline.com. Apress Media, LLC is a California LLC and the sole member (owner) is Springer Science + Business Media Finance Inc (SSBM Finance Inc). SSBM Finance Inc is a **Delaware** corporation.

For information on translations, please e-mail rights@apress.com or visit http://www.apress.com/rights-permissions.

Apress titles may be purchased in bulk for academic, corporate, or promotional use. eBook versions and licenses are also available for most titles. For more information, reference our Print and eBook Bulk Sales web page at http://www.apress.com/bulk-sales.

Any source code or other supplementary material referenced by the author in this book is available to readers on GitHub via the book's product page, located at www.apress.com/9781484226797. For more detailed information, please visit http://www.apress.com/source-code.

Printed on acid-free paper

For Tanya, my love, always.

Table of Contents

About the Author

Wessel Badenhorst is deeply passionate about the process of attaining mastery, especially in the field of programming. The combination of a bachelor's degree in computer science and extensive experience in the real world gives him a balanced and practical perspective on programming and the road every programmer must walk.

About the Technical Reviewer

 **Michael Thomas** has worked in software development for more than 20 years as an individual contributor, team lead, program manager, and vice president of engineering. Michael has more than ten years of experience working with mobile devices. His current focus is in the medical sector, which is using mobile devices to accelerate information transfer between patients and health care providers.

Acknowledgments

A very big thank you to Mark Powers and his team at Apress, without whom this book would not have seen the light of day. To Tanya, Lente, and Philip, for letting me do this when I could have spent time on other things, thank you. Thank you, Lord, for the grace to complete this project. To you, the reader, thank you for taking steps to make yourself a better programmer, thereby making the profession better.

CHAPTER 1

Before We Begin

Design patterns help you learn from others' successes instead of your own failures.

—Mark Johnson

The world is changing.

As you are reading this, people all over the world are learning to program, mostly poorly. There is a flood of "programmers" heading for the market, and there is nothing you can do to stop them. As with all things, you will soon see that as the supply of programmers increases, the cost of hiring programmers will decrease. Simply being able to write a few lines of code or change something in a piece of software will (like the role of spreadsheet or word-processing guru) become a basic skill.

If you plan on making a living as a programmer, this problem is made worse by the Internet. You have to worry not only about programmers in your own area, but also those from all over the world.

Do you know who does *not* worry about the millions of programmers produced by the hundreds of code boot camps that seem to spring up like mushrooms?

The Masters

While everyone can write, there are still the Hemingways of the world. While everyone can work Excel, there are still the financial modelers. And when everyone can code, there will still be the Peter Norvigs of the world.

Programming is a tool. For a time, simply knowing how to use this tool made you valuable. That time has come to an end. There is a new reality, the same one that a lot of industries have had to face over the years. When a tool is new, no one wants to use it. Then, some see the value, and it makes them twice as good as the ones who can't use the tool. Then, it becomes popular. Before you know it, everyone can use the Internet.

© Wessel Badenhorst 2017
W. Badenhorst, *Practical Python Design Patterns*, https://doi.org/10.1007/978-1-4842-2680-3_1

Suddenly, being able create a website becomes a lot less valuable. All the businesses that were consulting, charging big bucks for the service, get marginalized. However, the people who spent time mastering the tools are able to thrive no matter what happens in the market. They can do this because they are able to outproduce the average person on every level—quality of work, speed of development, and the beauty of the final result.

Right now, we see the popular uptake of that which is easy. The next step will be automating what is easy. Easy tasks, in every area of life, are easy because they do not require creativity and deep understanding, and as a result of these characteristics they are the exact tasks that will be handed over to computers first.

The reason you picked up this book is because you want to become a better programmer. You want to progress beyond the thousands of introductions to this and that. You are ready to take the next step, to master the craft.

In the new world of programming, you want to be able to solve big, complex problems. To do that, you need to be able to think on a higher level. Just like the chess grand-masters, who can digest the game in larger chunks than mere masters, you too need to develop the skill to solve problems in larger chunks. When you are able to look at a brand-new problem and rapidly deconstruct it into high-level parts, parts you have solved before, you become an exponential programmer.

When I began programming, I could not read the manual yet. There was a picture of *Space Invaders* on the cover, and it promised to teach you how to program a game yourself. It was a bit of a racket because the game ended up being a `for` loop and a single `if` statement, not *Space Invaders*. But I was in love. Passion drove me to learn everything I could about programming, which was not a lot. After mastering the basics, I stagnated, even while attaining a BS in computer science (cum laud). I felt like what I was learning was a simple rehashing of the basics. I did learn, but it felt slow and frustrating, like everybody was waiting for something.

In the "real world," it did not look a lot different. I came to realize that if I wanted to become an exponential programmer, I had to do something different. At first, I thought about getting a master's degree or Ph.D., but in the end I decided to dig deeper on my own.

I reread the old theory of computing books, and they gained new meaning and new life. I started regularly taking part in coding challenges and studied more idiomatic ways of writing code. Then, I began exploring programming languages and paradigms foreign to my own. Before I knew it, I was completely transformed in my thinking about programming. Problems that used to be hard became trivial, and some that seemed impossible became merely challenging.

I am still learning, still digging.

You can do it too. Start with this very book you are reading right now. In it you will find a number of tools and mental models to help you think and code better. After you have mastered this set of patterns, actively seek out and master different tools and techniques. Play with different frameworks and languages and figure out what makes them great. Once you can understand what makes someone love a different language than the one you use regularly, you may find a couple of ideas in it that you can integrate into your way of thinking. Study recipes and patterns wherever you find them and translate them into an abstract solution that you can use over and over. Sometimes, you can simply analyze a solution you already use: can you find a more elegant way to implement the idea, or is the idea flawed in some way? Constantly ask yourself how you can improve your tools, your skills, or yourself.

If you are ready to dig deep and master the art, you will find ideas in this book that will guide you along the road to mastery. We are going to explore a set of fundamental design patterns in a real-world context. While you are doing this, you will begin to realize how these design patterns can be seen as building blocks you can use when you encounter a specific type of problem in the future.

My hope is that you will use the design patterns in this book as a blueprint; that it will help you kick-start your own collection of problem–solution chunks. After you have read this book, you should be well on your way to reaching the next level in your journey as a programmer. You should also see how this set of abstract tools can be translated into any programming language you may encounter, and how you can use ideas and solutions from other languages and incorporate them into your mental toolbox.

Becoming a Better Programmer

To become a better programmer, you need to decide to obsess about mastery. Every day is a new opportunity to become better than the day before. Every line of code is an opportunity to improve. How do you do that?

- When you must work on a piece of existing code, leave the code better than you found it.

- Try to complete a quick problem-solving challenge every day.

- Look for opportunities to work with people who are better programmers than you are (open source projects are great for this).

- Focus on deliberate practice.

- Practice systems thinking whenever you can find an excuse.

- Collect and analyze mental models.

- Master your tools and understand what they are good for and what they should not be used for.

Deliberate Practice

Dr. Anders Erickson studied people who reached a level of performance we call mastery. He found that these people had a couple of things in common. The first, as popularized in Malcolm Gladwell's book *Outliers*, was that these people all seemed to have spent a significant amount of time working on the skill in question. The actual numbers vary, but the time invested approached about 10,000 hours. That is a significant amount of time, but simply spending 10,000 hours, or ten years, practicing is not enough. There is a very specific type of practice that was shown to be required for master-level performance. The key to world-dominating skill is *deliberate* practice.

We will look at how this relates to programming in a moment, but let's first look at what deliberate practice is.

Deliberate practice is slow, halting, anti-flow. If you are practicing the violin, deliberate practice would entail playing the piece extremely slowly, making sure you hit every note perfectly. If you are deliberately practicing tennis, this might mean doing the same shot over and over and over again with a coach, making small adjustments until you are able to perfectly hit that shot in that location time and time again.

The problem with knowledge work is that the standard deliberate practice protocols seem foreign. A sports task or playing an instrument is fairly simple when compared to the process involved in programming. It is a lot harder to deconstruct the process of designing and developing a software solution. It is hard to figure out how to practice a way of thinking. One of the reasons for this is that a solved problem tends to stay solved. What I mean by that is that as a developer you will very rarely be asked to write a piece of software that has already been written. Finding the "shot" to practice over and over is hard.

In programming, you want to learn different ways to solve problems. You want to find different challenges that force you to attack the same type of problem with different constraints. Keep working at it until you understand the problem and the set of possible solutions inside out.

In essence, deliberate practice has these components:

- Each practice session has a single focus.

- The distance (time) between attempt and feedback is as short as possible.

- Work on something that you cannot yet do.

- Follow in the path of those who have gone before you.

Single Focus

The reason you only want to focus on one thing during a specific training session is that you want devote all your attention to the element that you wish to improve. You want to do whatever it takes to do it perfectly, even if it is only once. Then, you want to repeat the process to get another perfect response, and then another. Every practice run is a single reinforcement of the skill. You want to reinforce the patterns that lead to the perfect result rather than those that have less desirable outcomes.

In the context of this book, I want you to target a single design pattern at a time. Really seek to understand not only how the pattern works, but also why it is used in the first place and how it applies to the problem at hand. Also, think about other problems that you might be able to solve using this design pattern. Next, try to solve some of these problems using the pattern you are working on.

You want to create a mental box for the problem and the pattern that solves it. Ideally, you will develop a sense for when problems would fit into one of the boxes you have mastered, and then be able to quickly and easily solve the problem.

Rapid Feedback

One of the pieces of deliberate practice that is often overlooked is the rapid-feedback loop. The quicker the feedback, the stronger the connection, and the more easily you learn from it. That is why things like marketing and writing are so hard to master. The time between putting letters on a page and getting feedback from the market is simply too long to really be able to see the effects of experiments. With programming this is not the case; you can write a piece of code and then run it for instant feedback. This allows you to course correct and ultimately reach an acceptable solution. If you go one step further and write solid tests for your code, you get even more feedback, and you are able to arrive at the solution much more quickly than if you had to test the process manually each time you made a change.

Another trick to help you learn from the process more rapidly is to make a prediction as to what the outcome of the block of code you want to write will be. Make a note as to why you expect this specific outcome. Now write the code and check the result against the expected result. If it does not match up, try to explain why this is the case and how you would verify your explanation with another block of code. Then, test that. Keep doing it until you have attained mastery.

You will find yourself getting feedback on different levels, and each has its own merit.

Level one is simply whether the solution works or not. Next, you might begin considering questions such as "How easy was the solution to implement?" or "Is this solution a good fit for the problem?" Later, you might seek out external feedback, which can take the form of simple code review, working on projects, or discussing solutions with like-minded people.

Stretch Yourself

What are the things that you shy away from? These are the areas of programming that cause you slight discomfort. It might be reading from a file on disk or connecting to a remote API. It makes no difference if it is some graphical library or a machine-learning setup, we all have some part of the craft that just does not sit comfortably. These are usually the things that you most need to work on. Here are the areas that will stretch you and force you to face your own weaknesses and blind spots. The only way to get over this discomfort is to dive deep into it, to use that tool so many times and in so many ways that you begin to get a feel for it. You must get so comfortable with it that you no longer have to look up that file open protocol on stack overflow; in fact, you have written a better one. You jump rope with the GUI and suck data out of a database with one hand tied behind your back.

There is no shortcut to this level of mastery; the only way is through the mountain. That is why so few people become true masters. Getting there means spending a lot of time on the things that are not easy, that do not make you feel like you are invincible. You spend so much time in these ego-destroying zones that very few masters of any craft have a lot of arrogance left in them.

So, what should you work on first? That thing you thought of as you read the previous two paragraphs.

Working your way through the design patterns in this book is another good way of finding potential growth areas. Just start with the singleton pattern and work your way through.

Stand on the Shoulders of Giants

There are people who do amazing things in the programming space. These people often give talks at developer conferences and sometimes have a presence online. Look at what these people are talking about. Try to understand how they approach a novel problem. Type along with them as they demonstrate solutions. Get into their head and figure out what makes them tick. Try to solve a problem like you imagine one of them would do it; how does the solution you come up with in this way differ from the one you came up with on your own?

Really great developers are passionate about programming, and it should not take a lot of prodding to get them to talk about the finer details of the craft. Seek out the user groups where this type of developer hangs out and strike up a lot of conversations. Be open and keep learning.

Pick personal projects that force you to use design patterns you have yet to master. Have fun with it. Most of all, learn to love the process, and don't get caught up on some perceived outcome rather than spending time becoming a better programmer.

How Do You Do This?

Begin the same way Leonardo da Vinci began when he decided to make painting his vocation.

Copy!

That is right. Begin by identifying some interesting problem, one that is already solved, and then blatantly copy the solution. Don't copy/paste. Copy the solution by typing it out yourself. Get your copy to work. Once you do, delete it all. Now try to solve the problem from memory, only referring to the original solution when your memory fails you. Do this until you are able to reproduce the solution flawlessly without looking at the original solution. If you are looking for solutions to problems that you can copy and learn from, Github is a gold mine.

Once you are comfortable with the solution as you found it, try to improve on the original solution. You need to learn to think about the solutions you find out there—what makes them good? How can you make them more elegant, more idiomatic, more simple? Always look for opportunities to make code better in one of these ways.

Next, you want to take your new solution out into the wild. Find places to use the solution. Practicing in the real world forces you to deal with different constraints, the kinds you would never dream up for yourself. It will force you to bend your nice, clean solution in ways it was never intended to be. Sometimes, your code will break, and you will learn to appreciate the way the problem was solved originally. Other times, you may find that your solution works better than the original. Ask yourself why one solution outperforms another, and what that teaches you about the problem and the solution.

Try using languages with different paradigms to solve similar problems, taking from each and shaping a solution yourself. If you pay attention to the process as much as you do to actually solving the problem, no project will leave you untouched.

The beauty of working on open source projects is that there is usually just the right mix of people who will help you along, and others who will tell you exactly what is wrong with your code. Evaluate their feedback, learn what you can, and discard the rest.

The Ability to Course Correct

When exploring a problem, you have two options: go on trying this way, or scrap everything and start over with what I have learned. Daniel Kahnamann, in his book *Thinking, Fast and Slow*, explains the sunk cost fallacy. It is where you keep investing in a poor investment because you have already invested so much in it. This is a deadly trap for a developer. The quickest way to make a two-day project take several months is to try to power your way through a poor solution. Often it feels like it would be a massive loss if we were to scrap a day, a week, or a month's work and start from nothing.

The reality is that we are never starting from scratch, and sometimes the last 10,000 lines of code you are deleting are the 10,000 lines of code you needed to write to become the programmer you need to be to solve the problem in 100 lines of code with a startlingly elegant solution.

You need to develop the mental fortitude to say enough is enough and start over, building a new solution using what you have learned.

No amount of time spent on a solution means anything if it is the wrong solution. The sooner you realize that the better.

This self-awareness gives you the ability to know when to try one more thing and when to head in a different direction.

Systems Thinking

Everything is a system. By understanding what elements make up the system, how they are connected, and how they interact with one another, you can understand the system. By learning to deconstruct and understand systems, you inevitably teach yourself how to design and build systems. Every piece of software out there is an expression of these three core components: the elements that make up the solution, and a set of connections and interactions between them.

At a very basic level, you can begin by asking yourself: "What are the elements of the system I want to build?" Write these down. Then, write down how they are connected to each other. Lastly, list all the interactions between these elements and what connections come into play. Do this, and you will have designed the system.

All design patterns deal with these three fundamental questions: 1) What are the elements and how are they created? 2) What are the connections between elements, or what does the structure look like? 3) How do the elements interact, or what does their behavior look like?

There are other ways to classify design patterns, but for now use the classical three groupings to help you develop your systems thinking skills.

Mental Models

Mental models are internal representations of the external world. The more accurate your models of the world are, the more effective your thinking is. The map is not the territory, so having more-accurate mental models makes your view of the world more accurate, and the more versatile your set of mental models is, the more diverse the set of problems you will be able to solve. Throughout this book you will learn a set of mental tools that will help you solve specific programming problems you will regularly come across in your career as a programmer.

Another way to look at mental models is to see them as a grouping of concepts into single unit of thought. The study of design patterns will aid you in developing new mental models. The structure of a problem will suggest the kind of solution you will need to implement in order to solve the problem in question. That is why it is important that you gain complete clarity into exactly what the problem is you are trying to solve.

The better—and by *better* I mean more complete—the problem definition or description is, the more hints you have of what a possible solution would look like. So, ask yourself dumb questions about the problem until you have a clear and simple problem statement.

Design patterns help you go from A (the problem statement) to C (the solution) without having to go through B and however many other false starts.

The Right Tools for the Job

To break down a brick wall, you need a hammer, but not just any hammer—you need a big, heavy hammer with a long handle. Sure, you can break down the wall with the same hammer you would use to put nails in a music box, but it will take you a couple of lifetimes to do what an afternoon's worth of hammering with the right tool will do.

With the wrong tools, any job becomes a mess and takes way longer than it should. Selecting the right tool for the job is a matter of experience. If you had no idea that there were hammers other than the tiny craft hammer you were used to, you would have a hard time imagining that someone could come along and take down a whole wall in a couple of hours. You might even call such a person a 10x wall breaker. The point I am trying to make is that with the right tool you will be able to do many times more work than someone who is trying to make do with what they have. It is worth the time and effort to expand your toolbox, and to master different tools, so that when you encounter a novel problem you will know which to select.

To become a master programmer, you need to consistently add new tools to your arsenal, not just familiarizing yourself with them, but mastering them. We already looked at the process for attaining mastery of the tools you decide on, but in the context of Python, let me make some specific suggestions.

Some of the beauties of the Python ecosystem are the packages available right out of the gate. There are a lot of packages, but more often than not you have one or two clear leaders for every type of problem you might encounter. These packages are valuable tools, and you should spend a couple of hours every week exploring them. Once you have mastered the patterns in this book, grab Numpy or Scipy and master them. Then, head off in any direction your imagination carries you. Download the package you are interested in, learn the basics, and then begin experimenting with it using the frameworks touched on already. Where do they shine, and what is missing? What kinds of problems are they especially good at solving? How can you use them in the future? What side project can you do that will allow you to try the package in question in a real-world scenario?

Design Patterns as a Concept

The Gang of Four's book on design patterns seems to be the place where it all started. They set forth a framework for describing design patterns (specifically for C++), but the description was focused on the solution in general, and as a result many of the patterns were translated into a number of languages. The goal of the 23 design patterns set forth in that book was to codify best-practice solutions to common problems encountered in object-oriented programming. As such, the solutions focus on classes and their methods and attributes.

These design patterns represent a single complete solution idea each, and they keep the things that change separate from the things that do not.

There are many people who are critical of the original design patterns. One of these critics, Peter Norvig, showed how 16 of the patterns could be replaced by language constructs in Lisp. Many of these replacements are possible in Python too.

In this book, we are going to look at several of the original design patterns and how they fit into real-world projects. We will also consider arguments about them in the context of the Python language, sometimes discarding the pattern for a solution that comes stock standard with the language, sometimes altering the GoF solution to take advantage of the power and expressiveness of Python, and other times simply implementing the original solution in a pythonic way.

What Makes a Design Pattern?

Design patterns can be a lot of things, but they all contain the following elements (credit: Peter Norvig, `http://norvig.com/design-patterns/ppframe.htm`):

- Pattern name

- Intent/purpose

- Aliases

- Motivation/context

- Problem

- Solution

- Structure

- Participants

- Collaborations

- Consequences/constraints

- Implementation

- Sample code

- Known uses

- Related patterns

In Appendix A, you can find all the design patterns we discuss in this book structured according to these elements. For the sake of readability and the learning process, the chapters on the design patterns themselves will not all follow this structure.

Classification

Design patterns are classified into different groupings to help us as programmers talk about categories of solutions with one another and to give us a common language when discussing these solutions. This allows us to communicate clearly and to be expressive in our discussions around the subject.

As mentioned earlier in this chapter, we are going to classify design patterns according to the original groupings of creational, structural, and behavioral patterns. This is done not only to stick to the general way things are done, but also to aid you, the reader, in looking at the patterns in the context of the systems they are found in.

Creational

The first category deals with the elements in the system—specifically, how they are created. As we are dealing with object-oriented programming, the creation of objects happens through class instantiation. As you will soon see, there are different characteristics that are desirable when it comes to solving specific problems, and the way in which an object is created has a significant effect on these characteristics.

Structural

The structural patterns deal with how classes and objects are composed. Objects can be composed using inheritance to obtain new functionality.

Behavioral

These design patterns are focused on the interaction between objects.

The Tools We Will Be Using

The world is shifting toward Python 3. This shift is slow and deliberate and, like a glacier, cannot be stopped. For the sake of this book, we will release Python 2 and embrace the future. That said, you should be able to make most of the code work with Python 2 without much trouble (this is less due to the code in the book and more a result of the brilliant work done by the Python core developers).

With Python, CPython (the default one) specifically, you get to use Pip, the Python Package Installer. Pip integrates with PyPI, the Python Package Index, and lets you download and install a package from the package index without manually downloading the package, uncompressing it, running python setup.py install and so on. Pip makes installing libraries for your environment a joy. Pip also deals with all the dependencies for you, so no need to run around after required packages you have not installed yet.

By the time you begin working on your third project, you are going to need a lot of packages. Not all of these packages are needed for all of your projects. You will want to keep every project's packages nicely contained. Enter VirtualEnv, a virtual Python interpreter that isolates the packages installed for that interpreter from others on the system. You get to keep each project in its own minimalist space, only installing the packages it needs in order to work, without interfering with the other projects you may be working on.

How to Read This Book

There are many ways to read a book, especially a programming book. Most people start a book like this hoping to read it from cover to cover and end up just jumping from code example to code example. We have all done it. With that in mind, there are ways you can read this book and gain optimal value from the time spent on it.

The first group of readers just wants a quick, robust reference of pythonic versions of the GoF design patterns. If this is you, skip ahead to Appendix A to see the formal definition of each of the design patterns. When you have time, you can then return to the relevant chapter and follow the exploration of the design pattern you are interested in.

The second group wants to be able to find specific solutions to specific problems. For those readers, each design pattern chapter starts with a description of the problem addressed by the pattern in question. This should help you decide if the pattern will be helpful in solving the problem you are faced with.

The last group wants to use this book to master their craft. For these readers, I suggest you begin at the beginning and code your way through the book. Type out every example. Tinker with every solution. Do all the exercises. See what happens when you alter the code. What breaks, and why? Make the solutions better. Tackle one pattern at a time and master it. Then, find other real-world contexts where you can apply your new knowledge.

Setting Up Your Python Environment

Let's begin by getting a working Python 3 environment running on your machine. In this section, we will look at installing Python 3 on Linux, Mac, and Windows.

On Linux

The commands we use are for *Ubuntu* with the *apt package manager*. For other distributions that do not work with apt, you can look at the process for installing Python 3 and `pip` using an alternative package manager, like yum, or installing the relevant packages from source.

The whole installation process will make use of the terminal, so you can go ahead and open it up now.

Let's begin by checking if you have a version of Python already installed on your system.

Just a note: For the duration of this book, I will indicate terminal commands with the leading $; you do not type this character or the subsequent space when entering the comment in your terminal.

```
$ python --version
```

If you have Python 3 (as is the case with Ubuntu 16.04 and up) already installed, you can skip ahead to the section on installing pip.

If you have either Python 2 or no Python installed on your system, you can go ahead and install Python 3 using the following command:

```
$ sudo apt-get install python3-dev
```

This will install Python 3. You can check the version of the Python install, as before, to verify that the right version was installed:

```
$ python3 --version
```

Python 3 should now be available on your system.

Next, we install build essentials and Python `pip`:

```
$ sudo apt-get install python-pip build-essential
```

Now, check that `pip` is working:

```
$ pip --version
```

You should see a version of `pip` installed on your system, and now you are ready to install the `virtualenv` package; please skip past the Mac and Windows installation instructions.

On Mac

macOS comes with a version of Python 2 installed by default, but we will not be needing this.

To install Python 3, we are going to use Homebrew, a command-line package manager for macOS. For this to work, we will need Xcode, which you can get for free from the Mac AppStore.

Once you have installed Xcode, open the Terminal app and install the command-line tools for Xcode:

```
$ xcode-select --install
```

Simply follow the prompt in the window that pops up to install the command-line tools for Xcode. Once that is done, you can install Homebrew:

```
$ ruby -e "$(curl -fsSL https://raw.githubusercontent.com/Homebrew/install/master/install)"
```

If you do not have XQuartz already installed, your macOS might encounter some errors. If this happens, you can download the XQuartz `.dmg` here: `https://www.xquartz.org/`. Then, check that you have successfully installed Homebrew and that it is working:

```
$ brew doctor
```

To run brew commands from any folder in the Terminal, you need to add the Homebrew path to your PATH environment variable. Open or create ~/.bash_profile and add the following line at the end of the file:

```
export PATH=/usr/local/bin:$PATH
```

Close and reopen Terminal. Upon reopening, the new PATH variable will be included in the environment, and now you can call brew from anywhere. Use brew to find the available packages for Python:

```
brew search python
```

You will now see all the Python-related packages, python3 being one of them. Now, install Python 3 using the following brew command:

```
$ brew install python3
```

Finally, you can check that Python 3 is installed and working:

```
python3 --version
```

When you install Python with Homebrew, you also install the corresponding package manager (pip), Setuptools, and pyvenv (an alternative to virtualenv, but for this book you will only need pip).

Check that pip is working:

```
$ pip --version
```

If you see the version information, it means that pip was successfully installed on your system, and you can skip past the Windows installation section to the section on using pip to install VirtualEnv.

On Windows

Begin by downloading the Python 3 Windows installer. You can download the installer here: https://www.python.org/.

When your download is done, run the installer and select the Customize option. Make sure that pip is selected to be installed. Also, select the option to add Python to your environment variables.

With the install, you also get IDLE, which is an interactive Python shell. This lets you run Python commands in a real-time interpreter, which is great for testing ideas or playing around with new packages.

Once you are done with the install, open your command-line interface:

```
windowsbutton-r
cmd
```

This will open a terminal similar to the ones available on Mac and Linux.

Now, check that Python is working:

```
$ python --version
```

If you see version information, Python is installed and linked to the path, as it should be.

Before we go on, check that pip is working:

```
$ pip --version
```

VirtualEnv

Before we begin installing VirtualEnv, let's make sure we have the latest version of pip installed:

```
$ pip install --upgrade pip
```

Windows users will see a command prompt like this:

```
c:\some\directory>
```

On Mac you have

```
#
```

On Linux it is

```
$
```

I will be using $ to indicate terminal commands for the duration of this book.

Use pip to install the virtualenv package:

```
$ pip install virtualenv
```

Now that you have the `virtualenv` package, let's use it to create an environment to use with this book.

In your terminal, go to the directory you will be working in. Next, create a virtual environment where you will install the packages needed for the projects in this book. Our virtual environment will be called ppdpenv; the env is just so we know that it is a virtual environment. Whenever we have this environment active and install a new package using the `pip` command, the new package will only be installed in this environment, and will only be available to programs while this environment is active.

```
$ virtualenv -p python3 ppdpenv
```

On Windows, you need a slightly different command:

```
$ virtualenv -p python ppdpenv
```

If Python 3 is not part of your PATH, you can use the full path to the Python executable you want to use inside your `virtualenv`.

After the installation process is concluded, you will have a new directory named ppdpenv in the directory you were in when you ran the `virtualenv` command.

To activate the virtual environment, run the following command on Mac and Linux:

```
$ source ./ppdpenv/bin/activate
```

And on Windows:

```
$ source ppdpenv\Scripts\activate
```

Lastly, check the version of Python to make sure that the right version is installed. That's it—you are all set up and ready to program in Python!

To exit the virtual environment, you run the following command:

```
$ deactivate
```

Editors

Any text editor that can save plain text files can be used to write Python programs. You could write the next Uber using nothing but Notepad, but it would be painful. Whenever you write a program of any length, you want an editor that highlights your code, marking different keywords and expressions with different colors so you can easily differentiate between them.

What follows is a short list of my favorite text editors, with a couple of notes on each.

Atom

Github made an editor, they called it Atom, and it is a simple, beautiful, and functional editor right out of the box. It offers simple git integration and a good package system (including a real-time markdown compiler). The fact that it is based on Electron means that you can take your editor with you no matter what platform you want to work on. If it can run Chromium, it will run Atom.

Get it here: `https://atom.io/`.

LightTable

This one is based on ClojureScript (a Lisp dialect that compiles down to JavaScript) with both Vim and Emacs modes, so you can free yourself from the mouse. Like most modern code editors, LightTable also offers direct git integration. It is open source and easy to customize.

Get it here: `http://lighttable.com/`.

PyCharm

Jetbrains made the industry standard when it comes to Python editors. It comes with great code completion, Python linter, unused import warnings, and a whole lot more, but for me the killer feature is the code spell checking that takes both Camel and Snake case into consideration.

The enterprise edition of PyCharm is not cheap, but they offer free student and community licenses.

Get it here: `https://www.jetbrains.com/pycharm/download`.

Vim

Most UNIX-based operating systems come with Vim already installed. Vim is sometimes called *The Editor You Can't Get Out Of* (tip: "`:q!`" gets you out). What gives Vim most of its power is that its shortcut keys do everything from selecting blocks to jumping to specific lines in code—everything without taking your hands off of the keyboard. Over the years, Vim accumulated a number of extensions, color themes, and every feature a full-fledged IDE would dream of. It has its own package manager and gives you total control over every aspect of code editing. It is free and is the quickest out of the blocks of any editor I have seen. For all its pros, Vim is hard to learn—very hard. I use Vim whenever I want to write a quick script or make a small change and do not want to wait for some other editor/IDE to start up.

Set up Vim for Python by going here: `https://realpython.com/blog/python/vim-and-python-a-match-made-in-heaven/`.

Emacs

An amazing operating system; if only it had a good text editor. Emacs is built on Emacs Lisp and is insanely customizable. You can do anything with it, from sending emails to having your coffee machine start, with a simple shortcut key combination. Like Vim, it is mouse free, but it has an even steeper learning curve. Those in the know swear by it, and with good reason. You have all the code-completion and split-screen options that a modern IDE offers with the ability to adapt the system as and when you feel the need to. You do not have to wait for some vendor to create a package to handle some new language feature; you can easily do it yourself. *Easily* is used very loosely. With Emacs you can make your editor do things the way you feel they ought to be done, and a large part of programming is being dissatisfied with the way things are currently done and taking it upon yourself to do it differently.

Set up Emacs for Python development by reading this: `https://realpython.com/blog/python/emacs-the-best-python-editor/`.

Sublime Text

This is more of an honorable mention than a real suggestion. Sublime used to be the best free (with nag screens every couple of saves) option available. It has a beautiful default color scheme, is fairly quick to start, and is extensible. It comes Python-ready, but its time has probably passed.

If you are interested in looking at it, you can get it here: `https://www.sublimetext.com/3`.

Summary

In the end, it does not matter which editor you choose to use. It must be something you feel comfortable with. Whatever you choose, take the time to master this tool. If you want to be productive, you must master any tool or process you have to use every day, no matter how mundane it may seem. What I suggest is that you pick one of these to learn inside out, and if it is not Vim or Emacs, at least learn enough Vim to edit text in it. It will make the time you spend on servers editing software much more enjoyable.

Now, you have your environment set up and isolated from the rest of your system. You also have your editor of choice installed and ready to go, so let's not waste any time. Let's start looking at some practical Python design patterns.

CHAPTER 2

The Singleton Pattern

There can be only one!–

—Connor MacLeod

The Problem

One of the first debugging techniques you learn is simply printing the values of certain variables to the console. This helps you see what is going on inside your program. When the programs you write become more complex, you reach a point where you cannot run the whole program in your mind effectively. This is when you need to print out the values of certain variables at specific times, especially when the program does not act as you expect it to. Looking at the output of your program at different points in its execution helps you locate and fix bugs swiftly.

Your code quickly becomes littered with `print` statements, and that's fine, until one fine day when you deploy your code. Running your code on a server, as a scheduled job on your own machine, or as a standalone piece of software on a client's computer means that you can no longer rely on the console for feedback when something goes wrong. You have no way of knowing what went wrong or how to replicate the issue. This takes debugging from the realm of science straight into gambling.

The simplest solution is to replace `print` statements with a command to write the output to a file instead of to the console, like this:

```python
with open("filename.log", "a") as log_file:
    log_file.write("Log message goes here.\n")
```

© Wessel Badenhorst 2017
W. Badenhorst, *Practical Python Design Patterns*, https://doi.org/10.1007/978-1-4842-2680-3_2

Now you can see what is happening in the program when things go wrong. Your log file is like a black box on an aircraft: it keeps a tally of your program's execution. When your program crashes, you can pop open the black box and see what happened leading up to the crash, as well as where you should start looking for a bug. One line is better than two, so create a function that handles opening and writing to the file:

```python
def log_message(msg):
  with open("filename.log", "a") as log_file:
    log_file.write("{0}\n".format(msg))
```

You can use this replacement for `print` statements wherever you want to record some state of your program for later review:

```python
log_message("save this for later")
```

The `log_message` function opens a file and appends the message passed to it to the file. This is the *DRY* principle in action. DRY? you ask. It stands for **don't repeat yourself**. At the most basic level, you should hear a little alarm go off in your mind whenever you feel tempted to copy and paste code. Whenever possible, you should repackage the code in such a way that you can reuse it without the need to copy and paste the lines somewhere else.

Why should you go through the effort of rethinking code that works? Why not copy it and just change one or two pieces? If your code is in one place, and you must change something, you only have to change it at that one place. If, for instance, you had the code for the logger scattered throughout your program, and you decided to change the name of the file you write the logs to, you would have to change the name in many places. You will find that this is a recipe for disaster; if you miss one line of output code, some of your log messages will go missing. In programming, the number one cause of mistakes is people. If you need to work on a project that spans thousands or even millions of lines of code, and you need to change something like a log file name, you can easily miss a line here or there during your update. Whenever possible, eliminate the number of human interactions with your code.

Good programmers write solid code; great programmers write code that makes average programmers produce solid code.

One way of making the code a bit more user-friendly is to have a file in your project that contains nothing but the logging function. This allows you to import the logging function into any file in your project. All changes to the way logging is done in the project need only be made in this one file.

Let's create a new file called logger.py and write the following code in the file:

logger.py

```python
def log_message(msg):
  with open("/var/log/filename.log", "a") as log_file:
    log_file.write("{0}\n".format(msg))
```

Now, we can use our new logger function to write log messages to the file system in our main_script.py file:

main_script.py

```python
import logger

for i in range(4):
  logger.log_message("log message {}".format(i))
```

The first line of the file-import logger tells Python to import the logger.py file (note that you do not add .py when you import the file). Importing a file allows you to use the functions defined in the logger.py file in the main_script.py file. In the preceding code snippet, we have a loop where we tell Python to write a message log message i every time the loop runs, where i is the index of the loop in the range.

Open the filename.log file and verify that the messages were indeed written as expected.

As the number of log messages increases, you will find you want to distinguish between them. The most useful distinction is the terms used to describe the severity of the event causing the message in question.

For the sake of our logger, we will handle the following levels:

- Critical

- Error

- Warning

- Info

- Debug

Luckily, we only have a single file to update (aren't you glad we moved this logger to its own file?).

In the log file, we want each message to be prepended with the level associated with the message. This helps us easily scan the file for specific types of messages. You can use this convention with certain command-line tools, like using grep in a *.nix environment to show only messages of a certain level.

After upgrading our logging function, it looks like this:

logger.py

```python
def critical(msg):
  with open("/var/log/filename.log", "a") as log_file:
    log_file.write("[CRITICAL] {0}\n".format(msg))

def error(msg):
  with open("/var/log/filename.log", "a") as log_file:
    log_file.write("[ERROR] {0}\n".format(msg))

def warn(msg):
  with open("/var/log/filename.log", "a") as log_file:
    log_file.write("[WARN] {0}\n".format(msg))

def info(msg):
  with open("/var/log/filename.log", "a") as log_file:
    log_file.write("[INFO] {0}\n".format(msg))

def debug(msg):
  with open("/var/log/filename.log", "a") as log_file:
    log_file.write("[DEBUG] {0}\n".format(msg))
```

You do not need to change the way you import the code; you just use the level of message you want to save, as follows:

test_error_log.py

```python
import logger

try:
  a = 1 / 0
except:
  logger.error("something went wrong")
```

If you look at the output of the _test_error_log.py__ function, you will see that the message now has the level added to the line as a prefix:

```
[ERROR] something went wrong
```

Our logging project now has some really useful functionality, but I bet there is something bothering you about the way the logger.py file is written. That alarm bell in your head just went off, did it not?

If it did, you are completely right!

We should not be copying the same instructions to open the file and append the message to the file, with only the prefix string differing for each function. Let's refactor our code so we don't repeat ourselves.

The part that is repeated is the part we want to extract from all the methods duplicating the code. The next step is to generalize the function enough so that every function can use it without losing any of its original functionality.

In each of the repeated functions, the prefix was the only thing that differed from function to function. So, if we were to write a function that takes the message and level as parameters, we could use this function in each of the other functions and reduce it to a single line of code in each case.

We now have a shorter, clearer logger to use in our other projects.

logger.py

```python
def write_log(level, msg):
  with open("/var/log/filename.log", "a") as log_file:
    log_file.write("[{0}] {1}\n".format(level, msg))

def critical(msg):
  write_log("CRITICAL",msg)

def error(msg):
  write_log("ERROR", msg)

def warn(msg):
  write_log("WARN", msg)

def info(msg):
  write_log("INFO", msg)

def debug(msg):
  write_log("DEBUG", msg)
```

This looks even better. It is simple and clean, as each function does only one thing. The write_log function just writes the message level and message text to the file. Each log writer simply calls the write_log function, adding the level of the message to the call.

I'm sure you are really beginning to like our little logger, but what bothers me most at the moment is that hardcoded filename.log that we use to persist all our log files in. You now know that logging makes you a better developer and saves you a lot of time. So, this being such a nice logger, you are sure to want to use it in several of your own projects. The last thing you want your logger to do is to write messages from different projects to the same file.

To circumvent this issue, we could just add the file name as a parameter on the functions we call when logging our messages.

Go ahead and implement this change. Note that the following code snippet is still incomplete, as the write_log function still takes a filename parameter.

logger.py

```python
def write_log(filename, level, msg):
  with open(filename, "a") as log_file:
    log_file.write("[{0}] {1}\n".format(level, msg))

  def critical(msg):
    write_log("CRITICAL",msg)

  def error(msg):
    write_log("ERROR", msg)

  def warn(msg):
    write_log("WARN", msg)

  def info(msg):
    write_log("INFO", msg)

  def debug(msg):
    write_log("DEBUG", msg)
```

The filename parameter does not change from call to call, so passing the same value over and over is not the right way to do things. The very reason we extracted the write_log function from the other functions is so that we would not have to repeat the same code. We want to set up the logger once, with the log file it should be logging to, and then use it without paying any more attention to the selection of the file to write to.

Enter the Objects

Classes in Python allow you to define logical groupings of data and functions. They also allow you to add some contextual data to the logger (like which file you want to write to).

To get the most out of classes, you need to think in a slightly new way.

This grouping of functions and data that relate to each other into a class forms a blueprint for creating specific instances (version) of the data combined with their associated functions. An instance of a class is called an *object*.

To help you understand this, consider for a moment the logger we have just developed. If we were able to generalize this logger in such a way that we could send it the name of the file to use when we use it, we would have a blueprint to create any logger (a class). The moment we make this call, we effectively create a new logger that writes to a specific file. This new logger is called an instance of the class.

Thinking about data and the functions that alter the data as a single entity is the basis for object-oriented programming.

We will now implement a simple Logger class as an example.

logger_class.py

```python
class Logger(object):
  """A file-based message logger with the following properties

  Attributes:
    file_name: a string representing the full path of the log file to which
this logger will write its messages
  """

  def __init__(self, file_name):
    """Return a Logger object whose file_name is *file_name*"""
    self.file_name = file_name

  def _write_log(self, level, msg):
    """Writes a message to the file_name for a specific Logger instance"""
    with open(self.file_name, "a") as log_file:
      log_file.write("[{0}] {1}\n".format(level, msg))

  def critical(self, level, msg):
    self._write_log("CRITICAL",msg)
```

```
def error(self, level, msg):
  self._write_log("ERROR", msg)

def warn(self, level, msg):
  self._write_log("WARN", msg)

def info(self, level, msg):
  self._write_log("INFO", msg)

def debug(self, level, msg):
  self._write_log("DEBUG", msg)
```

There is quite a lot happening here, so just look at the code for a minute before I show you how this new logger is implemented in another project.

The first big departure from our previous logger is the addition of the class keyword, which acts like the def keyword in that it tells Python that we are now going to define a new class. Then, we have the class name, which we will use when we want to create a new object of this class (called an instance, as you might have guessed).

One of the main benefits of object-oriented programming (OOP) is that once you define a class, you are able to reuse the class to create other classes. This process is called *inheritance*, since the child class inherits the traits (data and function blueprint) from the parent class (the class that is used to create the child). In Python, every class ultimately inherits from the object class. In the case of our logger, we have no other class we are using as a base, so here we just say that Logger only has object as its parent.

Next, we have a bit of text wrapped in """ characters, denoting that the text contained is a doc string. Certain integrated development environments (IDEs) and other programs know to look for these strings and use them to help guide programmers who want to use this class.

Classes are not the only structures that can make use of a doc string, and you will also see that functions can have their own doc strings, like the __init__ function.

The __init__ is called whenever a new Logger object is instantiated. In this case, it takes the name of a file as an argument and associates that with the instance that is being created. When we want to reference this file name, we have to tell the method in the object to look for the file_name in its own list of attributes. The self keyword is used to let the code know we are referring to an attribute or method associated with an object from which the call is made, and, as such, it should not be looking somewhere else for these elements.

Just a quick note with regards to the terms *attributes* and *methods*. *Attributes* are the pieces of data associated with an object as defined in the class blueprint. The functions that perform actions on these pieces of data are referred to as *methods*. When we use the `self` keyword together with a method, like this:

```
self.some_method()
```

what is really happening is that the Python interpreter calls the method `some_method` and passes the object itself as a variable into the function, which is why you have `self` as a parameter in the methods of the object, but do not explicitly pass it in when making the call.

Another thing to note is that when referencing an attribute in an object, as in

```
self.some_attribute
```

what Python does is call a method called __getattr__ and pass in the object itself together with the attribute name that it is requesting. You will see an example of this soon.

In the __init__ method, you will see that we set an attribute called `file_name`. This allows us to request the value of the `file_name` attribute that we set when we first created the class whenever we want to use the `_write_log` method.

The rest is close to what we had before, with the exception that we now also must make provision for the `self` parameter, which we discussed.

As a matter of good practice, the result of the __init__ method must be a fully initialized object. What that means is that the object must be ready for use; it should not require some other settings to be tweaked or methods to be executed before it can perform its function.

If you are wondering about the leading underscore in `_write_log`, it is just a convention to tell other programmers that this method should not be used by any outside program; it is said to be private.

Now, we can look at how this new `Logger` class of ours will be used.

new_script_with_logger.py

```
from logger_class import Logger

logger_object = Logger("/var/log/class_logger.log")

logger_object.info("This is an info message")
```

We can now import a specific class from a Python file by telling the interpreter which file we want to use, and then what class it should import. Importing from different packages can get more complex than this, but for now just realizing that you can import the specific class you want to use is enough. Packages are groups of Python files that live in the same folder on your computer and provide similar or related functions.

To create a new logger using the Logger blueprint (class), we simply use a name for the logger and set that equal to the class name, and then we pass in any parameters needed by the __init__ function. After instantiating the logger, we can simply use the object name with the relevant log function to write the log message to the correct file.

Running `new_script_with_logger.py` will result in the following message in the `/var/log/class_logger.log` file:

```
[INFO] This is an info message
```

Cleaning It Up

Now, you probably do not want to write to a unique log file for every part of your project that needs to write some log messages. So, what you want is some way to get the same logger that you already created if there is one, or create a new logger if none already exist.

You want to keep the benefits of object-oriented programming while taking control of the object-creation process out of the hands of the programmer using the logger. We do that by taking control of the process by which the logger object is created.

Consider the following way of taking control of the process:

singleton_object.py

```python
class SingletonObject(object):
  class __SingletonObject():
    def __init__(self):
      self.val = None

    def __str__(self):
      return "{0!r} {1}".format(self, self.val)

    # the rest of the class definition will follow here, as per the previous
    logging script

  instance = None
```

```
def __new__(cls):
  if not SingletonObject.instance:
    SingletonObject.instance = SingletonObject.__SingletonObject()

  return SingletonObject.instance

def __getattr__(self, name):
  return getattr(self.instance, name)

def __setattr__(self, name):
  return setattr(self.instance, name)
```

Don't panic.

At first, it seems like a lot is happening here. Let's walk through the code and see how this results in a single instance of a class being created, or being returned whenever the class is instantiated.

The elephant in the room is the class definition inside our SingletonObject class. The leading underscores tell other programmers that this is a private class, and they should not be using it outside of the original class definition. The private class is where we implement the functionality of the logger, which is left to you as an exercise at the end of the chapter. For the sake of the example, this class has an object attribute called val and two methods: __init__, which instantiates the object, and __str__, which is called when you use the object in a print statement.

Next, we see something called a *class attribute instance*, which is fixed for all objects instantiated from the SingletonObject class. This attribute is set to None, which means that when the script starts to execute there is no value for the instance.

The other thing we are not used to seeing is the use of the cls parameter and having no self parameter in the definition of the __new__ function. This is because __new__ is a class method. Instead of taking the object as a parameter, it receives the class as a parameter and then uses the class definition to construct a new instance of the class.

By now you have seen a number of these methods with two leading and two trailing underscores. What you need to know is that in the cases you have encountered up to now, these were used to indicate that these are *magic methods*, which are methods used by the Python interpreter without your calling them explicitly.

In the __new__ function, we see that whenever a programmer tries to instantiate an object of type SingletonObject, the interpreter will first check the class variable instance to see if there is such an instance in existence. If there is no existing instance, it creates a new instance of the private class and assigns it to the instance class variable. Finally, the __new__ function returns the class in the instance class variable.

We also alter the __getattr__ and __setattr__ functions to call the attributes found in the private class saved in the instance class variable. This relays the call to the object housed in the instance variable as if the outer object has the attributes.

The self.val attribute is set just to show that the object remains the same even though the script attempts to instantiate it more than once.

Good—now you can use the class to verify that the singleton implementation does what you would expect it to do.

test_singleton.py

```
from singleton_object import SingletonObject

obj1 = SingletonObject()

obj1.val = "Object value 1"
print("print obj1: ", obj1)

print("-----")
obj2 = SingletonObject()
obj2.val = "Object value 2"
print("print obj1: ", obj1)
print("print obj2: ", obj2)
```

Here is the output:

```
print obj1:  <__main__.SingletonObject._SingletonObject object at
0x7fda5524def0> Object value 1
-----
print obj1:  <__main__.SingletonObject._SingletonObject object at
0x7fda5524def0> Object value 2
print obj2:  <__main__.SingletonObject._SingletonObject object at
0x7fda5524def0> Object value 2
```

The main criticism of the singleton pattern is that it is just a pretty way to get a global state, which is one of the things you want to avoid when writing programs. One of the reasons why you want to avoid global state is that code in one part of your project may alter the global state and cause unexpected results in a completely unrelated piece of code.

That said, when you have parts of a project that do not affect the execution of your code, like logging, it is acceptable to use global state. Other places where global state may be used are in caching, load balancing, and route mapping. In all these cases, information flows in one direction, and the singleton instance itself is immutable (it does not change). No part of the program attempts to make a change in the singleton, and as such there is no danger of one part of a project interfering with another part of the project because of the shared state.

There you have it—you have discovered your first design pattern, which is called the *Singleton Pattern.* Congratulations!

Exercises

- Implement your own logger singleton.

- How would you create a logger using the singleton pattern?

(Credit: Inspiration for the singleton pattern code template was sparked by the singleton pattern implementation on `http://python-3-patterns-idioms-test.readthedocs.io/en/latest/Singleton.html` CC-BY-SA.)

CHAPTER 3

The Prototype Pattern

Reality doesn't care if you believe in it.

—Boba Fett, StarWars extended universe

The Problem

I can still remember the very first time I wanted to program anything. This was at a time when DOS could not address more than 20 MB at a time, and thus our massive 40 MB hard drive had to be partitioned into two drives. It was a beige Olivetti XT. The local library had a section with computer books in it. One of them, a very thin softcover, had a picture of a game character on it. The title promised to teach you to program your very own games. In a classic case of youthful ignorance swayed by false advertising, I worked through every example, typing out the characters one by one (I could not read English at the time, so I really had no idea what I was doing). After about the tenth time, I got everything entered correctly into the GW Basic interface that came with the computer. I did not know about saving and loading programs, so every mistake meant starting from scratch. My crowning moment fell completely flat. The "game" I had worked so hard on turned out to be a simple `for` loop and an `if` statement. The premise of the game was that you were in a runaway car and got three chances to guess a number before the car ended up in a dam. That was it— no graphics, no sound, no pretty colors, just the same text question three times and then: "You are dead." Getting it right resulted in a simple message: "Yay! You got it right."

Beyond the First Steps

Even though my first program was a complete let-down, that magical moment when I picked up the book for the first time and believed that I could program a game, or anything I could dream of, stuck with me.

W. Badenhorst, *Practical Python Design Patterns*, https://doi.org/10.1007/978-1-4842-2680-3_3

I guess a lot of people first become interested in programming in some derivative of interest in games and the desire to program games. Sadly, games tend to be vast and complex systems, and making a game that will be fun and popular is a massive undertaking without any guarantees of success. In the end, relatively few programmers pursue their initial interest in game programming. In this chapter, we will imagine that we are indeed part of this select group of programmers.

Base for an Actual Game

Suppose we want to write an RTS (short for real-time strategy game) like *StarCraft*, where you have a player that controls a group of characters. The player needs to construct buildings, generate units, and ultimately meet some sort of strategic objective. Let's consider one unit, a *Knight*. The Knight is produced in a building called the *Barracks*. A player can have multiple such buildings in a single scenario so as to create knight units more rapidly.

Looking at this description of the unit and its interaction with the building, a fairly obvious solution would involve defining a `Barracks` class that has a `generate_knight` function that returns a `Knight` object, which is an instance of the `Knight` class. We will be implementing the following basic properties for the `Knight` class:

- Life
- Speed
- Attack power
- Attack range
- Weapon

Generating a new `Knight` instance would simply involve instantiating an object from the `Knight` class and setting the values.

Here is the code for doing exactly that:

rts_simple.py

```python
class Knight(object):
  def __init__(
    self,
    life,
```

```python
        speed,
        attack_power,
        attack_range,
        weapon
    ):
        self.life = life
        self.speed = speed
        self.attack_power = attack_power
        self.attack_range = attack_range
        self.weapon = weapon

    def __str__(self):
        return  "Life: {0}\n" \
                "Speed: {1}\n" \
                "Attack Power: {2}\n" \
                "Attack Range: {3}\n" \
                "Weapon: {4}".format(
        self.life,
        self.speed,
        self.attack_power,
        self.attack_range,
        self.weapon
        )

class Barracks(object):
    def generate_knight(self):
        return Knight(400, 5, 3, 1, "short sword")
if __name__ == "__main__":
    barracks = Barracks()
    knight1 = barracks.generate_knight()
    print("[knight1] {}".format(knight1))
```

Running this code from the command line will create a barracks instance of the Barracks class, and will then use that instance to generate knight1, which is just an instance of the Knight class with values set for the properties we defined in the previous section. Running the code prints the following text to the terminal so you can check that the knight instance matches what you expect it to be based on the values set in the generate_knight function.

```
[knight1] Life: 400
Speed: 5
Attack Power: 3
Attack Range: 1
Weapon: short sword
```

Even though we do not have any draw logic or interaction code, it is quite easy to generate a new knight with some default values. For the rest of this chapter, we will be concerning ourselves with this generation code and will see what it teaches us about creating multiple objects that are almost exactly alike.

Note   If you are interested in learning more about game programming, I challenge you to look at the PyGame package; see the "Exercises" section of this chapter for more information.

If you have never played or seen an RTS before, it is important to know that a big part of the fun in these games comes from the many different units you can generate. Each unit has its own strengths and weaknesses, and how you leverage these unique characteristics shapes the strategy you end up adopting. The better you are at understanding trade-offs, the better you become at developing effective strategies.

The next step is to add one more character to the cast that can be generated by a barracks. For example, I am going to add an Archer class, but feel free to add some of your own unit types, giving them unique strengths and weaknesses. You get to create your dream cast of units. While you are at it, feel free to think of other attributes your units will need to add depth to the game. When you are done with this chapter, go through the code you have written and add these ideas. Not only will it make your RTS more interesting, but it will also help you better grasp the arguments presented throughout the chapter.

With the addition of the Archer class, our rts_simple.py now looks like this:

rts_simple.py

```
class Knight(object):
  def __init__(
    self,
    life,
    speed,
```

```python
      attack_power,
      attack_range,
      weapon
    ):
      self.unit_type = "Knight"
      self.life = life
      self.speed = speed
      self.attack_power = attack_power
      self.attack_range = attack_range
      self.weapon = weapon

  def __str__(self):
    return  "Type: {0}\n" \
            "Life: {1}\n" \
            "Speed: {2}\n" \
            "Attack Power: {3}\n" \
            "Attack Range: {4}\n" \
            "Weapon: {5}".format(
      self.unit_type,
      self.life,
      self.speed,
      self.attack_power,
      self.attack_range,
      self.weapon
    )

class Archer(object):
  def __init__(
    self,
    life,
    speed,
    attack_power,
    attack_range,
    weapon
    ):
```

```
    self.unit_type = "Archer"
    self.life = life
    self.speed = speed
    self.attack_power = attack_power
    self.attack_range = attack_range
    self.weapon = weapon

  def __str__(self):
    return  "Type: {0}\n" \
            "Life: {1}\n" \
            "Speed: {2}\n" \
            "Attack Power: {3}\n" \
            "Attack Range: {4}\n" \
            "Weapon: {5}".format(
      self.unit_type,
      self.life,
      self.speed,
      self.attack_power,
      self.attack_range,
      self.weapon
    )

class Barracks(object):
  def generate_knight(self):
    return Knight(400, 5, 3, 1, "short sword")

  def generate_archer(self):
    return Archer(200, 7, 1, 5, "short bow")

if __name__ == "__main__":
  barracks = Barracks()  knight1 = barracks.generate_knight()
  archer1 = barracks.generate_archer()
  print("[knight1] {}".format(knight1))
  print("[archer1] {}".format(archer1))
```

Next, you will see the result of running this program. We now have a knight and an archer, each with its very own unique values for the unit attributes. Read through the code and try to understand what each line is doing before you continue to the explanation of the results.

```
[knight1] Type: Knight
Life: 400
Speed: 5
Attack Power: 3
Attack Range: 1
Weapon: short sword
[archer1] Type: Archer
Life: 200
Speed: 7
Attack Power: 1
Attack Range: 5
Weapon: short bow
```

At the moment, there are only the two units to think about, but since you already had a moment to contemplate all the other units you are going to add to your unit generator, it should be pretty clear that having a separate function for each type of unit you plan on generating in a specific building is not a great idea. To hammer this point home a bit, imagine what would happen if you wanted to upgrade the units that a barracks could generate. As an example, consider upgrading the Archer class so that the weapon it gets created with is no longer a short bow but rather a long bow, and its attack range is upped by five points along with a two-point increase in attack power. Suddenly, you double the number of functions needed in the Barracks class, and you need to keep some sort of record of the state of the barracks and the units that it can generate to make sure you generate the right level of unit.

Alarm bells should be going off by now.

There must be a better way to implement unit generation, one that is aware of not only the type of unit you want it to generate, but also of the level of the unit in question. One way to implement this would be to replace the individual generate_knight and generate_archer methods with one method called generate_unit. This method would take as its parameters the type of unit to be generated along with the level of unit you wanted it to generate. The single method would use this information to split out into the units to be created. We should also extend the individual unit classes to alter the parameters used for the different unit attributes, based on a level parameter passed to the constructor when the unit is instantiated.

Your upgraded unit-generation code would now look like this:

rts_multi_unit.py

```python
class Knight(object):
  def __init__(self, level):
    self.unit_type = "Knight"
    if level == 1:
      self.life = 400
      self.speed = 5
      self.attack_power = 3
      self.attack_range = 1
      self.weapon = "short sword"
    elif level == 2:
      self.life = 400
      self.speed = 5
      self.attack_power = 6
      self.attack_range = 2
      self.weapon = "long sword"

  def __str__(self):
    return "Type: {0}\n" \
           "Life: {1}\n" \
           "Speed: {2}\n" \
           "Attack Power: {3}\n" \
           "Attack Range: {4}\n" \
           "Weapon: {5}".format(
      self.unit_type,
      self.life,
      self.speed,
      self.attack_power,
      self.attack_range,
      self.weapon
    )

class Archer(object):
  def __init__(self, level):
    self.unit_type = "Archer"
```

```python
    if level == 1:
      self.life = 200
      self.speed = 7
      self.attack_power = 1
      self.attack_range = 5
      self.weapon = "short bow"
    elif level == 2:
      self.life = 200
      self.speed = 7
      self.attack_power = 3
      self.attack_range = 10
      self.weapon = "long bow"

  def __str__(self):
   return "Type: {0}\n" \
          "Life: {1}\n" \
          "Speed: {2}\n" \
          "Attack Power: {3}\n" \
          "Attack Range: {4}\n" \
          "Weapon: {5}".format(
      self.unit_type,
      self.life,
      self.speed,
      self.attack_power,
      self.attack_range,
      self.weapon
    )

class Barracks(object):
  def build_unit(self, unit_type, level):
    if unit_type == "knight":
      return Knight(level)
    elif unit_type == "archer":
      return Archer(level)

if __name__ == "__main__":
  barracks = Barracks()
```

```
knight1 = barracks.build_unit("knight", 1)
archer1 = barracks.build_unit("archer", 2)
print("[knight1] {}".format(knight1))
print("[archer1] {}".format(archer1))
```

In the results that follow, you will see that the code generates a level 1 knight and a level 2 archer, and their individual parameters match what you would expect them to be, without the need for the Barracks class to keep track of every level of every unit and the relevant parameters associated with them.

```
[knight1] Type: Knight
Life: 400
Speed: 5
Attack Power: 3
Attack Range: 1
Weapon: short sword
[archer1] Type: Archer
Life: 200
Speed: 7
Attack Power: 3
Attack Range: 10
Weapon: long bow
```

I like this implementation a little more than the previous one, as we have reduced the methods needed and isolated the unit-level parameters inside the unit class, where it makes more sense to have them.

In modern RTS games, balance is a big issue—one of the main challenges facing game designers. The idea behind game balance is that sometimes users find a way to exploit a specific unit's characteristics in such a way that it overpowers every other strategy or situation in the game. Even though that sounds like exactly the type of strategy you would want to find, this is actually a guarantee that players will lose interest in your game. Alternatively, some characters might suffer from a weakness that makes it practically useless for the game. In both these cases, the unit in question (or the game as a whole) is said to be imbalanced. A game designer wants to make alterations to the parameters of each unit (like attack power) in order to address these imbalances.

Digging through hundreds of thousands of lines of code to find values for the parameters of each class and alter them, especially if the developers must do that hundreds of times throughout the development lifecycle. Imagine what a mess digging through lines upon lines of code would be for a game like *Eve Online*, which relies heavily on its Python base for game logic.

We could store the parameters in a separate JSON file or a database to allow game designers to alter unit parameters in a single place. It would be easy to create a nice GUI (Graphical User Interface) for game designers where they could quickly and easily make changes without even having to alter the file in a text editor.

When we want to instantiate a unit, we load the relevant file or entry, extract the values we need, and create the instance as before, like this:

knight_1.dat
400
5
3
1
short sword
archer_1.dat
200
7
3
10
Long bow

rts_file_based.py

```python
class Knight(object):
  def __init__(self, level):
    self.unit_type = "Knight"

    filename = "{}_{}.dat".format(self.unit_type, level)

    with open(filename, 'r') as parameter_file:
      lines = parameter_file.read().split("\n")
      self.life = lines[0]
      self.speed = lines[1]
```

```python
        self.attack_power = lines[2]
        self.attack_range = lines[3]
        self.weapon = lines[4]

    def __str__(self):
        return  "Type: {0}\n" \
                "Life: {1}\n" \
                "Speed: {2}\n" \
                "Attack Power: {3}\n" \
                "Attack Range: {4}\n" \
                "Weapon: {5}".format(
            self.unit_type,
            self.life,
            self.speed,
            self.attack_power,
            self.attack_range,
            self.weapon
        )


class Archer(object):

    def __init__(self, level):
        self.unit_type = "Archer"

        filename = "{}_{}.dat".format(self.unit_type, level)

        with open(filename, 'r') as parameter_file:
            lines = parameter_file.read().split("\n")
            self.life = lines[0]
            self.speed = lines[1]
            self.attack_power = lines[2]
            self.attack_range = lines[3]
            self.weapon = lines[4]
```

```python
    def __str__(self):
        return "Type: {0}\n" \
               "Life: {1}\n" \
               "Speed: {2}\n" \
               "Attack Power: {3}\n" \
               "Attack Range: {4}\n" \
               "Weapon: {5}".format(
            self.unit_type,
            self.life,
            self.speed,
            self.attack_power,
            self.attack_range,
            self.weapon
        )

class Barracks(object):
    def build_unit(self, unit_type, level):
        if unit_type == "knight":
            return Knight(level)
        elif unit_type == "archer":
            return Archer(level)

if __name__ == "__main__":
    barracks = Barracks()
    knight1 = barracks.build_unit("knight", 1)
    archer1 = barracks.build_unit("archer", 2)
    print("[knight1] {}".format(knight1))
    print("[archer1] {}".format(archer1))
```

Since the unit data files store the data in a predictable order, it makes it very easy to grab the file from disk and then read in the parameters needed to construct the relevant unit. The code still delivers the same result as before, but now we are ready to balance many different unit types and levels. In our example, the import from file looks the same for both the Archer and Knight classes, but we must keep in mind that we will have units that have to import different parameters from their file, so a single import file would be impractical in a real-world scenario.

You can verify that your results match these results:

```
[knight1] Type: Knight
Life: 400
Speed: 5
Attack Power: 3
Attack Range: 1
Weapon: short sword
[archer1] Type: Archer
Life: 200
Speed: 7
Attack Power: 3
Attack Range: 10
Weapon: long bow
```

Players will be able to build multiple versions of the same building, as we discussed before, and we want the levels and types of units that a specific building can generate to change based on the level of the building. A level 1 barracks generates only level 1 knights, but once the barracks is upgraded to level 2, it unlocks the archer unit, and as an added bonus it now generates level 2 knights instead of the level 1 knights from before. Upgrading one building only has an effect on the units that it is able to generate, and not on the capabilities of all the buildings of the same type that the player built. We cannot simply keep track of a single instance of a unit; now every building needs to track its own version of the unit.

Every time a building wants to create a unit, it needs to look up what units it can create and then issue a command to create the selected unit. The unit class then has to query the storage system to find the relevant parameters, which are then read from storage before they are passed into the class constructor of the instance being created. This is all very inefficient. If one building has to generate 500 units of the same type, you have to make 499 duplicate requests of the storage system you chose. Multiply this by the number of buildings, and then add the lookups each building needs to do to decide which units it should be capable of generating. A massive game like *Eve Online*, or any other modern RTS for that matter, will kill your system in short order if it is required to go through this process every time it needs to generate a unit or build a building. Some games take this a step further by allowing specific add-ons on buildings that give units generated in that building different capabilities from the general unit type, which would make the system even more resource hungry.

What we have here is a very real need to create a large number of objects that are mostly the same, with one or two small tweaks differentiating them. Loading these objects from scratch every time is not a scalable solution, as we saw.

Which brings us to . . .

Implementing the Prototype Pattern

In the prototype pattern, we favor composition over inheritance. Classes that are composed of parts allow you to substitute those parts at runtime, profoundly affecting the testability and maintainability of the system. The classes to instantiate are specified at runtime by means of dynamic loading. The result of this characteristic of the prototype pattern is that sub-classing is reduced significantly. The complexities of creating a new instance are hidden from the client. All of this is great, but the main benefit of this pattern is that it forces you to program to an interface, which leads to better design.

Note   Just beware that deep-cloning classes with circular references can and will cause issues. See the next section for more information on shallow versus deep copy.

We simply want to make a copy of some object we have on hand. To make sure the copy is set up the way it should be, and to isolate the functionality of the object from the rest of the system, the instance you are going to copy should provide the copying feature. A clone() method on the instance that clones the object and then modifies its values accordingly would be ideal.

The three components needed for the prototype pattern are as follows:

- Client creates a new object by asking a prototype to clone itself

- Prototype declares an interface for cloning itself

- Concrete prototype implements the operation for cloning itself

(Credit for the tree components of the prototype pattern: http://radek.io/2011/08/03/design-pattern-prototype/)

In the RTS example, every building should keep a list of the prototypes it can use to generate units, like a list of units of the same level, with the properties to match the current state of the building. When a building is upgraded, this list is updated to match the new capabilities of the building. We get to remove the 499 redundant calls from the equation. This is also the point where the prototype design pattern deviates from the abstract factory design pattern, which we will look at later in this book. By swapping the prototypes that a building can use at runtime, we allow the building to dynamically switch to generating completely different units without any form of sub-classing of the building class in question. Our buildings effectively become prototype managers.

The idea of a prototype pattern is great, but we need to look at one more concept before we can implement the pattern in our buildings.

Shallow Copy vs. Deep Copy

Python handles variables a little differently than do other programming languages you may have come across. Apart from the basic types, like integers and strings, variables in Python are closer to tags or labels than to the buckets other programming languages use as a metaphor. The Python variables are essentially pointers to addresses in memory where the relevant values are stored.

Let's look at the following example:

```
a = range(1,6)
print("[a] {}".format(a))
b = a
print("[b] {}".format(b))
b.append(6)
print("[a] {}".format(a))
print("[b] {}".format(b))
```

The first statement points the variable a to a list of numbers from 1 to 6 (excluding 6). Next, variable b is assigned to the same list of numbers that a is pointing to. Finally, the digit 6 is added to the end of list pointed to by b.

What do you expect the results of the print statements to be? Look at the following output. Does it match what you expected?

```
[a] [1, 2, 3, 4, 5]
[b] [1, 2, 3, 4, 5]
[a] [1, 2, 3, 4, 5, 6]
[b] [1, 2, 3, 4, 5, 6]
```

Most people find it surprising that the digit 6 was appended to the end of both the list a points to and the list b points to. If you remember that in fact a and b point to the same list, it is clear that adding an element to the end of that list should show the element added to the end of the list no matter which variable you are looking at.

Shallow Copy

When we want to make an actual copy of the list, and have two independent lists at the end of the process, we need to use a different strategy.

Just as before, we are going to load the same digits into a list and point the variable a at the list. This time, we are going to use the *slice operator* to copy the list.

```
a = range(1,6)
print("[a] {}".format(a))
b = a[:]
print("[b] {}".format(b))
b.append(6)
print("[a] {}".format(a))
print("[b] {}".format(b))
```

The slice operator is a very useful tool, since it allows us to cut up a list (or string) in many different ways. Want to get all the elements from a list, while leaving out the first two elements? No problem—just slice the list with [2:]. What about all elements but the last two? Slice does that: [:-2]. You could even ask the slice operator to only give you every second element. I challenge you to figure out how that is done.

When we assigned b to a[:], we told b to point to a slice created by duplicating the elements in list a, from the first to the last element, effectively copying all the values in list a to another location in memory and pointing the variable b to this list.

Does the result you see surprise you?

```
[a] [1, 2, 3, 4, 5]
[b] [1, 2, 3, 4, 5]
[a] [1, 2, 3, 4, 5]
[b] [1, 2, 3, 4, 5, 6]
```

The slice operator works perfectly when dealing with a shallow list (a list containing only actual values, not references to other complex objects like lists or dictionaries).

Dealing with Nested Structures

Look at the code that follows. What do you think the result will be?

```
lst1 = ['a', 'b', ['ab', 'ba']]
lst2 = lst1[:]
lst2[0] = 'c'
print("[lst1] {}".format(lst1))
print("[lst2] {}".format(lst2))
```

Here, you see an example of a deep list. Take a look at the results—do they match what you predicted?

```
[lst1] ['a', 'b', ['ab', 'ba']]
[lst2] ['c', 'b', ['ab', 'ba']]
```

As you might have expected from the shallow copy example, altering the first element of lst2 does not alter the first element of lst1, but what happens when we alter one of the elements in the list within the list?

```
lst1 = ['a', 'b', ['ab', 'ba']]
lst2 = lst1[:]
lst2[2][1] = 'd'
print("[lst1] {}".format(lst1))
print("[lst2] {}".format(lst2))
```

Can you explain the results we get this time?

```
[lst1] ['a', 'b', ['ab', 'd']]
[lst2] ['a', 'b', ['ab', 'd']]
```

Were you surprised to see what happened?

The list lst1 contained three elements, 'a', 'b', and a pointer to another list that looked like this: ['ab', 'ba']. When we did a shallow copy of lst1 to create the list that lst2 points to, only the elements in the list on one level were duplicated. The structures contained at the addresses for the element at position 2 in lst1 were not cloned; only the value pointing to the position of the list ['ab', 'ba'] in memory was. As a result, both lst1 and lst2 ended up pointing to separate lists containing the characters 'a' and 'b' followed by a pointer to the same list containing ['ab', 'ba'], which would result in an issue whenever some function changes an element at this list, since it would have an effect on the contents of the other list.

Deep Copy

Clearly, we will need another solution when making clones of objects. How can we force Python to make a complete copy, a deep copy, of everything contained in the list and its sub-lists or objects? Luckily, we have the copy module as part of the standard library. The copy contains a method, deep-copy, that allows a complete deep copy of an arbitrary list; i.e., shallow and other lists. We will now use deep copy to alter the previous example so we get the output we expect.

```
from copy import deepcopy

lst1 = ['a', 'b', ['ab', 'ba']]
lst2 = deepcopy(lst1)
lst2[2][1] = 'd'
print("[lst1] {}".format(lst1))
print("[lst2] {}".format(lst2))
```

resulting in:

```
[lst1] ['a', 'b', ['ab', 'ba']]
[lst2] ['a', 'b', ['ab', 'd']]
```

There. Now we have the expected result, and after that fairly long detour, we are ready to see what this means for the buildings in our RTS.

Using What We Have Learned in Our Project

At its heart, the prototype pattern is just a clone() function that accepts an object as an input parameter and returns a clone of it.

The skeleton of a prototype pattern implementation should declare an abstract base class that specifies a pure virtual clone() method. Any class that needs a *polymorphic constructor* (the class decides which constructor to use based on the number of arguments it receives upon instantiation) capability derives itself from the abstract base class and implements the clone() method. Every unit needs to derive itself from this abstract base class. The client, instead of writing code that invokes the new operator on a hard-coded class name, calls the clone() method on the prototype.

This is what the prototype pattern would look like in general terms:

prototype_1.py

```
from abc import ABCMeta, abstractmethod

class Prototype(metaclass=ABCMeta):
  @abstractmethod
  def clone(self):
    pass
```

concrete.py

```
from prototype_1 import Prototype
from copy import deepcopy

class Concrete(Prototype):
  def clone(self):
    return deepcopy(self)
```

Finally, we can implement our unit-generating building with the prototype pattern, using the same prototype_1.py file.

rts_prototype.py

```
from prototype_1 import Prototype
from copy import deepcopy
```

```python
class Knight(Prototype):
  def __init__(self, level):
    self.unit_type = "Knight"

    filename = "{}_{}.dat".format(self.unit_type, level)

    with open(filename, 'r') as parameter_file:
      lines = parameter_file.read().split("\n")
      self.life = lines[0]
      self.speed = lines[1]
      self.attack_power = lines[2]
      self.attack_range = lines[3]
      self.weapon = lines[4]

  def __str__(self):
    return  "Type: {0}\n" \
            "Life: {1}\n" \
            "Speed: {2}\n" \
            "Attack Power: {3}\n" \
            "Attack Range: {4}\n" \
            "Weapon: {5}".format(
      self.unit_type,
      self.life,
      self.speed,
      self.attack_power,
      self.attack_range,
      self.weapon
    )

  def clone(self):
    return deepcopy(self)

class Archer(Prototype):

  def __init__(self, level):
    self.unit_type = "Archer"

    filename = "{}_{}.dat".format(self.unit_type, level)
```

```python
    with open(filename, 'r') as parameter_file:
      lines = parameter_file.read().split("\n")
      self.life = lines[0]
      self.speed = lines[1]
      self.attack_power = lines[2]
      self.attack_range = lines[3]
      self.weapon = lines[4]

  def __str__(self):
    return  "Type: {0}\n" \
            "Life: {1}\n" \
            "Speed: {2}\n" \
            "Attack Power: {3}\n" \
            "Attack Range: {4}\n" \
            "Weapon: {5}".format(
      self.unit_type,
      self.life,
      self.speed,
      self.attack_power,
      self.attack_range,
      self.weapon
    )

  def clone(self):
    return deepcopy(self)

class Barracks(object):
  def __init__(self):
    self.units = {
      "knight": {
        1: Knight(1),
        2: Knight(2)
      },
      "archer": {
        1: Archer(1),
        2: Archer(2)
      }
    }
```

```
  def build_unit(self, unit_type, level):
    return self.units[unit_type][level].clone()

if __name__ == "__main__":
  barracks = Baracks()
  knight1 = barracks.build_unit("knight", 1)
  archer1 = barracks.build_unit("archer", 2)
  print("[knight1] {}".format(knight1))
  print("[archer1] {}".format(archer1))
```

When we extended the abstract base class in the unit classes, that forced us to implement the clone method, which we used when we had the barracks generate new units. The other thing we did was generate all the options that a Barracks instance can generate and keep it in a unit's array. Now, we can simply clone the unit with the right level without opening a file or loading any data from an external source.

```
[knight1] Type: Knight
Life: 400
Speed: 5
Attack Power: 3
Attack Range: 1
Weapon: short sword
[archer1] Type: Archer
Life: 200
Speed: 7
Attack Power: 3
Attack Range: 10
Weapon: long bow
```

Well done; you have not only taken your first steps to creating your very own RTS, but you have also dug deeply into a very useful design pattern.

Exercises

- Take the prototype example code and extend the Archer class to handle its upgrades.

- Experiment with adding more units to the barracks building.

- Add a second type of building.

- Take a look at the PyGame package (`http://pygame.org/hifi.html`). How can you extend your `Knight` class so it can draw itself in a game loop?

- As an exercise, you can look at the PyGame package and implement a `draw()` method for the `Knight` class to be able to draw it on a map.

- If you are interested, try to write your own mini RTS game with a barracks and two units using PyGame.

- Extend the `clone` method of each unit to generate a random name, so each cloned unit will have a different name.

CHAPTER 4

Factory Pattern

Quality means doing it right when no one is looking.

—Henry Ford

In Chapter 3, you started thinking about writing your own game. To make sure you don't feel duped by a text-only "game," let's take a moment and look at drawing something on the screen. In this chapter, we will touch on the basics of graphics using Python. We will use the PyGame package as our weapon of choice. We will be creating factory classes. Factory classes define objects that take a certain set of parameters and use that to create objects of some other class. We will also define abstract factory classes that serve as the template used to build these factory classes.

Getting Started

In a virtual environment, you can use pip to install PyGame by using this command:

```
pip install pygame
```

This should be fairly painless. Now, to get an actual window to work with:

graphic_base.py

```
import pygame

pygame.init()
screen = pygame.display.set_mode((800, 600))
```

Save graphic_base.py and run the file:

```
python graphic_base.py
```

A blank window that is 400 pixels wide and 300 pixels high will pop up on your screen and immediately vanish again. Congratulations, you have created your first

© Wessel Badenhorst 2017
W. Badenhorst, *Practical Python Design Patterns*, https://doi.org/10.1007/978-1-4842-2680-3_4

screen. Obviously, we want the screen to stay up a little longer, so let's just add a sleep function to graphic_base.py.

graphic_base.py

```
import pygame
from time import sleep

pygame.init()
screen = pygame.display.set_mode((800, 600))

sleep(10)
```

From the time package (part of the standard library) we import the sleep function, which suspends execution for a given number of seconds. A ten-second sleep was added to the end of the script, which keeps the window open for ten seconds before the script completes execution and the window vanishes.

I was very excited when I created a window on screen the first time, but when I called my roommate over to show him my window, he was completely underwhelmed. I suggest you add something to the window before showing off your new creation. Extend graphic_base.py to add a square to the window.

graphic_base.py

```
import pygame
import time

pygame.init()
screen = pygame.display.set_mode((800,600))

pygame.draw.rect(screen, (255, 0, 34), pygame.Rect(42, 15, 40, 32))
pygame.display.flip()

time.sleep(10)
```

The pygame.draw.rect function draws a rectangle to the screen variable that points to your window. The second parameter is a tuple containing the color used to fill the shape, and, lastly, the pygame rectangle is passed in with the coordinates of the top left and bottom right corners. The three values you see in the color tuple make up what is known as the RGB value (for Red Green Blue), and each component is a value out of 255, which indicates the intensity of the component color in the final color mix.

If you leave out the `pygame.display.flip()`, no shape is displayed. This is because PyGame draws the screen on a memory buffer and then flips the whole image onto the active screen (which is what you see). Every time you update the display, you have to call `pygame.display.flip()` to have the changes show up on the screen.

Experiment with drawing different rectangles in many colors on screen.

The Game Loop

The most basic concept in game programming is called the *game loop*. The idea works like this: the game checks for some input from the user, who does some calculation to update the state of the game, and then gives some feedback to the player. In our case, we will just be updating what the player sees on the screen, but you could include sound or haptic feedback. This happens over and over until the player quits. Every time the screen is updated, we run the `pygame.display.flip()` function to show the updated display to the player.

The basic structure for a game will then be as follows:

- Some initialization occurs, such as setting up the window and initial position and color of the elements on the screen.

- While the user does not quit the game, run the game loop.

- When the user quits, terminate the window.

In code, it could look something like this:

graphic_base.py

```python
import pygame

window_dimensions = 800, 600
screen = pygame.display.set_mode(window_dimensions)

player_quits = False

while not player_quits:
  for event in pygame.event.get():
    if event.type == pygame.QUIT:
      player_quits = True

  pygame.display.flip()
```

At the moment, this code does nothing but wait for the player to click the Close button on the window and then terminate execution. To make this more interactive, let's add a small square and have it move when the user presses one of the arrow keys.

For this, we will need to draw the square on the screen in its initial position, ready to react to arrow key events.

shape_game.py (see ch04_03.py)

```python
import pygame

window_dimensions = 800, 600
screen = pygame.display.set_mode(window_dimensions)

x = 100
y = 100

player_quits = False

while not player_quits:
    for event in pygame.event.get():
        if event.type == pygame.QUIT:
            player_quits = True

        pressed = pygame.key.get_pressed()
        if pressed[pygame.K_UP]: y -= 4
        if pressed[pygame.K_DOWN]: y += 4
        if pressed[pygame.K_LEFT]: x -= 4
        if pressed[pygame.K_RIGHT]: x += 4

        screen.fill((0, 0, 0))
        pygame.draw.rect(screen, (255, 255, 0), pygame.Rect(x, y, 20, 20))

    pygame.display.flip()
```

Play around with the code for a bit to see if you can get the block to not move out of the boundaries of the window.

Now that your block can move around the screen, how about doing all of this for a circle? And then for a triangle. And now for a game character icon. . . You get the picture; suddenly, there is a lot of display code clogging up the game loop. What if we cleaned this up a bit using an object-oriented approach to the situation?

shape_game.py

```python
import pygame

class Shape(object):
    def __init__(self, x, y):
        self.x = x
        self.y = y

    def draw(self):
        raise NotImplementedError()

    def move(self, direction):
        if direction == 'up':
            self.y -= 4
        elif direction == 'down':
            self.y += 4
        elif direction == 'left':
            self.x -= 4
        elif direction == 'right':
            self.x += 4

class Square(Shape):
    def draw(self):
        pygame.draw.rect(
            screen,
            (255, 255, 0),
            pygame.Rect(self.x, self.y, 20, 20)
        )

class Circle(Shape):
    def draw(self):
        pygame.draw.circle(
            screen,
            (0, 255, 255),
            (selfx, self.y),
            10
        )
```

```python
if __name__ == '__main__':
    window_dimensions = 800, 600
    screen = pygame.display.set_mode(window_dimensions)

    square = Square(100, 100)
    obj = square

    player_quits = False

    while not player_quits:
        for event in pygame.event.get():
            if event.type == pygame.QUIT:
                player_quits = True

            pressed = pygame.key.get_pressed()
            if pressed[pygame.K_UP]: obj.move('up')
            if pressed[pygame.K_DOWN]: obj.move('down')
            if pressed[pygame.K_LEFT]: obj.move('left')
            if pressed[pygame.K_RIGHT]: obj.move('right')

            screen.fill((0, 0, 0))
            obj.draw()

        pygame.display.flip()
```

Since you now have the circle and square objects available, think about how you would go about altering the program so that when you press the "C" key the object on screen turns into a circle (if it is not currently one). Similarly, when you press the "S" key the shape should change to a square. See how much easier it is to use the objects than it is to handle all of this inside the game loop.

Tip   Look at the keybindings for PyGame together with the code in this chapter.

There is still an improvement or two we could implement, such as abstracting things like move and draw that have to happen with each class so we do not have to keep track of what shape we are dealing with. We want to be able to refer to the shape in general and just tell it to draw itself without worrying about what shape it is (or if it is a shape, to begin with, and not some image or even a frame of animation).

Clearly, polymorphism is not a complete solution, since we would have to keep updating code whenever we create a new object, and in a large game this will happen in many places. The issue is the creation of the new types and not the use of these types.

Since you want to write better code, think about the following characteristics of good code as you try to come up with a better way of handling the expansion we want to add to our shapeshifter game.

Good code is

- easy to maintain,

- easy to update,

- easy to extend, and

- clear in what it is trying to accomplish.

Good code should make working on something you wrote a couple of weeks back as painless as possible. The last thing you want is to create these areas in your code you dread working on.

We want to be able to create objects through a common interface rather than spreading the creation code throughout the system. This localizes the code that needs to change when you update the types of shapes that can be created. Since adding new types is the most likely addition you will make to the system, it makes sense that this is one of the areas you have to look at first in terms of code improvement.

One way of creating a centralized system of object creation is by using the factory pattern. This pattern has two distinct approaches, and we will cover both, starting with the simpler factory method and then moving on to the abstract factory implementation. We will also look at how you could implement each of these in terms of our game skeleton.

Before we get into the weeds with the factory pattern, I want you to take note of the fact that there is one main difference between the prototype pattern and the factory pattern. The prototype pattern does not require sub-classing, but requires an `initialize` operation, whereas the factory pattern requires sub-classing but not initialization. Each of these has its own advantages and places where you should opt for one over the other, and over the course of this chapter this distinction should become clearer.

The Factory Method

When we want to call a method such that we pass in a string and get as a return value a *new object*, we are essentially calling a *factory method*. The type of the object is determined by the string that is passed to the method.

This makes it easy to extend the code you write by allowing you to add functionality to your software, which is accomplished by adding a new class and extending the factory method to accept a new string and return the class you created.

Let's look at a simple implementation of the factory method.

shape_factory.py

```python
import pygame

class Shape(object):
  def __init__(self, x, y):
      self.x = x
      self.y = y

  def draw(self):
      raise NotImplementedError()

  def move(self, direction):
      if direction == 'up':
          self.y -= 4
      elif direction == 'down':
          self.y += 4
      elif direction == 'left':
          self.x -= 4
      elif direction == 'right':
          self.x += 4

  @staticmethod
  def factory(type):
    if type == "Circle":
      return Circle(100, 100)
    if type == "Square":
      return Square(100, 100)
```

```python
        assert 0, "Bad shape requested: " + type

class Square(Shape):
    def draw(self):
        pygame.draw.rect(
            screen,
            (255, 255, 0),
            pygame.Rect(self.x, self.y, 20, 20)
        )

class Circle(Shape):
    def draw(self):
        pygame.draw.circle(
            screen,
            (0, 255, 255),
            (selfx, self.y),
            10
        )

if __name__ == '__main__':
    window_dimensions = 800, 600
    screen = pygame.display.set_mode(window_dimensions)

    obj = Shape.factory("square")

    player_quits = False

    while not player_quits:
        for event in pygame.event.get():
            if event.type == pygame.QUIT:
                player_quits = True

            pressed = pygame.key.get_pressed()
            if pressed[pygame.K_UP]: obj.move('up')
            if pressed[pygame.K_DOWN]: obj.move('down')
            if pressed[pygame.K_LEFT]: obj.move('left')
            if pressed[pygame.K_RIGHT]: obj.move('right')
```

```
        screen.fill((0, 0, 0))
        obj.draw()

    pygame.display.flip()
```

How much easier would it be to adapt this piece of code above to change from a square to a circle, or to any other shape or image you might want?

Some advocates of the factory method suggest that all constructors should be private or protected since it should not matter to the user of the class whether a new object is created or an old one recycled. The idea is that you decouple the request for an object from its creation.

This idea should not be followed as dogma, but try it out in one of your own projects and see what benefits you derive from it. Once you are comfortable with using factory methods, and possibly factory patterns, you are free to use your own discretion in terms of the usefulness of the pattern in the project at hand.

Whenever you add to your game a new class that needs to be drawn on the screen, you simply need to change the `factory()` method.

What happens when we need different kinds of factories? Maybe you would like to add sound effect factories or environmental elements versus player characters factories? You want to be able to create different types of factory sub-classes from the same basic factory.

The Abstract Factory

When you want to create a single interface to access an entire collection of factories, you can confidently reach for an abstract factory. Each abstract factory in the collection needs to implement a predefined interface, and each function on that interface returns another abstract type, as per the factory method pattern.

```
import abc

class AbstractFactory(object):
    __metaclass__ = abc.ABCMeta

    @abc.abstractmethod
    def make_object(self):
        return
```

```python
class CircleFactory(AbstractFactory):
  def make_object(self):
    # do something
    return Circle()

class SquareFactory(AbstractFactory):
  def make_object(self):
    # do something
    return Square()
```

Here, we used the built-in abc module, which lets you define an abstract base class. The abstract factory defines the blueprint for defining the concrete factories that then create circles and squares in this example.

Python is dynamically typed, so you do not need to define the common base class. If we were to make the code more pythonic, we would be looking at something like this:

```python
class CircleFactory(AbstractFactory):
  def make_object(self):
    # do something
    return Circle()

class SquareFactory(AbstractFactory):
  def make_object(self):
    # do something
    return Square()

def draw_function(factory):
  drawable = factory.make_object()
  drawable.draw()

def prepare_client():
  squareFactory = SquareFactory()
  draw_function(squareFactory)

  circleFactory = CircleFactory()
  draw_function(circleFactory)
```

In the barebones game we have set up so far, you could imagine the factory generating objects that contain a `play()` method, which you could run in the game loop to play sounds, calculate moves, or draw shapes and images on the screen. Another popular use for abstract factories is to create factories for the GUI elements of different operating systems. All of them use the same basic functions, but the factory that gets created gets selected based on the operating system the program is running on.

Congratulations! You just leveled up your ability to write great code. Using abstract factories, you can write code that is easier to modify, and code that can be tested easily.

Summary

When developing software, you want to guard against the nagging feeling that you should build something that will be able to cater to every possible future eventuality. Although it is good to think about the future of your software, it is often an exercise in futility to try to build a piece of software that is so generic that it will solve every possible future requirement. The simplest reason for this is that there is no way to envision where your software will go. I'm not saying you should be naive and not consider the immediate future of your code, but being able to evolve your code to incorporate new functionality is one of the most valuable skills you will learn as a software developer. There is always the temptation to throw out all the old code you have previously written and start from scratch to "do it right." That is a dream, and as soon as you "do it right" you will learn something new that will make your code look less than pretty, and so you will have to redo everything again, never finishing anything.

The general principle is YAGNI; you will probably come across this acronym in your career as a software developer. What does it mean? *You ain't gonna need it!* It is the principle that you should write code that solves the current problem well, and only when needed alter it to solve subsequent problems.

This is why many software designs start out using the simpler factory method, and only once the developer discovers where more flexibility is needed does he evolve the program to use the abstract factory, prototype, or builder patterns.

Exercises

- Add the functionality to switch between a circle, triangle, and square via key press.

- Try to implement an image object instead of just a shape.

- Enhance your image object class to switch between separate images to be drawn when moving up, down, left, and right, respectively.

- As a challenge, try to add animation to the image when moving.

CHAPTER 5

Builder Pattern

Can he fix it? Yes, he can!

—"Bob the Builder" Theme Song

If you work in software for any amount of time, you will have to deal with getting input from the user—anything from having a player enter their character name in a game to adding data to the cells on a spreadsheet. Forms are often the heart of an application. Actually, most applications are just a special case of the input, transform, and feedback flow of information. There are many input widgets and interfaces, but the most common remain the following:

- Text boxes

- Dropdown and Select lists

- Checkboxes

- Radio buttons

- File upload fields

- Buttons

These can be mixed and matched in many different ways to take different types of data as input from the user. What we are interested in for this chapter is how we can write a script that could ease the effort of generating these forms. For our use case, we will be generating HTML webforms, but the same technology can be used, with a couple of tweaks, to generate mobile app interfaces, JSON or XML representations of the form, or whatever else you can dream up. Let's begin by writing a simple function that will generate a little form for us.

© Wessel Badenhorst 2017
W. Badenhorst, *Practical Python Design Patterns*, https://doi.org/10.1007/978-1-4842-2680-3_5

basic_form_generator.py

```python
def generate_webform(field_list):
    generated_fields = "\n".join(
        map(
            lambda x: '{0}:<br><input type="text" name="{0}"><br>'.format(x),
            field_list
        )
    )
    return "<form>{fields}</form>".format(fields=generated_fields)

if __name__ == "__main__":
    fields = ["name", "age", "email", "telephone"]
    print(generate_webform(fields))
```

In this simplistic example, the code assumes that the list of fields contains only text fields. The field name is contained in the list as a string. The strings in the list are also the labels used in the form that is returned. For every element in the list, a single field is added to the webform. The webform is then returned as a string containing the HTML code for the generated webform.

If we go one step further, we could have a script take the generated response and build a regular HTML file from it, one you could open in your web browser.

html_form_generator.py

```python
def generate_webform(field_list):
    generated_fields = "\n".join(
        map(
            lambda x: '{0}:<br><input type="text" name="{0}"><br>'.format(x),
            field_list
        )
    )
    return "<form>{fields}</form>".format(fields=generated_fields)

def build_html_form(fields):
    with open("form_file.html", w) as f:
        f.write(
            "<html><body>{}</body></html>".format(generate_webform(fields))
        )
```

```
if __name__ == "__main__":
    fields = ["name", "age", "email", "telephone"]
    build_html_form(fields)
```

As I mentioned in the beginning of this chapter, webforms (and forms in general) could have many more field types than simple text fields. We could add more field types to the form using named parameters. Look at the following code, where we will add checkboxes.

html_form_generator.py

```
def generate_webform(text_field_list=[], checkbox_field_list=[]):
    generated_fields = "\n".join(
        map(
            lambda x: '{0}:<br><input type="text" name="{0}"><br>'.format(x),
            text_field_list
        )
    )

    generated_fields += "\n".join(
        map(
            lambda x: '<label><input type="checkbox" id="{0}" value="{0}">
            {0}<br>'.format(x),
            checkbox_field_list
        )
    )

    return "<form>{fields}</form>".format(fields=generated_fields)


def build_html_form(text_field_list=[], checkbox_field_list=[]):
    with open("form_file.html", 'w') as f:
        f.write(
            "<html><body>{}</body></html>".format(
                generate_webform(
                    text_field_list=text_field_list,
                    checkbox_field_list=checkbox_field_list
                )
            )
        )
```

```python
if __name__ == "__main__":
    text_fields = ["name", "age", "email", "telephone"]
    checkbox_fields = ["awesome", "bad"]
    build_html_form(text_field_list=text_fields, checkbox_field_list=checkbox_
    fields)
```

There are clear issues with this approach, the first of which is the fact that we cannot deal with fields that have different defaults or options or in fact any information beyond a simple label or field name. We cannot even cater for a difference between the field name and the label used in the form. We are now going to extend the functionality of the form-generator function so we can cater for a large number of field types, each with its own settings. We also have the issue that there is no way to interleave different types of fields. To show you how this would work, we are ripping out the named parameters and replacing them with a list of dictionaries. The function will look in each dictionary in the list and then use the contained information to generate the field as defined in the dictionary.

html_dictionary_form_generator.py

```python
def generate_webform(field_dict_list):
    generated_field_list = []

    for field_dict in field_dict_list:
        if field_dict["type"] == "text_field":
            generated_field_list.append(
                '{0}:<br><input type="text" name="{1}"><br>'.format(
                    field_dict["label"],
                    field_dict["name"]
                )
            )
        elif field_dict["type"] == "checkbox":
            generated_field_list.append(
                '<label><input type="checkbox" id="{0}" value="{1}">
                {2}<br>'.format(
                    field_dict["id"],
                    field_dict["value"],
                    field_dict["label"]
                )
            )
```

```python
    generated_fields = "\n".join(generated_field_list)

    return "<form>{fields}</form>".format(fields=generated_fields)

def build_html_form(field_list):
    with open("form_file.html", 'w') as f:
        f.write(
            "<html><body>{}</body></html>".format(
                generate_webform(field_list)
            )
        )

if __name__ == "__main__":
    field_list = [
        {
        "type": "text_field",
        "label": "Best text you have ever written",
        "name": "best_text"
        },
        {
        "type": "checkbox",
        "id": "check_it",
        "value": "1",
        "label": "Check for one",
        },
        {
        "type": "text_field",
        "label": "Another Text field",
        "name": "text_field2"
        }
    ]

    build_html_form(field_list)
```

The dictionary contains a type field, which is used to select which type of field to add. Then, you have some optional elements as part of the dictionary, like label, name, and options (in the case of a select list). You could use this as a base to create a form generator that would generate any form you could imagine. By now you should be picking up a bad smell. Stacking loops and conditional statements inside and on top of each other quickly becomes unreadable and unmaintainable. Let's clean up the code a bit.

We are going to take the meat of each field's generation code and place that into a separate function that takes the dictionary and returns a snippet of HTML code that represents that field. The key in this step is to clean up the code without changing any of the functionality, input, or output of the main function.

cleaned_html_dictionary_form_generator.py

```python
def generate_webform(field_dict_list):
    generated_field_list = []

    for field_dict in field_dict_list:
        if field_dict["type"] == "text_field":
            field_html = generate_text_field(field_dict)
        elif field_dict["type"] == "checkbox":
            field_html = generate_checkbox(field_dict)

        generated_field_list.append(field_html)

    generated_fields = "\n".join(generated_field_list)

    return "<form>{fields}</form>".format(fields=generated_fields)

def generate_text_field(text_field_dict):
    return '{0}:<br><input type="text" name="{1}"><br>'.format(
        text_field_dict["label"],
        text_field_dict["name"]
    )

def generate_checkbox(checbox_dict):
    return '<label><input type="checkbox" id="{0}" value="{1}"> {2}<br>'.
    format(
        checkbox_dict["id"],
        checkbox_dict["value"],
        checkbox_dict["label"]
    )
```

```python
def build_html_form(field_list):
    with open("form_file.html", 'w') as f:
        f.write(
            "<html><body>{}</body></html>".format(
                generate_webform(field_list)
            )
        )

if __name__ == "__main__":
    field_list = [
        {
        "type": "text_field",
        "label": "Best text you have ever written",
        "name": "best_text"
        },
        {
        "type": "checkbox",
        "id": "check_it",
        "value": "1",
        "label": "Check for one",
        },
        {
        "type": "text_field",
        "label": "Another Text field",
        "name": "text_field2"
        }
    ]

    build_html_form(field_list)
```

The if statements are still there, but at least now the code is a little cleaner. These sprawling if statements will keep growing as we add more field types to the form generator. Let's try to better the situation by using an object-oriented approach. We could use polymorphism to deal with some of the specific fields and the issues we are having in generating them.

oop_html_form_generator.py

```python
class HtmlField(object):
    def __init__(self, **kwargs):
        self.html = ""

        if kwargs['field_type'] == "text_field":
            self.html = self.construct_text_field(kwargs["label"],
            kwargs["field_name"])

        elif kwargs['field_type'] == "checkbox":
            self.html = self.construct_checkbox(kwargs["field_id"],
            kwargs["value"], kwargs["label"])

    def construct_text_field(self, label, field_name):
        return '{0}:<br><input type="text" name="{1}"><br>'.format(
            label,
            field_name
        )

    def construct_checkbox(self, field_id, value, label):
        return '<label><input type="checkbox" id="{0}" value="{1}">
        {2}<br>'.format(
            field_id,
            value,
            label
            )

    def __str__(self):
        return self.html

def generate_webform(field_dict_list):
    generated_field_list = []
    for field in field_dict_list:
        try:
            generated_field_list.append(str(HtmlField(**field)))
        except Exception as e:
            print("error: {}".format(e))
```

```python
    generated_fields = "\n".join(generated_field_list)

    return "<form>{fields}</form>".format(fields=generated_fields)

def build_html_form(field_list):
    with open("form_file.html", 'w') as f:
        f.write(
            "<html><body>{}</body></html>".format(
                generate_webform(field_list)
            )
        )

if __name__ == "__main__":
    field_list = [
        {
            "field_type": "text_field",
            "label": "Best text you have ever written",
            "field_name": "Field One"
        },
        {
            "field_type": "checkbox",
            "field_id": "check_it",
            "value": "1",
            "label": "Check for on",
        },
        {
            "field_type": "text_field",
            "label": "Another Text field",
            "field_name": "Field One"
        }
    ]

    build_html_form(field_list)
```

For every alternative set of parameters, we need another constructor, so our code very quickly breaks down and becomes a mess of constructors, which is commonly known as the telescoping constructor anti-pattern. Like design patterns, anti-patterns are mistakes you will see regularly due to the nature of the software design and development process in the real world. With some languages, like Java, you can overload the constructor with many different options in terms of the parameters accepted and what is then constructed in turn. Also, notice that the `if` conditional in the constructor `__init__()` could be defined more clearly.

I'm sure you have a lot of objections to this implementation, and you should. Before we clean it up a little more, we are going to quickly look at anti-patterns.

Anti-Patterns

An anti-pattern is, as the name suggests, the opposite of a software pattern. It is also something that appears regularly in the process of software development. Anti-patterns are usually a general way to work around or attempt to solve a specific type of problem, but are also the wrong way to solve the problem. This does not mean that design patterns are always the right way. What it means is that our goal is to write clean code that is easy to debug, easy to update, and easy to extend. Anti-patterns lead to code that is exactly the opposite of these stated goals. They produce bad code.

The problem with the telescoping constructor anti-pattern is that it results in several constructors, each with a specific number of parameters, all of which then delegate to a default constructor (if the class is properly written).

The builder pattern does not use numerous constructors; it uses a builder object instead. This builder object receives each initialization parameter step by step and then returns the resulting constructed object as a single result. In the webform example, we want to add the different fields and get the generated webform as a result. An added benefit of the builder pattern is that it separates the construction of an object from the way the object is represented, so we could change the representation of the object without changing the process by which it is constructed.

In the builder pattern, the two main players are the `Builder` and the `Director`.

The `Builder` is an abstract class that knows how to build all the components of the final object. In our case, the `Builder` class will know how to build each of the field types. It can assemble the various parts into a complete form object.

The `Director` controls the process of building. There is an instance (or instances) of `Builder` that the `Director` uses to build the webform. The output from the `Director` is a fully initialized object—the webform, in our example. The `Director` implements the set of instructions for setting up a webform from the fields it contains. This set of instructions is independent of the types of the individual fields passed to the director.

A generic implementation of the builder pattern in Python looks like this:

form_builder.py

```python
from abc import ABCMeta, abstractmethod

class Director(object, metaclass=ABCMeta):

    def __init__(self):
        self._builder = None

    @abstractmethod
    def construct(self):
        pass

    def get_constructed_object(self):
        return self._builder.constructed_object

class Builder(object, metaclass=ABCMeta):

    def __init__(self, constructed_object):
        self.constructed_object = constructed_object

class Product(object):
    def __init__(self):
        pass

    def __repr__(self):
        pass

class ConcreteBuilder(Builder):
    pass

class ConcreteDirector(Director):
    pass
```

You see we have an abstract class, `Builder`, which forms the interface for creating objects (product). Then, the `ConcreteBuilder` provides an implementation for `Builder`. The resulting object is able to construct other objects.

Using the builder pattern, we can now redo our webform generator.

```python
from abc import ABCMeta, abstractmethod

class Director(object, metaclass=ABCMeta):

    def __init__(self):
        self._builder = None

    def set_builder(self, builder):
        self._builder = builder

    @abstractmethod
    def construct(self, field_list):
        pass

    def get_constructed_object(self):
        return self._builder.constructed_object

class AbstractFormBuilder(object, metaclass=ABCMeta):

    def __init__(self):
        self.constructed_object = None

    @abstractmethod
    def add_text_field(self, field_dict):
        pass

    @abstractmethod
    def add_checkbox(self, checkbox_dict):
        pass

    @abstractmethod
    def add_button(self, button_dict):
        pass

class HtmlForm(object):
    def __init__(self):
        self.field_list = []
```

```python
    def __repr__(self):
        return "<form>{}</form>".format("".join(self.field_list))

class HtmlFormBuilder(AbstractFormBuilder):

    def __init__(self):
        self.constructed_object = HtmlForm()

    def add_text_field(self, field_dict):
        self.constructed_object.field_list.append(
            '{0}:<br><input type="text" name="{1}"><br>'.format(
                field_dict['label'],
                field_dict['field_name']
            )
        )

    def add_checkbox(self, checkbox_dict):
        self.constructed_object.field_list.append(
            '<label><input type="checkbox" id="{0}" value="{1}"> {2}<br>'.
            format(
                checkbox_dict['field_id'],
                checkbox_dict['value'],
                checkbox_dict['label']
            )
        )

    def add_button(self, button_dict):
        self.constructed_object.field_list.append(
            '<button type="button">{}</button>'.format(
                button_dict['text']
            )
        )

class FormDirector(Director):

    def __init__(self):
        Director.__init__(self)
```

```python
    def construct(self, field_list):
        for field in field_list:
            if field["field_type"] == "text_field":
                self._builder.add_text_field(field)
            elif field["field_type"] == "checkbox":
                self._builder.add_checkbox(field)
            elif field["field_type"] == "button":
                self._builder.add_button(field)

if __name__ == "__main__":
    director = FormDirector()
    html_form_builder = HtmlFormBuilder()
    director.set_builder(html_form_builder)

    field_list = [
        {
            "field_type": "text_field",
            "label": "Best text you have ever written",
            "field_name": "Field One"
        },
        {
            "field_type": "checkbox",
            "field_id": "check_it",
            "value": "1",
            "label": "Check for on",
        },
        {
            "field_type": "text_field",
            "label": "Another Text field",
            "field_name": "Field One"
        },
        {
            "field_type": "button",
            "text": "DONE"
        }
    ]
```

```
    director.construct(field_list)

    with open("form_file.html", 'w') as f:
        f.write(
            "<html><body>{0!r}</body></html>".format(
                director.get_constructed_object()
            )
        )
```

Our new script can only build forms with text fields, checkboxes, and a basic button. You can add more field types as an exercise.

One of the `ConcreteBuilder` classes has the logic needed for the creation of the webform you want. `Director` calls the `create()` method. In this way, the logic for creating different kinds of products gets abstracted. Note how the builder pattern focuses on building the form step by step. This is in stark contrast to the abstract factory, where a family of products can be created and returned immediately using polymorphism.

Since the builder pattern separates the construction of a complex object from its representation, you can now use the same construction process to create forms in different representations, from native app interface code to a simple text field.

An added benefit of this separation is a reduction in object size, which leads to cleaner code. We have better control over the construction process and the modular nature allow us to easily make changes to the internal representation of objects.

The biggest downside is that this pattern requires that we create `ConcreteBuilder` builders for each type of product that you want to create.

So, when should you *not* use the builder pattern? When you are constructing mutable objects that provide a means of modifying the configuration values after the object has been constructed. You should also avoid this pattern if there are very few constructors, the constructors are simple, or there are no reasonable default values for any of the constructor parameters and all of them must be specified explicitly.

A Note on Abstraction

When we talk about abstraction, in the most basic terms we refer to the process of associating names to things. Machine code is abstracted in C using labels for the Machine instructions, which are a set of hexadecimal instructions, which in turn is an abstraction of the actual binary numbers in the machine. With Python, we have a further level of abstraction in terms of objects and functions (even though C also has functions and libraries).

Exercises

- Implement a radio group generation function as part of your form builder.

- Extend the form builder to handle post-submit data and save the incoming information in a dictionary.

- Implement a version of the form builder that uses a database table schema to build a form interface to the database table.

- Code up an admin interface generator that auto-generates forms to deal with information to and from a database. You can pass a schema in as a string to the form builder and then have it return the HTML for the form, plus some submit URL.

- Extend the form builder so you have two new objects, one to create an XML version of the form and another to generate a JSON object containing the form information.

CHAPTER 6

Adapter Pattern

It is not the strongest of the species that survives, nor the most intelligent.
It is the one that is most adaptable to change.

—Charles Darwin

Sometimes you do not have the interface you would like to connect to. There could be many reasons for this, but in this chapter, we will concern ourselves with what we can do to change what we are given into something that is closer to what we would like to have.

Let's say you want to build your own marketing software. You begin by writing some code to send emails. In the larger system, you might make a call like this:

send_email.py

```python
import smtplib
from email.mime.text import MIMEText

def send_email(sender, recipients, subject, message):
    msg = MIMEText(message)
    msg['Subject'] = subject
    msg['From'] = sender
    msg['To'] = ",".join(recipients)

    mail_sender = smtplib.SMTP('localhost')
    mail_sender.send_message(msg)
    mail_sender.quit()

if __name__ == "__main__":
    response = send_email(
        'me@example.com',
        ["peter@example.com", "paul@example.com", "john@example.com"],
        "This is your message", "Have a good day"
    )
```

© Wessel Badenhorst 2017
W. Badenhorst, *Practical Python Design Patterns*, https://doi.org/10.1007/978-1-4842-2680-3_6

Next, you implement an email sender as a class, since by now you suspect that if you are going to build larger systems you will need to work in an object-oriented way. The EmailSender class handles the details of sending a message to a user. Users are stored in a comma-separated values (CSV) file, which you load as needed.

users.csv

```
name, surname, email
peter, potter, peter@example.comma
...
```

Here is what your email-sending class might look like on a first pass:

mail_sender.py

```python
import csv
import smtplib
from email.mime.text import MIMEText

class Mailer(object):
  def send(sender, recipients, subject, message):
      msg = MIMEText(message)
      msg['Subject'] = subject
      msg['From'] = sender
      msg['To'] = [recipients]

      s = smtplib.SMTP('localhost')
      s.send_message(recipient)
      s.quit()

if __name__ == "__main__":
  with open('users.csv', 'r') as csv_file:
    reader = csv.DictReader(csv_file)
    users = [x for row in reader]

  mailer = Mailer()
  mailer.send(
  'me@example.com',
  [x["email"] for x in users],
  "This is your message", "Have a good day"
  )
```

For this to work, you might need some sort of email service set up on your operating system. Postfix is a good free option should you need it. Before we continue with the example, I would like to introduce two design principles that you will see many times in this book. These principles provide a clear guide to writing better code.

Don't Repeat Yourself (DRY)

Design principles like DRY are guiding lights in the forest of problems and challenges you need to overcome in any software project. They are little voices in the back of your head, guiding you toward a clean, clear, and maintainable solution. You will be tempted to skip over them, but doing so should leave you feeling uncomfortable. When you have dark corners in your code where no one likes to go, it is probably because the original developer did not follow these guidelines. I will not lie to you; in the beginning, it is hard. It often takes a little longer to do things the right way, but in the long run, it is worth it.

In the *Gang of Four* book (the original tome on object-oriented design patterns), the two main principles proposed by the authors for solving common problems are as follows:

- Program to an interface, not an implementation

- Favor object composition over inheritance

Keeping the first principle in mind, we would like to change the way we get user data so that we no longer deal with the implementation of data fetching inside the EmailSender class. We want to move this part of the code out into a separate class in such a way that we are no longer concerned with how the data is retrieved. This will allow us to swap out the file system for a database of some sort, or even a remote microservice, should that be required in the future.

Separation of Concern

Programming to an interface allows us to create better separation between the code that gets user details and the code that sends the message. The more clearly you separate your system into distinct units, each with its own concern or task, and the more independent of one another these sections are, the easier it becomes to maintain and extend the system. As long as you keep the interface fixed, you are able to switch to newer and better ways of doing things without requiring a complete overall of your existing system. In the real world, this can mean the difference between a system that is stuck with a COBOL base and magnetic tape and one that moves with the times. It also has the added bonus of allowing you to course correct more easily should you find that one or more design decisions you made early on were sub-optimal.

This design principle is called Separation of Concern (SoC), and sooner or later you will either be very thankful you adhered to it or very sorry that you did not. You have been warned.

Let's follow our own advice and separate the retrieval of user information from the EmailSender class.

user_fetcher.py

```python
class UserFetcher(object):
  def __init__(source):
    self.source = source

  def fetch_users():
    with open(self.source, 'r') as csv_file:
      reader = csv.DictReader(csv_file)
      users = [x for row in reader]

    return rows
```

mail_sender.py

```python
import csv
import smtplib
from email.mime.text import MIMEText

class Mailer(object):
  def send(sender, recipients, subject, message):
      msg = MIMEText(message)
      msg['Subject'] = subject
      msg['From'] = sender
      msg['To'] = [recipients]

      s = smtplib.SMTP('localhost')
      s.send_message(recipient)
      s.quit()
```

```python
if __name__ == "__main__":
    user_fetcher = UserFetcher('users.csv')
    mailer = Mailer()

    mailer.send(
        'me@example.com',
        [x["email"] for x in user_fetcher.fetch_users()],
        "This is your message", "Have a good day"
    )
```

Can you see how it might take a bit of effort to get this right, but how much easier it will be when we want to drop in Postgres, Redis, or some external API without changing the code that does the actual sending of the email?

Now that you have this beautiful piece of code that sends emails to users, you might get a request for your code to be able to send status updates to a social media platform like Facebook or Twitter. You do not want to change your working email-sending code, and you found a package or program online that can handle the other side of the integration for you. How could you create some sort of messaging interface that would allow you to send messages to many different platforms without changing the code doing the sending to fit each target, or reinventing the wheel to fit your needs?

The more general problem we want to solve is: *The interface I have is not the interface I want!*

As with most common software problems, there is a design pattern for that. Let's work on a sample problem first so we can develop a bit of intuition about the solution before we implement it for the problem we have at hand.

Let's begin by oversimplifying the problem. We want to plug one piece of code into another, but the plug does not fit the socket. When trying to charge your laptop when traveling to another country, you need to get some sort of adapter to adapt your charger plug to the wall socket. In our everyday lives, we have adapters for switching between two-pronged plugs and three-pronged sockets, or for using VGA screens with HDMI outputs or other physical devices. These are all physical solutions for the problem of *The interface I have is not the interface I want!*

When you are building everything from the ground up, you will not face this problem, because you get to decide the level of abstraction you are going to use in your system and how the different parts of the system will interact with one another. In the real world, you rarely get to build everything from scratch. You have to use the plugin

95

packages and tools available to you. You need to extend code you wrote a year ago in a way that you never considered, without the luxury to go back and redo everything you did before. Every few weeks or months, you will realize that you are no longer the programmer you were before—you became better—but you still need to support the projects (and mistakes) you previously made. You will need interfaces you do not have. You will need adapters.

Sample Problem

We said that we want an adapter, whenever really we want a specific interface that we do not have.

```python
class WhatIHave(object):
  def provided_function_1(self): pass
  def provided_function_2(self): pass

class WhatIWant(object):
  def required_function(): pass
```

The first solution that comes to mind is simply changing what we want to fit what we have. When you only need to interface with a single object, you are able to do this, but let's imagine we want to also use a second service, and now we have a second interface. We could begin by using an if statement to direct the execution to the right interface:

```python
class Client(object)
  def __init__(some_object):
    self.some_object = some_object

  def do_something():
    if self.some_object.__class__ == WhatIHave:
      self.some_object.provided_function_2()
      self.some_object.provided_function_1()
    else if self.some_object.__class__ == WhatIWant:
      self.some_object.required_function()
    else:
      print("Class of self.some_object not recognized")
```

In a system where we have only two interfaces, this is not a bad solution, but by now you know that very rarely will it stay just the two systems. What also tends to happen is that different parts of your program might make use of the same service. Suddenly, you have multiple files that need to be altered to fit every new interface you introduce. In the previous chapter, you realized that adding to a system by creating multiple, often telescoping, if statements all over the place is rarely the way to go.

You want to create a piece of code that goes between the library or interface you have and makes it look like the interface you want. Adding another similar service will then simply entail adding another interface to that service, and thus your calling object becomes decoupled from the provided service.

Class Adapter

One way of attacking this problem is to create several interfaces that use polymorphism to inherit both the expected and the provided interfaces. So, the target interface can be created as a pure interface class.

In the example that follows, we import a third-party library that contains a class called WhatIHave. This class contains two methods, provided_function_1 and provided_function_2, which we use to build the function required by the client object.

```
from third_party import WhatIHave

class WhatIWant:
    def required_function(self): pass

class MyAdapter(WhatIHave, WhatIWant):
  def __init__(self, what_i_have):
    self.what_i_have = what_i_have

  def provided_function_1(self):
    self.what_i_have.provided_function_1

  def provided_function_2(self):
    self.what_i_have.profided_function_2

  def required_function(self):
    self.provided_function_1()
    self.provided_function_2()
```

```python
class ClientObject():

  def __init__(self, what_i_want):
    self.what_i_want = what_i_want

  def do_something():
    self.what_i_want.required_function()

if __name__ == "__main__":
  adaptee = WhatIHave()
  adapter = MyAdapter(adaptee)
  client = ClientObject(adapter)

  client.do_something()
```

Adapters occur at all levels of complexity. In Python, the concept of adapters extends beyond classes and their instances. Often, callables are adapted via decorators, closures, and functools.

There is yet another way that you could adapt one interface to another, and this one is even more Pythonic at its core.

Object Adapter Pattern

Instead of using inheritance to wrap a class, we could make use of composition. An adapter could then contain the class it wraps and make calls to the instance of the wrapped object. This approach further reduces the implementation complexity.

```python
class ObjectAdapter(InterfaceSuperClass):
  def __init__(self, what_i_have):
    self.what_i_have = what_i_have

  def required_function(self):
    return self.what_i_have.provided_function_1()

  def __getattr__(self, attr):
    # Everything else is handled by the wrapped object
    return getattr(self.what_i_have, attr)
```

Our adapter now only inherits from InterfaceSuperClass and takes an instance as a parameter in its constructor. The instance is then stored in self.what_i_have.

It implements a `required_function` method, which returns the result of calling the `provided_function_1()` method of its wrapped `WhatIHave` object. All other calls on the class are passed to its `what_i_have` instance via the `__getattr__()` method.

You still only need to implement the interface you are adapting. `ObjectAdapter` does not need to inherit the rest of the `WhatIHave` interface; instead, it supplies `__getattr__()` to provide the same interface as the `WhatIHave` class, apart from the methods it implements itself.

The `__getattr__()` method, much like the `__init__()` method, is a special method in Python. Often called *magic methods*, this class of methods is denoted by leading and trailing double underscores, sometimes referred to as *double under* or *dunder*. When the Python interpreter does an attribute lookup on the object but can't find it, the `__getattr__()` method is called, and the attribute lookup is passed to the `self.what_i_have` object.

Since Python uses a concept called *duck typing*, we can simplify our implementation some more.

Duck Typing

Duck typing says that if an animal walks like a duck and quacks like a duck, it is a duck.

Put in terms we can understand, in Python we only care about whether an object offers the interface elements we need. If it does, we can use it like an instance of the interface without the need to declare a common parent. `InterfaceSuperClass` just lost its usefulness and can be removed.

Now, consider the `ObjectAdapter` as it makes full use of duck typing to get rid of the `InterfaceSuperClass` inheritance.

```
from third_party import WhatIHave

class ObjectAdapter(object):
  def __init__(self, what_i_have):
    self.what_i_have = what_i_have

  def required_function(self):
    return self.what_i_have.provided_function_1()

  def __getattr__(self, attr):
    # Everything else is handeled by the wrapped object
    return getattr(self.what_i_have, attr)
```

The code does not look any different, other than having the default *object* instead of `InterfaceSuperClass` as a parent class of the `ObjectAdapter` class. This means that we never have to define some super class to adapt one interface to another. We followed the intent and spirit of the adapter pattern without all the run-around caused by less-dynamic languages.

Remember, you are not a slave to the way things were defined in the classic texts of our field. As technology grows and changes, so too must we, the implementers of that technology.

Our new version of the adapter pattern uses composition rather than inheritance to deliver a more Pythonic version of this structural design pattern. Thus, we do not require access to the source code of the interface class we are given. This, in turn, allows us to not violate the *open/closed* principle proposed by Bertrand Meyer, creator of the Eiffel programming language, and the idea of design by contract.

The open/closed principle states: *Software entities (classes, modules, functions, etc.) should be open for extension, but closed for modification.*

You want to extend the behavior of an entity without ever modifying its source code.

When you want to learn something new, especially when it is not a trivial bit of information, you need to understand the information on a deep level. An effective strategy for gaining deeper understanding is to deconstruct the big picture into smaller parts and then simplify those into digestible chunks. You then use these simple chunks to develop an intuitive sense of the problem and its solution. Once you gain confidence in your ability, you let in more of the complexity. Once you have a deep understanding of the parts, you continue to string them back together, and you will find that you have a much clearer sense of the whole. You can use the process we just followed whenever you want to begin exploring a new idea.

Implementing the Adapter Pattern in the Real World

Since you now have a feel for a clear, pythonic, implementation of the adapter pattern, let's apply that intuition to the case we looked at in the beginning of this chapter. We are going to create an adapter that will allow us to write text to the command line in order to show you what the adapter pattern looks like in action. As part of the exercises, you will be challenged to create an adapter to one of the social network libraries for Python and integrate that with the code that follows.

```python
import csv
import smtplib
from email.mime.text import MIMEText

class Mailer(object):
    def send(sender, recipients, subject, message):
        msg = MIMEText(message)
        msg['Subject'] = subject
        msg['From'] = sender
        msg['To'] = [recipients]

        s = smtplib.SMTP('localhost')
        s.send_message(recipient)
        s.quit()

class Logger(object):
    def output(message):
        print("[Logger]".format(message))

class LoggerAdapter(object):
    def __init__(self, what_i_have):
        self.what_i_have = what_i_have

    def send(sender, recipients, subject, message):
        log_message = "From: {}\nTo: {}\nSubject: {}\nMessage: {}".format(
            sender,
            recipients,
            subject,
            message
        )
        self.what_i_have.output(log_message)

    def __getattr__(self, attr):
        return getattr(self.what_i_have, attr)

if __name__ == "__main__":
    user_fetcher = UserFetcher('users.csv')
    mailer = Mailer()        mailer.send(
        'me@example.com',
```

```
    [x["email"] for x in user_fetcher.fetch_users()],
    "This is your message", "Have a good day"
)
```

You may just as well use the Logger class you developed in Chapter 1. In the preceding example, the Logger class is just used as an example.

For every new interface you want to adapt, you need to write a new AdapterObject type class. Each of these is constructed with two arguments in its constructor, one of which is an instance of the adaptee. Each of the adapters also needs to implement the send_message(self, topic, message_body) method with the required parameters so it can be called using the desired interface from anywhere in the code.

If the parameters we pass to each provided_function remain the same as those of the required_function, we could create a more generic adapter that no longer needs to know anything about the adaptee; we simply supply it an object and the provided_function, and we're done.

This is what the generic implementation of the idea would look like:

```
class ObjectAdapter(object):
    def __init__(self, what_i_have, provided_function):
        self.what_i_have = what_i_have
        self.required_function = provided_function

    def __getattr__(self, attr):
        return getattr(self.what_i_have, attr)
```

Implementing the message-sending adapter in this way is also one of the exercises at the end of this chapter. By now you may have realized that you have to do more and more of the implementation yourself. This is by design. The aim is to guide you in the learning process. You should be implementing the code so you gain more intuition about the concepts they address. Once you have a working version, fiddle with it, break it, then improve upon it.

Parting Shots

You saw that adapters are useful when you need to make things work after they are designed. It is a way of providing a different interface to subjects to which the interface are provided from the interface provided.

The adapter pattern has the following elements:

- *Target* - Defines the domain-specific *interface* the client uses

- *Client* - Uses objects that conform to the *Target* interface

- *Adaptee* - The interface you have to alter because the object does not conform to the *Target*

- *Adapter* - The code that changes what we have in the *Adaptee* to what we want in the *Client*

To implement the adapter pattern, follow this simple process:

1. Define what the components are that you want to accommodate.

2. Identify the interfaces the client requires.

3. Design and implement the adapters to map the client's required interface to the adaptee's provided interface.

The client is decoupled from the adaptee and coupled to the interface. This gives you extensibility and maintainability.

Exercises

- Extend the user-fetcher class to be able to fetch from a CSV file or a SQLite database.

- Pick any modern social network that provides an API to interact with the network and post messages of some sort. Now, install the Python library for that social network and create a class and an object adapter for said library so the code you have developed in this chapter can be used to send a message to that social network. Once done, you can congratulate yourself on building the basis of many large businesses that offer scheduled social media messages.

- Rewrite your code from the previous exercise to make use of the generic adapter for all of the interfaces you implemented.

CHAPTER 7

Decorator Pattern

Time abides long enough for those who make use of it.

—Leonardo da Vinci

As you become more experienced, you will find yourself moving beyond the type of problems that can easily be solved with the most general programming constructs. At such a time, you will realize you need a different tool set. This chapter focuses on one such tool.

When you are trying to squeeze every last drop of performance out of your machine, you need to know exactly how long a specific piece of code takes to execute. You must save the system time before you initiate the code to be profiled, then execute the code; once it has concluded, you must save the second system timestamp. Finally, subtract the first time from the second to obtain the time elapsed during the execution. Look at this example for calculating Fibonacci numbers.

fib. py

```
import time
n = 77

start_time = time.time()
fibPrev = 1
fib = 1

for num in range(2, n):
    fibPrev, fib = fib, fib + fibPrev

end_time = time.time()

print("[Time elapsed for n = {}] {}".format(n, end_time - start_time))
print("Fibonacci number for n = {}: {}".format(n, fibIter(n)))
```

© Wessel Badenhorst 2017
W. Badenhorst, *Practical Python Design Patterns*, https://doi.org/10.1007/978-1-4842-2680-3_7

Every system is different, but you should get a result shaped like the one here:

```
[Time elapsed for n = 77] 8.344650268554688e-06
Fibonacci number for n = 77: 5527939700884757
```

We now extend our Fibonacci code so we can request the number of elements in the Fibonacci sequence we wish to retrieve. We do this by encapsulating the Fibonacci calculation in a function.

fib_function.py

```python
import time

def fib(n):
    start_time = time.time()
    if n < 2:
        return

    fibPrev = 1
    fib = 1

    for num in range(2, n):
        fibPrev, fib = fib, fib + fibPrev

    end_time = time.time()
    print("[Time elapsed for n = {}] {}".format(n, end_time - start_time))

    return fib

if __name__ == "__main__":
    n = 77
    print("Fibonacci number for n = {}: {}".format(n, fib(n)))
```

In the preceding code, the profiling takes place outside of the function itself. This is fine when you only want to look at a single function, but this is not usually the case when you are optimizing a program. Luckily, functions are first-class citizens in Python, and as such we can pass the function as a parameter to another function. So, let's create a function to time the execution of another function.

fib_func_profile_me.py

```python
import time

def fib(n):
    if n < 2:
        return

    fibPrev = 1
    fib = 1

    for num in range(2, n):
        fibPrev, fib = fib, fib + fibPrev

    return fib

def profile_me(f, n):
    start_time = time.time()
    result = f(n)
    end_time = time.time()
    print("[Time elapsed for n = {}] {}".format(n, end_time - start_time))

    return result

if __name__ == "__main__":
    n = 77
    print("Fibonacci number for n = {}: {}".format(n, profile_me(fib, n)))
```

Whenever we want to get the time it takes to execute a function, we can simply pass the function into the profiling function and then run it as usual. This approach does have some limitations, since you must pre-define the parameters you want applied to the timed function. Yet again, Python comes to the rescue by allowing us to also return functions as a result. Instead of calling the function, we now return the function with the profiling added on.

base_profiled_fib.py

```python
import time

def fib(n):
    if n < 2:
        return
```

```
        fibPrev = 1
        fib = 1

        for num in range(2, n):
            fibPrev, fib = fib, fib + fibPrev

        return fib

def profile_me(f, n):
    start_time = time.time()
    result = f(n)
    end_time = time.time()
    print("[Time elapsed for n = {}] {}".format(n, end_time - start_time))

    return result

def get_profiled_function(f):
    return lambda n: profile_me(f, n)

if __name__ == "__main__":
    n = 77
    fib_profiled = get_profiled_function(fib)
    print("Fibonacci number for n = {}: {}".format(n, fib_profiled(n)))
```

This method works a lot better but still requires some effort when trying to profile several functions, as this causes interference with the code executing the function. There has to be a better way. Ideally, we want a way to tag a specific function as one to be profiled, and then not worry about the call that initiates the function call. We will do this using the decorator pattern.

The Decorator Pattern

To decorate a function, we need to return an object that can be used as a function. The classic implementation of the decorator pattern uses the fact that the way Python implements regular procedural functions these functions can be seen as classes with some kind of execution method. In Python, everything is an object; functions are objects with a special __call__() method. If our decorator returns an object with a __call__() method, the result can be used as a function.

The classic implementation of the decorator pattern does not use decorators in the sense that they are available in Python. Once again, we will opt for the more pythonic implementation of the decorator pattern, and as such we will leverage the power of the built-in syntax for decorators in Python, using the @ symbol.

class_decorated_profiled_fib.py

```python
import time

class ProfilingDecorator(object):

    def __init__(self, f):
        print("Profiling decorator initiated")
        self.f = f

    def __call__(self, *args):
        start_time = time.time()
        result = self.f(*args)
        end_time = time.time()
        print("[Time elapsed for n = {}] {}".format(n, end_time -
        start_time))

        return result

@ProfilingDecorator
def fib(n):
    print("Inside fib")
    if n < 2:
        return

    fibPrev = 1
    fib = 1

    for num in range(2, n):
        fibPrev, fib = fib, fib + fibPrev

    return fib

if __name__ == "__main__":
    n = 77
    print("Fibonacci number for n = {}: {}".format(n, fib(n)))
```

The print statement inside the fib function is just there to show where the execution fits relative to the profiling decorator. Remove it once you see it in action so as to not influence the actual time taken for the calculation.

```
Profiling decorator initiated
Inside fib
[Time elapsed for n = 77] 1.1682510375976562e-05
Fibonacci number for n = 77: 5527939700884757
```

In the class definition, we see that the decorated function is saved as an attribute of the object during initialization. Then, in the call function, the actual running of the function being decorated is wrapped in time requests. Just before returning, the profile value is printed to the console. When the compiler comes across the _@ProfilingDecorator_, it initiates an object and passes in the function being wrapped as an argument to the constructor. The returned object has the __call__() function as a method, and as such duck typing will allow this object to be used as a function. Also, note how we used *args in the __call__() method's parameters to pass in arguments. *args allows us to handle multiple arguments coming in. This is called *packing*, as all the parameters coming in are packed into the args variable. Then, when we call the stored function in the f attribute of the decorating object, we once again use *args. This is called *unpacking*, and it turns all the elements of the collection in args into individual arguments that are passed on to the function in question.

The decorator is a *unary function* (a function that takes a single argument) that takes a function to be decorated as its argument. As you saw earlier, it then returns a function that is the same as the original function with some added functionality. This means that all the code that interacts with the decorated function can remain the same as when the function was undecorated. This allows us to stack decorators. So, in a silly example, we could profile our Fibonacci function and then output the result string as HTML.

stacked_fib.py

```python
import time

class ProfilingDecorator(object):

    def __init__(self, f):
        print("Profiling decorator initiated")
        self.f = f
```

```python
    def __call__(self, *args):
        print("ProfilingDecorator called")
        start_time = time.time()
        result = self.f(*args)
        end_time = time.time()
        print("[Time elapsed for n = {}] {}".format(n, end_time -
        start_time))

        return result

class ToHTMLDecorator(object):

    def __init__(self, f):
        print("HTML wrapper initiated")
        self.f = f

    def __call__(self, *args):
        print("ToHTMLDecorator called")
        return "<html><body>{}</body></html>".format(self.f(*args))

@ToHTMLDecorator
@ProfilingDecorator
def fib(n):
    print("Inside fib")
    if n < 2:
        return

    fibPrev = 1
    fib = 1

    for num in range(2, n):
        fibPrev, fib = fib, fib + fibPrev

    return fib

if __name__ == "__main__":
    n = 77
    print("Fibonacci number for n = {}: {}".format(n, fib(n)))
```

This results in the following output. When decorating a function, be careful to take note what the output type of the function you wrap is and also what the output type of the result of the decorator is. More often than not, you want to keep the type consistent so functions using the undecorated function do not need to be changed. In this example, we change the type from a number to an HTML string as an example, but it is not something you usually want to do.

```
Profiling decorator initiated
HTML wrapper initiated
ToHTMLDecorator called
ProfilingDecorator called
Inside fib
[Time elapsed for n = 77] 1.52587890625e-05
Fibonacci number for n = 77: <html><body>5527939700884757</body></html>
```

Remember that we were able to use a class to decorate a function because in Python everything is an object as long as the object has a __call__() method, so it can be used like a function. Now, let's explore using this property of Python in reverse. Instead of using a class to decorate a function, let's use a function directly to decorate our fib function.

function_decorated_fib.py

```python
import time

def profiling_decorator(f):
    def wrapped_f(n):
        start_time = time.time()
        result = f(n)
        end_time = time.time()
        print("[Time elapsed for n = {}] {}".format(n, end_time -
            start_time))

        return result

    return wrapped_f

@profiling_decorator
def fib(n):
```

```
    print("Inside fib")
    if n < 2:
        return

    fibPrev = 1
    fib = 1

    for num in range(2, n):
        fibPrev, fib = fib, fib + fibPrev

    return fib

if __name__ == "__main__":
    n = 77
    print("Fibonacci number for n = {}: {}".format(n, fib(n)))
```

Get ready for a bit of a mind bender. The decorator function must return a function to be used when the decorated function is called. The returned function is used to wrap the decorated function. The `wrapped_f()` function is created when the function is called, so it has access to all the arguments passed to the `profiling_decorator()` function. This technique by which some data (in this case, the function passed to the `profiling_decorator()` function) gets attached to code is called a *closure* in Python.

Closures

Let's look at the `wrapped_f()` function that accesses the non-local variable f that is passed in to the `profiling_decorator()` function as a parameter. When the `wrapped_f()` function is created, the value of the non-local variable f is stored and returned as part of the function, even though the original variable moves out of scope and is removed from the namespace once the program exits the `profiling_decorator()` function.

In short, to have a closure, you have to have one function returning another function nested within itself, with the nested function referring to a variable within the scope of the enclosing function.

Retaining Function __name__ and __doc__ Attributes

As noted before, you ideally do not want any function using your decorator to be changed in any way, but the way we implemented the wrapper function in the previous section caused the __name__ and __doc__ attributes of the function to change to that of the wrapped_f() function. Look at the output of the following script to see how the __name__ attribute changes.

func_attrs.py

```python
def dummy_decorator(f):
    def wrap_f():
        print("Function to be decorated: ", f.__name__)
        print("Nested wrapping function: ", wrap_f.__name__)
        return f()

        return wrap_f

@dummy_decorator
def do_nothing():
    print("Inside do_nothing")

if __name__ == "__main__":
    print("Wrapped function: ",do_nothing.__name__)

    do_nothing()
```

Check the following results; the wrapped function took on the name of the wrap function.

```
Wrapped function:  wrap_f
Function to be decorated:  do_nothing
Nested wrapping function:  wrap_f
Inside do_nothing
```

In order to keep the __name__ and __doc__ attributes of the function being wrapped, we must set them to be equal to the function that was passed in before leaving the scope of the decorator function.

```python
def dummy_decorator(f):
    def wrap_f():
        print("Function to be decorated: ", f.__name__)
        print("Nested wrapping function: ", wrap_f.__name__)
        return f()

    wrap_f.__name__ = f.__name__
    wrap_f.__doc__ = wrap_f.__doc__
    return wrap_f

@dummy_decorator
def do_nothing():
    print("Inside do_nothing")

if __name__ == "__main__":
    print("Wrapped function: ",do_nothing.__name__)

    do_nothing()
```

Now there is no longer a difference between the do_nothing() function and the decorated do_nothing() function.

The Python standard library includes a module that allows retaining the __name__ and __doc__ attributes without setting it ourselves. What makes it even better in the context of this chapter is that the module does so by applying a decorator to the wrapping function.

```python
from functools import wraps

def dummy_decorator(f):

    @wraps(f)
    def wrap_f():
        print("Function to be decorated: ", f.__name__)
        print("Nested wrapping function: ", wrap_f.__name__)
        return f()

    return wrap_f

@dummy_decorator
def do_nothing():
    print("Inside do_nothing")
```

```
if __name__ == "__main__":
    print("Wrapped function: ",do_nothing.__name__)

    do_nothing()
```

What if we wanted to select the unit that the time should be printed in, as in seconds rather than milliseconds? We would have to find a way to pass arguments to the decorator. To do this, we will use a decorator factory. First, we create a decorator function. Then, we expand it into a decorator factory that modifies or replaces the wrapper. The factory then returns the updated decorator.

Let's look at our Fibonacci code with the functools wrapper included.

```
import time
from functools import wraps

def profiling_decorator(f):
    @wraps(f)
    def wrap_f(n):
        start_time = time.time()
        result = f(n)
        end_time = time.time()

        elapsed_time = (end_time - start_time)
        print("[Time elapsed for n = {}] {}".format(n, elapsed_time))

        return result

    return wrap_f

@profiling_decorator
def fib(n):
    print("Inside fib")
    if n < 2:
        return

    fibPrev = 1
    fib = 1
```

```
    for num in range(2, n):
        fibPrev, fib = fib, fib + fibPrev

    return fib

if __name__ == "__main__":
    n = 77
    print("Fibonacci number for n = {}: {}".format(n, fib(n)))
```

Now, let's extend the code so we can pass in an option to display the elapsed time in either milliseconds or seconds.

```
import time
from functools import wraps

def profiling_decorator_with_unit(unit):
    def profiling_decorator(f):
        @wraps(f)
        def wrap_f(n):
            start_time = time.time()
            result = f(n)
            end_time = time.time()
            if unit == "seconds":
                elapsed_time = (end_time - start_time) / 1000
            else:
                elapsed_time = (end_time - start_time)

            print("[Time elapsed for n = {}] {}".format(n, elapsed_time))

            return result

        return wrap_f
    return profiling_decorator

@profiling_decorator_with_unit("seconds")
def fib(n):
    print("Inside fib")
    if n < 2:
        return
```

```
    fibPrev = 1
    fib = 1

    for num in range(2, n):
        fibPrev, fib = fib, fib + fibPrev

    return fib

if __name__ == "__main__":
    n = 77
    print("Fibonacci number for n = {}: {}".format(n, fib(n)))
```

As before, when the compiler reaches the \@profiling_decorator_with_unit it calls the function, which returns the decorator, which is then applied to the function being decorated. You should also note that once again we used the closure concept to handle parameters passed to the decorator.

Decorating Classes

If we wanted to profile every method call in a specific class, our code would look something like this:

```
class DoMathStuff(object):
    @profiling_decorator
    def fib(self):

        ...
    @profiling_decorator
    def factorial(self):

        ...
```

Applying the same method to each method in the class would work perfectly fine, but it violates the DRY principle (Don't Repeat Yourself). What would happen if we decided we were happy with the performance and needed to take the profiling code out of a number of sprawling classes? What if we added methods to the class and forgot to decorate these newly added methods? There has to be a better way, and there is.

What we want to be able to do is decorate the class and have Python know to apply the decoration to each method in the class.

The code we want should look something like this:

```
@profile_all_class_methods
class DoMathStuff(object):

    def fib(self):
        ...
    @profiling_decorator
    def factorial(self):
        ...
```

In essence, what we want is a class that looks exactly like the DoMathStuff class from the outside, with the only difference being that every method call should be profiled.

The profiling code we wrote in the previous section should still be of use, so let's take that and make the wrapping function more general so it will work for any function passed to it.

```
import time

def profiling_wrapper(f):
    @wraps(f)
    def wrap_f(*args, **kwargs):
        start_time = time.time()
        result = f(*args, **kwargs)
        end_time = time.time()
        elapsed_time = end_time - start_time
        print("[Time elapsed for n = {}] {}".format(n, elapsed_time))

        return result

    return wrap_f
```

We received two packed arguments: a list of regular arguments and a list of arguments mapped to keywords. Between them, these two arguments will capture any form of argument that can be passed to a Python function. We also unpack both as we pass them on to the function to be wrapped.

Now, we want to create a class that would wrap a class and apply the decorating function to every method in that class and return a class that looks no different from the class it received. This is achieved through the __getattribute__() magic method. Python uses this method to retrieve methods and attributes for an object, and by overriding this method we can add the decorator as we wanted. Since __getattribute__() returns methods and values, we also need to check that the attribute requested is a method.

class_profiler.py

```python
import time

def profiling_wrapper(f):
    @wraps(f)
    def wrap_f(*args, **kwargs):
        start_time = time.time()
        result = f(*args, **kwargs)
        end_time = time.time()
        elapsed_time = end_time - start_time
        print("[Time elapsed for n = {}] {}".format(n, elapsed_time))

        return result

    return wrap_f

def profile_all_class_methods(Cls):
    class ProfiledClass(object):
        def __init__(self, *args, **kwargs):
            self.inst = Cls(*args, **kwargs)

        def __getattribute__(self, s):
            try:
                x = super(ProfiledClass, self).__getattribute__(s)
            except AttributeError:
                pass
            else:
                x = self.inst.__getattribute__(s)
                if type(x) == type(self.__init__):
                    return profiling_wrapper(x)
                else:
                    return x

    return ProfiledClass
```

```
@profile_all_class_methods
class DoMathStuff(object):

    def fib(self):
        ...
    @profiling_decorator
    def factorial(self):
        ...
```

There you have it! You can now decorate both classes and functions. It would be helpful to you if you download and read the Flask source code (download form the official website: `http://flask.pocoo.org/`), specifically noting how they make use of decorators to handle routing. Another package that you may find interesting is the Django Rest Framework (form the official website: `http://www.django-rest-framework.org/`), which uses decorators to alter return values.

Parting Shots

The decorator pattern differs from both the adapter and facade pattern in that the interface does not change, but new functionality is somehow added. So, if you have a specific piece of functionality that you want to attach to a number of functions to alter these functions without changing their interface, a decorator may be the way to go.

Exercises

- Extend the Fibonacci function wrapper so it also returns the time elapsed in minutes and hours, printed "hrs:minutes:seconds. milliseconds".

- Make a list of ten common cases you can think of in which you could implement decorators.

- Read the Flask source code and write down every interesting use of decorators you come across.

CHAPTER 8

Facade Pattern

The Phantom of the Opera is there, inside my mind.

—Christine

In this chapter, we will look at another way to hide the complexity of a system from the users of that system. All the moving parts should look like a single entity to the outside world.

All systems are more complex than they seem at first glance. Take, for instance, a point of sale (POS) system. Most people only ever interact with such a system as a customer on the other side of the register. In a simple case, every transaction that takes place requires a number of things to happen. The sale needs to be recorded, the stock levels for each item in the transaction need to be adjusted, and you might even have to apply some sort of loyalty points for regular customers. Most of these systems also allow for specials that take into account the items in the transaction, like buy two and get the cheapest one for free.

Point of Sale Example

There are a number of things involved in this transaction process, things like the loyalty system, the stock system, specials or promotions system, any payment systems, and whatever else is needed to make the process flow the way it should. For each of these interactions, we will have different classes providing the functionality in question.

© Wessel Badenhorst 2017
W. Badenhorst, *Practical Python Design Patterns*, https://doi.org/10.1007/978-1-4842-2680-3_8

It would not be hard to imagine an implementation of the process transaction that would work like this:

```python
import datetime
import random

class Invoice(object):
  def __init__(self, customer):
    self.timestamp = datetime.datetime.now()
    self.number = self.generate_number()
    self.lines = []
    self.total = 0
    self.tax = 0
    self.customer = customer

  def save(self):
    # Save the invoice to some sort of persistent storage
    pass

  def send_to_printer(self):
    # Send invoice representation to external printer
    pass

  def add_line(self, invoice_line):
    self.lines.append(invoice_line)
    self.calculate()

  def remove_line(self, line_item):
    try:
      self.lines.remove(line_item)
    except ValueError as e:
      print("could not remove {} because there is no such item in the
      invoice".format(line_item))

  def calculate(self):
    self.total = sum(x.total * x.amount for x in self.lines)
    self.tax = sum(x.total * x.tax_rate for x in self.lines)
```

```python
    def generate_number(self):
        rand = random.randint(1, 1000)
        return "{}{}".fomat(self.timestamp, rand)

class InvoiceLine(object):
    def __init__(self, line_item):
        # turn line item into an invoice line containing the current price etc
        pass

    def save(self):
        # save invoice line to persistent storage
        pass

class Receipt(object):
    def __init__(self, invoice, payment_type):
        self.invoice = invoice
        self.customer = invoice.customer
        self.payment_type = payment_type
        pass

    def save(self):
        # Save receipt to persistent storage
        pass

class Item(object):
    def __init__(self):
        pass

    @classmethod
    def fetch(cls, item_barcode):
        # fetch item from persistent storage
        pass

    def save(self):
        # Save item to persistent storage
        pass
```

```
class Customer(object):
  def __init__(self):
    pass

  @classmethod
  def fetch(cls, customer_code):
    # fetch customer from persistent storage
    pass

  def save(self):
    # save customer to persistent storage
    pass

class LoyaltyAccount(object):
  def __init__(self):
    pass

  @classmethod
  def fetch(cls, customer):
    # fetch loyaltyAccount from persistent storage
    pass

  def calculate(self, invoice):
    # Calculate the loyalty points received for this purchase
    pass

  def save(self):
    # save loyalty account back to persistent storage
    pass
```

If you want to process a sale, you have to interact with all of these classes.

```
def complex_sales_processor(customer_code, item_dict_list, payment_type):
  customer = Customer.fetch_customer(customer_code)
  invoice = Invoice()

  for item_dict in item_dict_list:
    item = Item.fetch(item_dict["barcode"])
    item.amount_in_stock - item_dict["amount_purchased"]
    item.save()
```

```
    invoice_line = InvoiceLine(item)
    invoice.add_line(invoice_line)

  invoice.calculate()
  invoice.save()

  loyalt_account = LoyaltyAccount.fetch(customer)
  loyalty_account.calculate(invoice)
  loyalty_account.save()

  receipt = Receipt(invoice, payment_type)
  receipt.save()
```

As you can see, whatever system is tasked with processing a sale needs to interact with a very large number of classes specific to the point of sale sub-system.

Systems Evolution

Systems evolve—that is a fact of life—and as they grow they can become very complex. To keep the whole system simple, we want to hide all the functionality from the client. I know you smelled it the moment you saw the preceding snippet. Everything is tightly coupled, and we have a large number of classes to interact with. When we want to extend our POS with some new technology or functionality, we will need to dig into the internals of the system. We might just forget to update some small hidden piece of code, and our whole system will thus come crashing down. We want to simplify this system without losing any of the system's power.

Ideally, we want our transaction processor to look something like this:

```
def nice_sales_processor(customer_code, item_dict_list, payment_type):
  invoice = SomeInvoiceClass(customer_code)

  for item_dict in item_dict_list:
    invoice.add_item(item_dict["barcode"], item_dict_list["amount_
    purchased"])

  invoice.finalize()
  invoice.generate_receipt(payment_type)
```

This makes the code much cleaner and easier to read. A simple rule of thumb in object-oriented programming is that whenever you encounter an ugly or messy system, hide it in an object.

You can imagine that this problem of complex or ugly systems is one that regularly comes up in the life of a programmer, so you can be certain that there are several opinions on how to best solve this issue. One such the solution is to use a design pattern called the facade pattern. This pattern is specifically used to create a complexity-limiting interface to a sub-system or collection of sub-systems. Look at the following piece of code to get a better feel for how this abstraction via the facade pattern should happen.

simple_facade.py

```python
class Invoice:
  def __init__(self, customer): pass
class Customer:
  # Altered customer class to try to fetch a customer on init or creates a new one
  def __init__(self, customer_id): pass
class Item:
  # Altered item class to try to fetch an item on init or creates a new one
  def __init__(self, item_barcode): pass

class Facade:
  @staticmethod
  def make_invoice(customer): return Invoice(customer)

  @staticmethod
  def make_customer(customer_id): return Customer(customer_id)

  @staticmethod
  def make_item(item_barcode): return Item(item_barcode)

  # ...
```

Before you read on, try to implement a facade pattern for the POS system on your own.

What Sets the Facade Pattern Apart

One key distinction with regards to the facade pattern is that the facade is used not just to encapsulate a single object but also to provide a wrapper that presents a simplified interface to a group of complex sub-systems that is easy to use without unneeded functions or complexity. Whenever possible, you want to limit the amount of knowledge and or complexity you expose to the world outside the system. The more you allow access to and interaction with a system, the more tightly coupled that system becomes. The ultimate result of allowing greater depth of access to your system is a system that can be used like a black box, with a clear set of expected inputs and well-defined outputs. The facade should decide which internal classes and representations to use. It is also within the facade that you will make changes in terms of functions to be assigned to external or updated internal systems when the time comes to do so.

Facades are often used in software libraries since the convenient methods provided by the facade make the library easier to understand and use. Since interaction with the library happens via the facade, using facades also reduces the dependencies from outside the library on its inner workings. As for any other system, this allows more flexibility when developing the library.

Not all APIs are created equal, and you will have to deal with poorly designed collections of APIs. However, using the facade pattern, you can wrap these APIs in a single well-designed API that is a joy to work with.

One of the most useful habits you can develop is that of creating solutions to your own problems. If you have a system you need to work with that is less than ideal, build a facade for it to make it work in your context. If your IDE misses a tool you love, code up your own extension to provide this function. Stop waiting for other people to come along and provide a solution. You will feel more empowered every day that you take an action to shape your world to fit your needs.

Let's implement our POS backend as just such a facade. Since we do not want to build the whole system, several the functions defined will be stubs, which you could expand if you chose to.

```python
class Sale(object):
  def __init__(self):
    pass
```

```python
@staticmethod
def make_invoice(customer_id):
  return Invoice(Customer.fetch(customer_id))

@staticmethod
def make_customer():
  return Customer()

@staticmethod
def make_item(item_barcode):
  return Item(item_barcode)

@staticmethod
def make_invoice_line(item):
  return InvoiceLine(item)

@staticmethod
def make_receipt(invoice, payment_type):
  return Receipt(invoice, payment_type)

@staticmethod
def make_loyalty_account(customer):
  return LoyaltyAccount(customer)

@staticmethod
def fetch_invoice(invoice_id):
  return Invoice(customer)

@staticmethod
def fetch_customer(customer_id):
  return Customer(customer_id)

@staticmethod
def fetch_item(item_barcode):
  return Item(item_barcode)

@staticmethod
def fetch_invoice_line(line_item_id):
  return InvoiceLine(item)
```

```
@staticmethod
def fetch_receipts(invoice_id):
  return Receipt(invoice, payment_type)

@staticmethod
def fetch_loyalty_account(customer_id):
  return LoyaltyAccount(customer)

@staticmethod
def add_item(invoice, item_barcode, amount_purchased):
  item = Item.fetch(item_barcode)
  item.amount_in_stock - amount_purchased
  item.save()
  invoice_line = InvoiceLine.make(item)
  invoice.add_line(invoice_line)

@staticmethod
def finalize(invoice):
  invoice.calculate()
  invoice.save()

  loyalt_account = LoyaltyAccount.fetch(invoice.customer)
  loyalty_account.calculate(invoice)
  loyalty_account.save()

@staticmethod
def generate_receipt(invoice, payment_type):
  receipt = Receipt(invoice, payment_type)
  receipt.save()
```

Using this new Sales class, which serves as a facade for the rest of the system, the ideal function we looked at earlier now looks like this:

```
def nice_sales_processor(customer_id, item_dict_list, payment_type):
  invoice = Sale.make_invoice(customer_id)

  for item_dict in item_dict_list:
    Sale.add_item(invoice, item_dict["barcode"], item_dict_list["amount_
    purchased"])
```

```
Sale.finalize(invoice)
Sale.generate_receipt(invoice, payment_type)
```

As you can see, not a lot has changed.

The code for `Sales` results in a single entry point to the more complex business system. We now have a limited set of functions to call via the facade that allows us to interact with the parts of the system we need access to, without overburdening us with all the internals of the system. We also have a single class to interact with, so we no longer have to go digging through the whole class diagram to find the correct place to hook into the system.

In the sub-system, a third-party stock-management system or loyalty program could replace internal systems without having the clients using the facade class change a single line of code. Our code is thus more loosely coupled and easier to extend. The POS clients do not care if we decide to hand off the stock and accounting to a third-party provider or build and run an internal system. The simplified interface remains blissfully unaware of the complexity under the hood without reducing the power inherent in the sub-system.

Parting Shots

There is not much to the facade pattern. You start out by feeling the frustration of a sub-system or group of sub-systems that does not work the way you want it to, or you find yourself having to look up interactions in many classes. By now, you know something is not right, so you decide to clean up this mess, or at least hide it behind a single, elegant interface. You design your wrapper class to turn the ugly sub-system into a black box that deals with the interactions and complexities for you. The rest of your code, and other potential client code, only deals with this facade. The world is now just a tiny bit better for your efforts—well done.

Exercises

- Facades are often implemented as singletons when they do not have to keep track of state. Alter the facade implementation in the last section of code so it uses the singleton pattern from Chapter 2.

- Expand the point of sale system outlined in this chapter until you have a system that you could use in the real world.

- Pick your favorite social media platform and create your own facade that allows you to interact with their API.

CHAPTER 9

Proxy Pattern

Do you bite your thumb at us, sir?

—Abram, *Romeo and Juliet*

As programs grow, you often find that there are functions that you call very often. When these calculations are heavy or slow, your whole program suffers.

Consider the following example for calculating the Fibonacci sequence for a number *n*:

```python
def fib(n):
  if n < 2:
    return 1

  return fib(n - 2) + fib(n - 1)
```

This fairly simple recursive function has a serious flaw, especially as *n* becomes really large. Can you figure out what the problem might be?

If you thought that it is the fact that the value of some $f(x)$ would have to be calculated multiple times whenever you want to calculate a Fibonacci number for an *n* larger than 2, you are spot on.

There are multiple ways we could handle this problem, but I want to use a very specific way, called *memoization*.

Memoization

Whenever we have a function being called multiple times, with the value repeated, it would be useful to store the response of the calculation so we do not have to go through the process of calculating the value again; we would rather just grab the value we already calculated and return that. This act of saving the result of a function call for later use is called *memoization*.

© Wessel Badenhorst 2017
W. Badenhorst, *Practical Python Design Patterns*, https://doi.org/10.1007/978-1-4842-2680-3_9

Now, let's see what effect memoization would have on our simple example case.

```
import time

def fib(n):
    if n < 2:
        return 1

    return fib(n - 2) + fib(n - 1)

if __name__ == "__main__":
    start_time = time.time()
    fib_sequence = [fib(x) for x in range(1,80)]
    end_time = time.time()

    print(
        "Calculating the list of {} Fibonacci numbers took {}"
        seconds".format(
            len(fib_sequence),
            end_time - start_time
        )
    )
```

Let this run for some time; see the amount of time elapsed just to calculate Fibonacci numbers from 0 to 40.

On my computer, I got the following result:

```
Calculating the list of 80 Fibonacci numbers took 64.29540348052979 seconds
```

Some new systems laugh at a mere 80 Fibonacci numbers. If you are in that situation, you could try increasing the numbers in orders of magnitude—80, 800, 8000—until you hit upon a number that shows load without taking forever to complete. Use this number throughout the rest of the chapter.

If we were to cache the results of each call, how would that affect the calculation?

Let's implement the same function as before, but this time we will make use of an extra dictionary to keep track of requests we have calculated before.

```python
import time

def fib_cached1(n, cache):
    if n < 2:
        return 1

    if n in cache:
        return cache[n]

    cache[n] = fib_cached1(n - 2, cache) + fib_cached1(n - 1, cache)
    return cache[n]

if __name__ == "__main__":
    cache = {}
    start_time = time.time()
    fib_sequence = [fib_cached1(x, cache) for x in range(0, 80)]
    end_time = time.time()

    print(
        "Calculating the list of {} Fibonacci numbers took {}"
        "seconds".format(
            len(fib_sequence),
            end_time - start_time
        )
    )
```

Run this code. On my machine, the same series of calculations now gives the following output:

```
Calculating the list of 80 Fibonacci numbers took 4.7206878662109375e-05
seconds
```

This is such a good result that we want to create a `calculator` object that does several mathematical series calculations, including calculating the Fibonacci numbers. See here:

```python
class Calculator(object):

    def fib_cached(self, n, cache):
        if n < 2:
            return 1

        try:
            result = cache[n]
        except:
            cache[n] = fib_cached(n - 2, cache) + fib_cached(n - 1, cache)
            result = cache[n]

        return result
```

You know that most users of your object will not know what they should do with the cache variable, or what it means. Having this variable in your method definition for the `calculator` method might cause confusion. What you want instead is to have a method definition that looks like the first piece of code we looked at, but with the performance benefits of caching.

In an ideal situation, we would have a class that functions as an interface to the `calculator` class. The client should not be aware of this class, in that the client only codes toward the interface of the original class, with the proxy providing the same functionality and results as the original class.

The Proxy Pattern

A proxy provides the same interface as the original object, but it controls access to the original object. As part of this control, it can perform other tasks before and after the original object is accessed. This is especially helpful when we want to implement something like memoization without placing any responsibility on the client to understand caching. By shielding the client from the call to the `fib` method, the proxy allows us to return the calculated result.

Duck typing allows us to create such a proxy by copying the object interface and then using the proxy class instead of the original class.

```python
import time

class RawCalculator(object):

    def fib(self, n):
        if n < 2:
            return 1

        return self.fib(n - 2) + self.fib(n - 1)

def memoize(fn):
    __cache = {}

    def memoized(*args):
        key = (fn.__name__, args)
        if key in __cache:
            return __cache[key]

        __cache[key] = fn(*args)
        return __cache[key]

    return memoized

class CalculatorProxy(object):

    def __init__(self, target):
        self.target = target

        fib = getattr(self.target, 'fib')
        setattr(self.target, 'fib', memoize(fib))

    def __getattr__(self, name):
        return getattr(self.target, name)
```

```
if __name__ == "__main__":
    calculator = CalculatorProxy(RawCalculator())

    start_time = time.time()
    fib_sequence = [calculator.fib(x) for x in range(0, 80)]
    end_time = time.time()

    print(
        "Calculating the list of {} Fibonacci numbers took {}
        seconds".format(
            len(fib_sequence),
            end_time - start_time
        )
    )
```

I must admit, this is not a trivial piece of code, but let's step through it and see what is happening.

First, we have the RawCalculator class, which is our imagined calculation object. At the moment, it only contains the Fibonacci calculation, but you could imagine it containing many other recursively defined series and sequences. As before, this method uses a recursive call.

Next, we define a closure that wraps the function call, but let's leave that for later.

Finally, we have the CalculatorProxy class, which upon initialization takes the target object as a parameter, sets an attribute on the proxy object, and then proceeds to override the fib method of the target object with a memoized version of the fib method. Whenever the target object calls its fib() method, the memoized version gets called.

Now, the memoize function takes a function as a parameter. Next, it initializes an empty dictionary. We then define a function that takes a list of arguments, gets the name of the function passed to it, and creates a tuple containing the function name and received arguments. This tuple then forms the key to the __cache dictionary. The value represents the value returned by the function call.

The memoized function first checks if the key is already in the cache dictionary. If it is, there is no need to recalculate the value, and the value is returned. If the key is not found, the original function is called, and the value is added to the dictionary before it is returned.

The `memoize` function takes a regular old function as a parameter, then it records the result of calling the received function. If needed it calls the function and receives the newly calculated values before returning a new function with the result saved if that value should be needed in future.

The final result is seen here:

```
Calculating the list of 80 Fibonacci numbers took 8.20159912109375e-05
seconds
```

I really like the fact that the `memoize` function can be used with any function passed to it. Having a generic piece of code like this is helpful, as it allows you to memoize many different functions without altering the code. This is one of the main aims of object-oriented programming. As you gain experience, you should also build up a library of interesting and useful pieces of code you can reuse. Ideally, you want to package these into your own libraries so you can do more in less time. It also helps you to keep improving.

Now that you understand the proxy pattern, let's look at the different types of proxies available to us. We already looked at a cache proxy in detail, so what remains are the following:

- Remote proxy
- Virtual proxy
- Protection proxy

Remote Proxy

When we want to abstract the location of an object, we can use a remote proxy. The remote object appears to be a local resource to the client. When you call a method on the proxy, it transfers the call to the remote object. Once the result is returned, the proxy makes this result available to the local object.

Virtual Proxy

Sometimes objects may be expensive to create, and they may not be needed until later in the program's execution. When it is helpful to delay object creation, a proxy can be used. The target object can then be created only once it is needed.

Protection Proxy

Many programs have different user roles with different levels of access. By placing a proxy between the target object and the client object, you can restrict access to information and methods on the target object.

Parting Shots

You saw how a proxy could take many forms, from the cache proxy we dealt with in this chapter to the network connection. Whenever we want to control how an object or resource is accessed in a way that is transparent from the client's perspective, the proxy pattern should be considered. In this chapter you saw how the proxy pattern wraps other objects and alters the way they execute in a way that is invisible to the user of these functions, since they still take the same parameters as input and returns the same results as output.

The proxy pattern typically has three parts:

- The *client* that requires access to some object

- The *object* the client wants to access

- The *proxy* that controls access to the object

The client instantiates the proxy and makes calls to the proxy as if it were the object itself.

Because Python is dynamically typed, we are not concerned with defining some common interface or abstract class, since we are only required to provide the same attributes as the target object in order for the proxy to be treated exactly like the target object by the client code.

It is helpful to think about proxies in terms we are already familiar with, like a web proxy. Once connected to the proxy, you, the client, are not aware of the proxy; you can access the Internet and other network resources as if there were no proxy. This is the key differentiator between the proxy pattern and the adapter pattern. With the proxy pattern, you want the interface to remain constant, with some actions taking place in the background. Conversely, the adapter pattern is targeted at changing the interface.

Exercises

- Add more functions to the RawCalculator class so it can create other sequences.

- Expand the CalculatorProxy class to handle the new series-generation functions you added. Do they also use the memoize function out of the box?

- Alter the __init__() function to iterate over the attributes of the target object and automatically memoize the callable attributes.

- Count how many times each of the RawCalculator methods is called during a program; use this to calculate how many calls are made to the fib() method.

- Check the Python standard library for other ways to memoize functions.

CHAPTER 10

Chain of Responsibility Pattern

It wasn't me.

—Shaggy, "It Wasn't Me"

Web apps are complex beasts. They need to interpret incoming requests and decide what should be done with them. When you think about creating a framework to help you build web apps more quickly, you stand a very real chance of drowning in the complexity and options involved with such a project. Python is home to many a web framework since the language is popular among developers of cloud applications. In this chapter, we are going to explore one component of web frameworks called the *middleware layer*.

The middleware sits in the middle, between the client making requests of the app and the actual application. It is a layer that both the requests from the client and the responses from the main application functions need to pass through. In the middleware, you can do things like log incoming requests for troubleshooting. You can also add some code to capture and save the response from the app that goes back to the user. Often, you will find code to check the user's access and whether they should be allowed to execute the request they are making on the system. You might want to translate the incoming request body into a data format that is easy to handle, or escape all input values to protect the system from hackers injecting code into the app. You could also think of the routing mechanism of the app as part of the middleware. The routing mechanism determines what code should be used to respond to requests directed at a specific endpoint.

© Wessel Badenhorst 2017
W. Badenhorst, *Practical Python Design Patterns*, https://doi.org/10.1007/978-1-4842-2680-3_10

Most web frameworks create a request object that is used throughout the system. A simple Request object might look like this:

```
class Request(object):
  def __init__(self, headers, url, body, GET, POST):
    self.headers
    self.url
    self.body
    self.GET
    self.POST
```

At the moment, you have no extra functionality associated with the request, but this limited object should be a good start for you to build up some intuition about the way middleware is used in handling client requests to a web app.

Web frameworks need to return some sort of response to the client. Let's define a basic Response object:

```
class Response(object):
  def __init__(self, headers, status_code, body):
    self.headers
    self.status_code
    self.body
```

If you look at the documentation of one of the more popular frameworks, like Django or Flask, you will see that the objects are way more involved that the simple ones just defined, but these will serve our purpose.

One of the things we would like our middleware to do is check for a token in the Request object's headers and then add the User object to the object. This will allow the main app to access the currently logged-in user to alter the interface and information displayed as needed.

Let's write a basic function that will grab the user token and load a User object from a database. The function will then return a User object that can be attached to the request object.

```
import User

def get_user_object(username, password):
  return User.find_by_token(username, password)
```

You could easily create a User class that gets stored in a database. As an exercise, look at the SQLAlchemy project (https://www.sqlalchemy.org/) and create an interface to an SQLite database where you store basic user data. Make sure the User class has a class function that finds a user based on the user token field, which is unique.

Setting Up a WSGI Server

Let's make this a little more practical.

Since you already have pip running on your system, install uWSGI on your virtual environment:

```
pip install uwsgi
```

Windows users might receive an error message, *AttributeError: module 'os' has no attribute 'uname'*, for this chapter, and in Chapter 12 you will need to install Cygwin. Make sure to select the python3 interpreter, pip3, gcc-core, python3-devel (check that you select your Windows version— 32-bit/64-bit), libcrypt-devel, and wget from the options during the Cygwin install process. You can get it at http://cygwin.com/install.html. Cygwin is a Linux-like terminal for Windows.

You can navigate using default Linux commands, such as the pip3 install uwsgi command. You could also follow the virtualenv setup instructions from Chapter 1 to set up a virtual environment in Cygwin (the activate command is located in YOURENVNAME/Scripts).

If all of this seems like way too much effort, you would do well to install virtualbox and run Ubuntu on the box. Then, you can follow the Linux path completely, without any changes in your day-to-day environment.

Let's test that the server works and can serve up websites on your machine. The following script returns a very simple status 200 success and Hello World message in the body (from the uWSGI documentation at http://uwsgi-docs.readthedocs.io/en/latest/WSGIquickstart.html).

hello_world_server.py

```
def application(env, start_response):
    start_response('200 OK', [('Content-Type','text/html')])
    return [b"Hello World"]
```

In your command line, with the virtual environment active, start the server, with `hello_world_server.py` set as the application to handle requests.

```
uwsgi --http :9090 --wsgi-file hello_world_server.py
```

If you point your browser to `http://localhost:9090`, you should see the message `Hello World` in the window.

Congratulations! You have your very own web server running; you could even deploy it on a server, point a URL at it, and let the world send requests to it. What we want to do next is see how the middleware fits into the flow from request to response by building it from the ground up.

Since the server is already up and running, let's add a function to check if the user token is set in the headers. We are going to follow a convention that is used by a number of bigger APIs you might find online.

Authentication Headers

The idea is that the client includes an `Authorization` header, where the header value is set to the word `Basic` followed by a space, followed by a base64-encoded string. The string that gets encoded has the following form, `USERNAME:PASSWORD`, which will be used to identify and verify the user on the system.

Before we continue building up the functionality, it is important to note that by including the `Authentication` header whenever you make a call to the app, and having the app check for the `Authorization` header, you remove the need for the app to keep track of which user is making the calls, and instead you get to attach the user to the request when that request happens.

The easiest way to test URL endpoints is to install a tool like postman on your system. It allows you to request URLs from the app and interpret the results. The free postman app can be downloaded here: `https://www.getpostman.com/`.

Once the postman install concludes, open the app.

First, enter the same URL you entered in your browser into the postman address bar and click *Send* or press *Enter*. You should see `Hello World` in the box at the bottom of the screen. This tells you that postman is working and your app is still running.

Right below the address bar, you will see a box with a couple of tabs attached to it. One of these tabs is *Authorization*. Click it and select *Basic Auth* from the dropdown box. Now username and password fields are added to the interface. Postman allows you to enter the username and password in these boxes, and it will then encode the string for you.

To see what the Request object you receive from uWSGI looks like, you need to change the script you used to return the Hello World message to the browser.

hello_world_request_display.py

```
import pprint

pp = pprint.PrettyPrinter(indent=4)

def application(env, start_response):
    pp.pprint(env)

    start_response('200 OK', [('Content-Type','text/html')])
    return [b"Hello World "]
```

The pprint module included in the Python standard library prints data types like dictionaries and lists and is an easy-to-read format. It is a valuable tool when you are debugging complex datatypes, like the request received from a web server.

When you restart your uWSGI server and send with postman the request including the Authorization headers, you will see a dictionary printed in the console. One of the keys in the dictionary will be HTTP_AUTHORIZATION, which is the field containing the word Basic followed by a space, followed by a base64-encoded string.

To retrieve the User object from the database, this string needs to be decoded and then split into the username and password respectively. We can do all of this by updating the server application. We will begin by obtaining the value of the HTTP_AUTHORIZATION header. Then, we will split that value on a space, giving us the word Basic and the base64-encoded string. We will then proceed to decode the string and split on the :, which will result in an array with the username at index 0 and the password for the user at index 1. We will then send this to a simple function that returns a User object, which we just construct inline for the sake of this example, but you are welcome to plug in your function that gets a user from your local SQLite database.

user_aware_server.py

```python
import base64

class User(object):
    def __init__(self, username, password, name, email):
        self.username = username
        self.password = password
        self.name = name
        self.email = email

    @classmethod
    def get_verified_user(cls, username, password):
        return User(
            username,
            password,
            username,
            "{}@demo.com".format(username)
        )

def application(env, start_response):
    authorization_header = env["HTTP_AUTHORIZATION"]
    header_array = authorization_header.split()
    encoded_string = header_array[1]
    decoded_string = base64.b64decode(encoded_string).decode('utf-8')
    username, password = decoded_string.split(":")

    user = User.get_verified_user(username, password)

    start_response('200 OK', [('Content-Type', 'text/html')])
    response = "Hello {}!".format(user.name)
    return [response.encode('utf-8')]
```

In our example, we created a user based on the request. This is clearly not correct, but the fact that we separated it into its own class allows us to take the code and change the get_verified_user method to get the user based on username. We then verify that the password for that user is correct. Then, you might want to add some code to handle the instance where the user does not exist in the database.

At this time, we already see a lot of code relevant only to the process of checking user credentials in the main server application. This feels wrong. Let's emphasize just how wrong it is by adding the most basic routing code possible. Our router will look for a header, which tells us which endpoint was requested by the client. Based on this information, we will print a hello message for all cases, except if the path contains the substring goodbye, in which case the server will return a goodbye message.

When we print out the request contents, we see that the path information is captured in the PATH_INFO header. The header starts with a leading "/" followed by the rest of the path.

You can split the path on "/" and then check if the path contains the word goodbye.

```python
import base64

from pprint import PrettyPrinter
pp = PrettyPrinter(indent=4)

class User(object):
    def __init__(self, username, password, name, email):
        self.username = username
        self.password = password
        self.name = name
        self.email = email

    @classmethod
    def get_verified_user(cls, username, password):
        return User(
            username,
            password,
            username,
            "{}@demo.com".format(username)
        )
```

```
def application(env, start_response):
    authorization_header = env["HTTP_AUTHORIZATION"]
    header_array = authorization_header.split()
    encoded_string = header_array[1]
    decoded_string = base64.b64decode(encoded_string).decode('utf-8')
    username, password = decoded_string.split(":")

    user = User.get_verified_user(username, password)

    start_response('200 OK', [('Content-Type', 'text/html')])

    path = env["PATH_INFO"].split("/")
    if "goodbye" in path:
        response = "Goodbye {}!".format(user.name)
    else:
        response = "Hello {}!".format(user.name)

    return [response.encode('utf-8')]
```

I'm sure your code sense is making a lot of noise right now. The `application` function is clearly doing three different things right now. It starts out getting the `User` object. Then, it decides what endpoint the client is requesting and composes the relevant message based on that path. Lastly, it returns the encoded message to the client who made the request.

Whenever more functionality is required between the initial request from the user and the actual response, the `application` function becomes more complex. In short, your code is bound to become a mess if you continue down this path.

We want each function to ideally do one and only one thing.

The Chain of Responsibility Pattern

The idea that every piece of code does one thing and only one thing is called the *single responsibility principle*, which is another handy guideline when you are working on writing better code.

If we wanted to adhere to the single responsibility principle in the preceding example, we would need a piece of code to handle the user retrieval and another piece of code to validate that the user matches the password. Yet another piece of code would generate a message based on the path of the request, and, finally, some piece of code would return the response to the browser.

Before we attempt to write the code for the server, we will build up some intuition about the solution using a sample application.

In our sample application, we have four functions, each of which simply prints out a message.

```python
def function_1():
  print("function_1")

def function_2():
  print("function_2")

def function_3():
  print("function_3")

def function_4():
  print("function_4")

def main_function():
  function_1()
  function_2()
  function_3()
  function_4()

if __name__ == "__main__":
  main_function()
```

From our discussion in the beginning of this section, we know that it is not ideal to have the main_function call each of the functions in order, since in a real-world scenario this leads to the messy code we encountered in the previous section.

What we want is to create some sort of way for us to make a single call and then have the functions called dynamically.

```python
class CatchAll(object):
    def __init__(self):
        self.next_to_execute = None

    def execute(self):
        print("end reached.")

class Function1Class(object):
    def __init__(self):
        self.next_to_execute = CatchAll()

    def execute(self):
        print("function_1")
        self.next_to_execute.execute()

class Function2Class(object):
    def __init__(self):
        self.next_to_execute = CatchAll()

    def execute(self):
        print("function_2")
        self.next_to_execute.execute()

class Function3Class(object):
    def __init__(self):
        self.next_to_execute = CatchAll()

    def execute(self):
        print("function_3")
        self.next_to_execute.execute()

class Function4Class(object):
    def __init__(self):
        self.next_to_execute = CatchAll()

    def execute(self):
        print("function_4")
        self.next_to_execute.execute()
```

```
def main_function(head):
  head.execute()

if __name__ == "__main__":
    hd = Function1Class()

    current = hd
    current.next_to_execute = Function2Class()

    current = current.next_to_execute
    current.next_to_execute = Function3Class()

    current = current.next_to_execute
    current.next_to_execute = Function4Class()

    main_function(hd)
```

Even though the amount of code written is significantly more than in the first instance, you should begin to see how cleanly this new program separates the execution of each function from the others.

To illustrate this further, we now extend the main execute function to include a request string. The string is a series of digits, and if the digit from the function name is included in the digit string, the function prints its name together with the request string before it removes all instances of the digit in question from the request string and passes the request on to the rest of the code for processing.

In our original context, we could solve this new requirement as follows:

```
def function_1(in_string):
    print(in_string)
    return "".join([x for x in in_string if x != '1'])

def function_2(in_string):
    print(in_string)
    return "".join([x for x in in_string if x != '2'])

def function_3(in_string):
    print(in_string)
    return "".join([x for x in in_string if x != '3'])
```

153

```python
def function_4(in_string):
    print(in_string)
    return "".join([x for x in in_string if x != '4'])

def main_function(input_string):
    if '1' in input_string:
        input_string = function_1(input_string)
    if '2' in input_string:
        input_string = function_2(input_string)
    if '3' in input_string:
        input_string = function_3(input_string)
    if '4' in input_string:
        input_string = function_4(input_string)

    print(input_string)

if __name__ == "__main__":
    main_function("1221345439")
```

Yes, you are right—all the functions do exactly the same thing, but this is just because of the way the sample problem is set up. If you were to refer to the original problem, you would see that this is not always the case.

What should also feel off is the series of if statements that will only grow in length as more functions are added to the execution queue.

Finally, you may have noted how closely coupled the main_function is to each of the functions being executed.

Implementing Chain of Responsibility in Our Project

Now, let's solve the same problem using the idea we began to build earlier.

```python
class CatchAll(object):
    def __init__(self):
        self.next_to_execute = None

    def execute(self, request):
        print(request)
```

```python
class Function1Class(object):
    def __init__(self):
        self.next_to_execute = CatchAll()

    def execute(self, request):
        print(request)
        request = "".join([x for x in request if x != '1'])
        self.next_to_execute.execute(request)

class Function2Class(object):
    def __init__(self):
        self.next_to_execute = CatchAll()

    def execute(self, request):
        print(request)
        request = "".join([x for x in request if x != '2'])
        self.next_to_execute.execute(request)

class Function3Class(object):
    def __init__(self):
        self.next_to_execute = CatchAll()

    def execute(self, request):
        print(request)
        request = "".join([x for x in request if x != '3'])
        self.next_to_execute.execute(request)

class Function4Class(object):
    def __init__(self):
        self.next_to_execute = CatchAll()

    def execute(self, request):
        print(request)
        request = "".join([x for x in request if x != '4'])
        self.next_to_execute.execute(request)
```

```
def main_function(head, request):
    head.execute(request)

if __name__ == "__main__":
    hd = Function1Class()

    current = hd
    current.next_to_execute = Function2Class()

    current = current.next_to_execute
    current.next_to_execute = Function3Class()

    current = current.next_to_execute
    current.next_to_execute = Function4Class()

    main_function(hd, "1221345439")
```

Already it is clear that we have a much cleaner solution at hand. We did not have to make any changes to the way each class is connected to the next, and apart from passing on the request, we did not require any changes to be made to the individual execute functions or the main function in order to accommodate the way each class executes the request. We have clearly separated each function into its own unit of code that can be plugged into, or removed from, the chain of classes dealing with the request.

Each handler cares only about its own execution and ignores what happens when another handler executes because of the query. The handler decides in the moment if it should do anything as a result of the request it receives, which leads to increased flexibility in determining which handlers should execute as a result of a query. The best part of this implementation is that handlers can be added and removed at runtime, and when the order is unimportant in terms of the execution queue, you could even shuffle the order of the handlers. This only goes to show, once again, that loosely coupled code is more flexible than tightly coupled code.

To further illustrate this flexibility, we extend the previous program so each class will only do something if it sees that the digit associated with the class name is in the request string.

```python
class CatchAll(object):
    def __init__(self):
        self.next_to_execute = None

    def execute(self, request):
        print(request)

class Function1Class(object):
    def __init__(self):
        self.next_to_execute = CatchAll()

    def execute(self, request):
        if '1' in request:
            print("Executing Type Function1Class with request [{}]".
            format(request))
            request = "".join([x for x in request if x != '1'])

        self.next_to_execute.execute(request)

class Function2Class(object):
    def __init__(self):
        self.next_to_execute = CatchAll()

    def execute(self, request):
        if '2' in request:
            print("Executing Type Function2Class with request [{}]".
            format(request))
            request = "".join([x for x in request if x != '2'])

        self.next_to_execute.execute(request)

class Function3Class(object):
    def __init__(self):
        self.next_to_execute = CatchAll()
```

```python
    def execute(self, request):
        if '3' in request:
            print("Executing Type Function3Class with request [{}]".
            format(request))
            request = "".join([x for x in request if x != '3'])

        self.next_to_execute.execute(request)

class Function4Class(object):
    def __init__(self):
        self.next_to_execute = CatchAll()

    def execute(self, request):
        if '4' in request:
            print("Executing Type Function4Class with request [{}]".
            format(request))
            request = "".join([x for x in request if x != '4'])

        self.next_to_execute.execute(request)

def main_function(head, request):
  head.execute(request)

if __name__ == "__main__":
    hd = Function1Class()

    current = hd
    current.next_to_execute = Function2Class()

    current = current.next_to_execute
    current.next_to_execute = Function3Class()

    current = current.next_to_execute
    current.next_to_execute = Function4Class()

    main_function(hd, "12214549")
```

Note that this time we do not have any 3 digits in the request, and as a result the code for the instance of `Function3Class` is not executed before the request is passed on to the instance of `Function4Class`. Also, note that we had no change in the code for the setup of the execution chain or in `main_function`.

This chain of handlers is the essence of the Chain of Responsibility pattern.

A More Pythonic Implementation

In the classic implementation of this pattern, you would define some sort of generic handler type that would define the concept of the `next_to_execute` object as well as the `execute` function. As we have seen before, the duck-typing system in Python frees us from having to add the extra overhead. As long as we define the relevant parts for each handler we want to use in the chain, we do not need to inherit from some shared base. This not only saves a lot of time otherwise spent writing boilerplate code, but also enables you, the developer, to easily evolve these types of ideas as your application or system calls for it.

In more constrained languages, you do not have the luxury of evolving the design on the fly. Changing direction like this often requires a large redesign, with a lot of code requiring a rewrite. To avoid the pain of redesigning the whole system or rebuilding large parts of the application, engineers and developers try to cater to every eventuality they can dream up. This approach is flawed in two critical ways. First, human knowledge of the future is imperfect, so even if you were to design the perfect system for today (a near impossibility), it would be impossible to account for every way in which clients might use your system, or for where the market might drive your application. The second is that, for the most part, *You Ain't Gonna Need It* (YAGNI), or, stated differently, most of the potential futures that get covered in the design of such a system will never be needed, and as such it is time and effort that has gone to waste. Once again, Python provides the capability to start with a simple solution to a simple problem and then grow the solution as the use cases change and evolve. Python moves with you, changing and growing as you do. Much like the game of Go, Python is easy to pick up, but you can devote a lifetime to mastering its many possibilities.

Here is a simple implementation of the Chain of Responsibility pattern, with all of the extras stripped away. All that is left is the general structure that we will be implementing on our web app.

```python
class EndHandler(object):
    def __init__(self):
        pass

    def handle_request(self, request):
        pass

class Handler1(object):
    def __init__(self):
        self.next_handler = EndHandler()

    def handle_request(self, request):

        self.next_handler.handle_request(request)

def main(request):
    concrete_handler = Handler1()

    concrete_handler.handle_request(request)

if __name__ == "__main__":
    # from the command line we can define some request
    main(request)
```

We will now use this very minimal skeleton to significantly improve our web app from the beginning of this chapter. The new solution will adhere to the single responsibility principle much more closely. You will also note that you could add many more functions and extensions to the process.

```python
import base64

class User(object):
    def __init__(self, username, password, name, email):
        self.username = username
        self.password = password
```

```python
        self.name = name
        self.email = email

    @classmethod
    def get_verified_user(cls, username, password):
        return User(
            username,
            password,
            username,
            "{}@demo.com".format(username)
        )

class EndHandler(object):
    def __init__(self):
        pass

    def handle_request(self, request, response=None):
        return response.encode('utf-8')

class AuthorizationHandler(object):
    def __init__(self):
        self.next_handler = EndHandler()

    def handle_request(self, request, response=None):
        authorization_header = request["HTTP_AUTHORIZATION"]
        header_array = authorization_header.split()
        encoded_string = header_array[1]
        decoded_string = base64.b64decode(encoded_string).decode('utf-8')
        username, password = decoded_string.split(":")
        request['username'] = username
        request['password'] = password

        return self.next_handler.handle_request(request, response)

class UserHandler(object):
    def __init__(self):
        self.next_handler = EndHandler()
```

```python
    def handle_request(self, request, response=None):
        user = User.get_verified_user(request['username'],
        request['password'])
        request['user'] = user

        return self.next_handler.handle_request(request, response)

class PathHandler(object):
    def __init__(self):
        self.next_handler = EndHandler()

    def handle_request(self, request, response=None):
        path = request["PATH_INFO"].split("/")
        if "goodbye" in path:
            response = "Goodbye {}!".format(request['user'].name)
        else:
            response = "Hello {}!".format(request['user'].name)

        return self.next_handler.handle_request(request, response)

def application(env, start_response):
    head = AuthorizationHandler()

    current = head
    current.next_handler = UserHandler()

    current = current.next_handler
    current.next_handler = PathHandler()

    start_response('200 OK', [('Content-Type', 'text/html')])
    return [head.handle_request(env)]
```

Another alternative implementation of the Chain of Responsibility pattern is to instantiate a main object to dispatch handlers from a list passed into the dispatcher on instantiation.

```
class Dispatcher(object):

  def __init__(self, handlers=[]):
    self.handlers = handlers

    def handle_request(self, request):
      for handler in self.handlers:
        request = handler(request)

      return request
```

The Dispatcher class takes advantage of the fact that everything in Python is an object, including functions. Since functions are first-class citizens (which means they can be passed to a function and be returned from a function) we can instantiate the dispatcher and pass in a list of functions, which can be saved like any other list. When the time comes to execute the functions, we iterate over the list and execute each function in turn.

Implementing the sample code we have been using in this section using the Dispatcher looks like this:

```
class Dispatcher(object):

    def __init__(self, handlers=[]):
        self.handlers = handlers

    def handle_request(self, request):
        for handle in self.handlers:
            request = handle(request)

        return request

def function_1(in_string):
    print(in_string)
    return "".join([x for x in in_string if x != '1'])

def function_2(in_string):
    print(in_string)
    return "".join([x for x in in_string if x != '2'])
```

```python
def function_3(in_string):
    print(in_string)
    return "".join([x for x in in_string if x != '3'])

def function_4(in_string):
    print(in_string)
    return "".join([x for x in in_string if x != '4'])

def main(request):
    dispatcher = Dispatcher([
        function_1,
        function_2,
        function_3,
        function_4
    ])

    dispatcher.handle_request(request)

if __name__ == "__main__":
    main("1221345439")
```

As an exercise, I suggest you use this structure to implement the process for the web app.

Before we wrap up this chapter, I want you to think about the discussion on middleware that we started with. Can you see how you would use the Chain of Responsibility pattern to implement a middleware for your web app by adding handlers to the queue?

Parting Shots

As we have seen throughout this chapter, the request is the central object around which the pattern is built, and as such care should be taken when constructing and altering the request object as it gets passed from one handler to the next.

Since the Chain of Responsibility pattern affords us the opportunity to shuffle and alter the handlers used at runtime, we can apply some performance-enhancing ideas to the chain. We could move a handler to the front of the chain every time it is used, resulting in more regularly used handlers taking the early positions in the chain followed by the less frequently used handlers (use this only when the order of execution of the handlers does not matter). When the order of the handlers has some sort of meaning, you could get some improved performance using ideas from the previous chapter and caching the results of certain handled requests.

We never want to completely ignore a request, so you must make sure to have some sort of end handler serving as a catch-all for the chain to, at the very least, alert you that the request was not handled by any of the handlers in your chain.

In the examples from this chapter, we had the chain execute until all the handlers had a look at the request. This does not have to be the case; you can break the chain at any point and return a result.

The Chain of Responsibility pattern can serve to encapsulate a processing of elements into a pipeline (like a data pipeline).

Finally, a good rule of thumb is to use the Chain of Responsibility pattern wherever you have more than one potential handler for a request, and thus do not know beforehand which handler or handlers would best handle the requests you will receive.

Exercises

- Look at SQLAlchemy and create an interface to an SQLite database where you store basic user data.

- Expand the User class function that retrieves the user so it uses the SQLite database, as in the previous exercise.

- Add the logger you built in chapter 2, on the singleton pattern, to the chain of responsibility of your web application so you can log the incoming request and the responses sent back to the client.

- Implement your web app from this chapter using the Dispatcher implementation of the Chain of Responsibility.

CHAPTER 11

Command Pattern

I'll be back.

—Terminator

The robots are coming.

In this chapter, we are going to look at how we can control a robot using Python code. For our purposes, we will be using the `turtle` module included in the Python standard library. This will allow us to handle commands like move forward, turn left, and turn right without the need to build an actual robot, although you should be able to use the code developed in this chapter, combined with a board like the Raspberry Pi and some actuators, to actually build a robot you could control with code.

Controlling the Turtle

Let's begin by doing something simple, like drawing a square on the screen using the turtle module.

turtle_basic.py

```python
import turtle

turtle.color('blue', 'red')

turtle.begin_fill()

for _ in range(4):
    turtle.forward(100)
    turtle.left(90)

turtle.end_fill()
turtle.done()
```

© Wessel Badenhorst 2017
W. Badenhorst, *Practical Python Design Patterns*, https://doi.org/10.1007/978-1-4842-2680-3_11

The turtle is a simple line-and-fill tool that helps to visualize what the robot is doing. In the preceding code, we import the `turtle` library. Next, we set the line color to blue and the background color to red. Then, we tell the turtle to record the current point as the start of a polygon that will be filled later. Then, the loop draws the four sides of the square. Finally, the `end_fill()` method fills the polygon with red. The `done()` method keeps the program from terminating and closing the window once the process is completed.

If you are using an Ubuntu system and get an error message regarding `python3-tk,` you need to install the package.

```
sudo apt-get install python3-tk
```

Run the code, and you should see a little triangle (the turtle) move on the screen.

This approach works while we are trying to draw shapes and lines on the screen, but since the turtle is just a metaphor for our robot, drawing pretty shapes does not have a lot of use. We are going to extend our robot control script to accept four commands (start, stop, turn left 10 degrees, and turn right 10 degrees), which we will map to keyboard keys.

turtle_control.py

```python
import turtle

turtle.setup(400, 400)

screen = turtle.Screen()
screen.title("Keyboard drawing!")

t = turtle.Turtle()
distance = 10

def advance():
    t.forward(distance)

def turn_left():
    t.left(10)

def turn_right():
    t.right(10)
```

```
def retreat():
    t.backward(10)

def quit():
    screen.bye()

screen.onkey(advance, "w")
screen.onkey(turn_left, "a")
screen.onkey(turn_right, "d")
screen.onkey(retreat, "s")
screen.onkey(quit, "Escape")

screen.listen()
screen.mainloop()
```

What you are essentially doing is creating an interface with which to control the turtle. In the real world, this would be akin to a remote control car that takes one signal to mean turn left, another for turn right, a third for accelerate, and a fourth for decelerate. If you were to build an RC sender that translated the signals that usually come from the remote to now take input from a keyboard using some electronics and your USB port, you would be able to use code similar to the code we have here to control the remote control car. In the same way, you could control a robot via remote control.

In essence, we are sending commands from one part of our system to another.

The Command Pattern

Whenever you want to send an instruction or set of instructions from one object to another, while keeping these objects loosely coupled, it is wise to encapsulate everything needed to execute the instructions in some kind of data structure.

The *client* that initiates the execution does not have to know anything about the way in which the instruction will be executed; all it is required to do is to set up all the required information and hand off whatever needs to happen next to the system.

Since we are dealing with an object-oriented paradigm, the data structure used to encapsulate the instruction will be an object. The class of objects used to encapsulate information needed by some other method in order to execute is called a *command*. The client object instantiates a command containing the method it wishes to execute, along with all the parameters needed to execute the method, as well as some target object that has the method.

This target object is called the *receiver*. The receiver is an instance of a class that can execute the method given the encapsulated information.

All of this relies on an object called an *invoker* that decides when the method on the receiver will execute. It might help to realize that invocations of methods are similar to instances of classes.

Without any actual functionality, the command pattern can be implemented like this:

```python
class Command:
    def __init__(self, receiver, text):
        self.receiver = receiver
        self.text = text

    def execute(self):
        self.receiver.print_message(self.text)

class Receiver(object):
    def print_message(self, text):
      print("Message received: {}".format(text))

class Invoker(object):
    def __init__(self):
        self.commands = []

    def add_command(self, command):
        self.commands.append(command)

    def run(self):
        for command in self.commands:
            command.execute()

if __name__ == "__main__":
    receiver = Receiver()

    command1 = Command(receiver, "Execute Command 1")
    command2 = Command(receiver, "Execute Command 2")
```

```
invoker = Invoker()
invoker.add_command(command1)
invoker.add_command(command2)
invoker.run()
```

Now you would be able to queue up commands to be executed even if the receiver were busy executing another command. This is a very useful concept in distributed systems where incoming commands need to be captured and handled, but the system may be busy with another action. Having all the information in an object in the queue allows the system to deal with all incoming commands without losing important commands while executing some other command. You essentially get to dynamically create new behavior at runtime. This process is especially useful when you want to set up the execution of a method at one time and then sometime later execute it.

Think about the implication for a robot like the Mars Rover if operatives were only able to send a single command to be executed and then had to wait for the command to finish execution before they could transmit the next command. It would make doing anything on Mars extremely time-consuming to the point of being impossible. What can be done instead is to send a sequence of actions to the rover. The rover can then invoke each command in turn, allowing it to get more work done per unit of time, and potentially negating much of the effect of the time lag between transmission and receipt of commands between the rover and Earth. This string of commands is called a *macro*.

Macros are also useful when running automated tests where you want to mimic user interaction with the system, or when you want to automate certain tasks that you do repeatedly. You could create a command for each step in the process and then string them up before letting some invoker handle the execution. The decoupling allows you to swap out direct human intervention via the keyboard for generated computer input.

Once we begin stringing commands together, we can also look at undoing the commands that were executed. This is another area where the command pattern is particularly useful. By pushing an undo command onto a stack for every command that gets invoked, we get multi-level undo for free, much like you see in everything from modern word processors to video-editing software.

To illustrate how you could go about using the command pattern to build a multi-level undo stack, we are going to build a very simple calculator that can do addition, subtraction, multiplication, and division. For the sake of keeping the example simple, we will not concern ourselves with the case where we have multiplication by zero.

```python
class AddCommand(object):
    def __init__(self, receiver, value):
        self.receiver = receiver
        self.value = value

    def execute(self):
        self.receiver.add(self.value)

    def undo(self):
        self.receiver.subtract(self.value)

class SubtractCommand(object):
    def __init__(self, receiver, value):
        self.receiver = receiver
        self.value = value

    def execute(self):
        self.receiver.subtract(self.value)

    def undo(self):
        self.receiver.add(self.value)

class MultiplyCommand(object):
    def __init__(self, receiver, value):
        self.receiver = receiver
        self.value = value

    def execute(self):
        self.receiver.multiply(self.value)

    def undo(self):
        self.receiver.divide(self.value)

class DivideCommand(object):
    def __init__(self, receiver, value):
        self.receiver = receiver
        self.value = value

    def execute(self):
        self.receiver.divide(self.value)
```

```python
    def undo(self):
        self.receiver.multiply(self.value)

class CalculationInvoker(object):
    def __init__(self):
        self.commands = []
        self.undo_stack = []

    def add_new_command(self, command):
        self.commands.append(command)

    def run(self):
        for command in self.commands:
            command.execute()
            self.undo_stack.append(command)

    def undo(self):
        undo_command = self.undo_stack.pop()
        undo_command.undo()

class Accumulator(object):
    def __init__(self, value):
        self._value = value

    def add(self, value):
        self._value += value

    def subtract(self, value):
        self._value -= value

    def multiply(self, value):
        self._value *= value

    def divide(self, value):
        self._value /= value

    def __str__(self):
        return "Current Value: {}".format(self._value)
```

```python
if __name__ == "__main__":
    acc = Accumulator(10.0)

    invoker = CalculationInvoker()
    invoker.add_new_command(AddCommand(acc, 11))
    invoker.add_new_command(SubtractCommand(acc, 12))
    invoker.add_new_command(MultiplyCommand(acc, 13))
    invoker.add_new_command(DivideCommand(acc, 14))

    invoker.run()

    print(acc)

    invoker.undo()
    invoker.undo()
    invoker.undo()
    invoker.undo()

    print(acc)
```

Just note that the __str()__ method is used when Python casts the accumulator object to a string when printing it.

As we have seen a couple of times now, the duck typing in Python allows us to skip defining an overarching base class to inherit from. As long as our commands have execute() and undo() methods and take a receiver and value as parameters on construction, we can use any command we feel like.

In the preceding code, we push every command that gets executed by the invoker onto a stack. Then, when we want to undo a command, the last command is popped from the stack and the undo() method of that command is executed. In the case of the calculator, the inverse calculation is executed to return the value of the accumulator back to what it would have been before the command was executed.

All implementations of the Command class in the command pattern will have a method such as execute() that is called by the invoker to execute the command. The instance of the Command class keeps a reference to the receiver, the name of the method to be executed, and the values to be used as parameters in the execution. The receiver is the only object that knows how to execute the method kept in the command, and it manages its own internal state independent of the other objects in the system. The client has no knowledge of the implementation details of the command, and neither do the command or the invoker. To be clear, the command object does not execute anything; it is just a container. By implementing this pattern, we have added a layer of abstraction between the action to be executed and the object that invokes that action. The added abstraction leads to better interaction between different objects in the system, and looser coupling between them, making the system easier to maintain and update.

The heart of this design pattern is the translation of method calls into data that can be saved in a variable, passed to a method or function as a parameter, and returned from a function as a result. The result of applying this pattern is that functions or methods become first-class citizens. When functions are first class citizens variables can point to functions, functions can be passed as a parameter to other functions, and they can be returned as the result from executing a function.

What is interesting about the command pattern, specifically this ability to turn behavior into a first-class citizen, is that we could use this pattern to implement a functional programming style with lazy evaluation, meaning that functions could be passed to other functions and could be returned by functions. All functions get passed all that is needed for execution, with no global state, and functions are only executed when an actual result needs to be returned. This is a fairly shallow description of functional programming, but the implications are deep.

The interesting twist in our tale is that in Python everything is a function, and as such we could also do away with the class that encapsulates the function call and just pass the function with the relevant parameters to the invoker.

```python
def text_writer(string1, string2):
    print("Writing {} - {}".format(string1, string2))

class Invoker(object):
    def __init__(self):
        self.commands = []

    def add_command(self, command):
        self.commands.append(command)

    def run(self):
        for command in self.commands:
            command["function"](*command["params"])
```

```python
if __name__ == "__main__":
    invoker = Invoker()
    invoker.add_command({
        "function": text_writer,
        "params": ("Command 1", "String 1")
    })
    invoker.add_command({
        "function": text_writer,
        "params": ("Command 2", "String 2")
    })
    invoker.run()
```

For a simple case like this, you could just define a lambda function, and you would not even have to write the function definition.

```python
class Invoker(object):
    def __init__(self):
        self.commands = []

    def add_command(self, command):
        self.commands.append(command)

    def run(self):
        for command in self.commands:
            command["function"](*command["params"])

if __name__ == "__main__":
    f = lambda string1, string2: print("Writing {} - {}".format
    (string1, string2))

    invoker = Invoker()
    invoker.add_command({
        "function": f,
        "params": ("Command 1", "String 1")
    })
    invoker.add_command({
        "function": f,
```

```
    "params": ("Command 2", "String 2")
})
invoker.run()
```

Once the function you want to execute gets more complicated, you have two options other than the method we used in the previous program. You could just wrap the command's `execute()` function in a lambda, letting you avoid creating a class. Even though it is a nifty trick, your code will probably be more clear if you just create a class for the complex case, which is the second option. So, a good rule of thumb is that when you need to create a command for anything more complex than a piece of code you can wrap in a single-line lambda function, create a class for it.

Parting Shots

Whether you are building a self-driving car or sending messages to outer space, decoupling the request for execution from the actual execution allows you to not only buffer actions that need to be executed, but also exchange the mode of input.

It is important that the command pattern isolates the invoker from the receiver. It also separates the time the execution is set up from the time it is processed.

Exercises

- Use the command pattern to create a command-line word-replacement script that can replace every instance of a given word in a given text file with some other word. Then, add a command to undo the last replace action.

CHAPTER 12

Interpreter Pattern

Silvia Broome: What do you do when you can't sleep? Tobin Keller: I stay awake.

—The Interpreter

Sometimes it makes sense to not use Python to describe a problem or the solution to such a problem. When we need a language geared toward a specific problem domain, we turn to something called a domain-specific language.

Domain-Specific Languages

Some languages, like Python, were created to tackle any type of problem. Python belongs to a whole family of languages, called general-purpose languages, designed to be used to solve any problem. On rare occasions, it makes more sense to create a language that does only one thing, but that does it extremely well. These languages, which belongto a family called domain-specific languages (DSLs), are helpful for people who are experts in some specific domain but are not programmers.

You have probably already encountered DSLs in your programming career. If you ever tinkered on a website, you know CSS, which is a DSL for defining how HTML should be rendered in a browser.

style.css

```css
body {
  color: #00ff00;
}
```

© Wessel Badenhorst 2017
W. Badenhorst, *Practical Python Design Patterns*, https://doi.org/10.1007/978-1-4842-2680-3_12

This little bit of CSS code tells a browser to render all the text inside the body tag of the web page that uses this CSS file in green. The code needed by the browser to do this is a lot more complex than this simple snippet of code, yet CSS is simple enough for most people to pick up in a couple of hours. HTML itself is a DSL that is interpreted by the browser and displayed as a formatted document with a fairly intricate layout.

Alternatively, you may have used Aloe in behavior-driven development, where you define acceptance criteria for a project in human-readable sentences.

```
Install the aloe framework using pip
$ pip install aloe
```

Now, we can write some tests.

zero.feature

```
Feature: Compute factorial
  In order to play with aloe
  As beginners
  We'll implement factorial

  Scenario: Factorial of 0
    Given I have the number 0
    When I compute its factorial
    Then I see the number 1
```

Next, you map these steps to some Python code so the Aloe framework can understand the behavior described.

steps.py

```python
from aloe import *

@step(r'I have the number (\d+)')
def have_the_number(step, number):
  world.number = int(number)

@step('I compute its factorial')
def compute_its_factorial(step):
  world.number = factorial(world.number)
```

```
@step(r'I see the number (\d+)')
def check_number(step, expected):
  expected = int(expected)
  assert world.number == expected, \
    "Got %d" % world.number

def factorial(number):
  return -1
```

This code lets you define the outcome of the program in terms that a non-technical person can understand and then maps those terms to actual code, which makes sure that they execute as described in the features file. The description in the .feature file is the DSL, and the Python code in the steps.py file is used to change the words and phrases in the DSL into something a computer can understand.

When you decide to create a DSL (practice domain engineering), you are enabling clear communication between domain experts and developers. Not only will the experts be able to express themselves more clearly, but the developers will understand what they require, and so will the computer. What you will generally find is that a domain expert will describe a problem, or the solution to a problem, from their domain to a developer, who will then immediately write down the description in the domain-specific language. Domain experts can understand this description of the problem or solution as presented by the developer and will be able to suggest changes or expansions to the description. Descriptions can thus be turned into functioning solutions during the course of a meeting, or over a couple of days at most, greatly increasing the productivity of everyone involved.

Let's make this practical.

You have been contracted to create a system restaurants can use to define their specials. These specials sometimes have simple rules like *Buy one get one free*, but other times they are a lot more complex, like *If you buy three pizzas on a Tuesday, the cheapest one is free*. The challenge is that these rules change often, and as such redeploying the code for every change just does not make sense. If you did not care about being forced to change the code every week when your customer decides to change the rules for specials, the potential magnitude of the if statement this would result in should be enough to scare you off.

Since we have been talking about DSLs, you might suspect that creating a DSL for the restaurant is the solution. Any changes or additions to the criteria for a special could then be stored independent of the main application and only be interpreted when called upon.

In a very informative talk, Neil Green, Technical Lead at ICE, suggested the following process for developing a DSL:

1. Understand your domain.

2. Model your domain.

3. Implement your domain.

If we were to follow Neil's guidance, we would go talk to the restaurant owner. We would try to learn how he or she expresses the rules for specials, and then try to capture these rules in a language that makes sense to us as well as to the owner. We would then draw some sort of diagram based on our conversation. If the owner agrees that we captured the essence of what he or she was saying, we get to write some code to implement our model.

DSLs come in two flavors: *internal* and *external*. External DSLs have code written in an external file or as a string. This string or file is then read and parsed by the application before it gets used. CSS is an example of an external DSL, where the browser is tasked with reading, parsing, and interpreting the textual data that represents how HTML elements should be displayed. Internal DSLs, on the other hand, use features of the language—Python, in this case—to enable people to write code that resembles the domain syntax, an example would be how numpy uses Python to allow mathematicians to describe linear algebra problems.

The interpreter pattern specifically caters to internal DSLs.

The idea is to create a syntax that is significantly less comprehensive than a general-purpose language, yet significantly more expressive, specifically as it relates to the domain in question.

Have a look at the following code, which defines rules for specials run by our imaginary restaurant and is written as conditionals in Python.

```python
pizzas = [item for tab.items if item.type == "pizza"]
if len(pizzas) > 2 and day_of_week == 4:
    cheapest_pizza_price = min([pizza.price for pizza in pizzas])
    tab.add_discount(cheapest_pizza_price)

drinks = [item for tab.items if item.type == "drink"]
if 17 < hour_now < 19:
    for item in tab.items:
        if item.type == "drink":
            item.price = item.price * 0.90
```

```
if tab.customer.is_member():
    for item in tab.items:
        item.price = item.price * 0.85
```

Now, look at the stark contrast between the previous code snippet and the definition of the same rules in a simple DSL for defining specials.

```
If tab contains 2 pizzas on Wednesdays cheapest one is free
Every day from 17:00 to 19:00 drinks are less 10%
All items are less 15% for members
```

We will not yet look at the interpretation, which will come a little later. What I want you to notice is how much more clearly the DSL communicates how the rules of the specials will be applied. It is written in a way that will make sense to a business owner and will allow them to either affirm that it does indeed fit their intent or that a mistake was made and corrections will be needed. Ambiguity is reduced, and adding new rules or specials becomes more simple—a win on both counts.

Advantages of DSLs

The level of understanding and communication with regards to the domain for which the DSL is created is greatly elevated. Domain experts can reason about the expression of both the problem and the solution in the DSL without their having a software engineering background. The development of business information systems can thus move from software developers to the domain experts. This results in richer, more accurate systems expressed in terms the experts being aided by the system can understand.

Disadvantages of DSLs

Before you head out and begin creating DSLs for every problem domain you can dream of, remember that there is a cost involved in learning a DSL, even if it makes sense for the domain experts. Someone new may understand what your DSL is expressing, but they will still need to learn the language implementation in order to be able to work with it. The deeper and richer your DSL, the more knowledge the domain expert needs to operate the language, which might have an impact on the number of people who will be able to use and maintain the system. Keep in mind that the use of a DSL should aid the business, not hamper it, or it will discard the language in the long run, if it ever adopts it in the first place.

We have considered the pros and cons of having a DSL and decide to move forward with one for specifying rules for the restaurant specials.

On a macro level, you want to accomplish two tasks. First, you want to define the language. Specifically, you want to define the semantics (meaning) and syntax (structure) of the language. Next, you want to write code that will be able to take the language as input and translate it into a form that a machine can understand and action.

Based on your conversations with customers, extract the things that are involved in the process as well as the actions taken by every entity involved. After this, isolate common words or phrases that have a specific meaning in the domain under consideration. Use these three elements to construct a grammar, which you will discuss with the domain experts before implementing it.

Before we look at an example of this process in the context of the restaurant specials, I want you start thinking of yourself as a tool maker. Whenever you encounter a frustration or problem, you should begin thinking of how you would go about solving this problem and what tools you would code to make the process ten times easier or faster. This is the mindset that sets the best software developers and engineers apart from the rest of the field.

In our example case, we started by having a series of conversations with the restaurant owner (the domain expert) and identified the following rules for specials:

```
Members always get 15% off their total tab
During happy hour, which happens from 17:00 to 19:00 weekdays, all drinks
are less 10%
Mondays are buy one get one free burger nights
Thursday are 'eat all you can' ribs
Sunday nights after 18:00 buy three pizzas and get the cheapest one free
when you buy 6 you get the two cheapest ones free and so on for every three
additional pizzas
```

Then, we identified the things that were mentioned:

```
members
tabs
happy hour
```

```
drinks
weekdays
Mondays
burgers
Thursday
ribs
Sunday
pizzas
```

We also identified the actions that could take place:

```
get 15% discount
get 10% discount
get one free
eat all you can
```

Finally, we recognized the key ideas as they relate to specials in the restaurant:

```
If a customer is of a certain type they always get a fixed % off their total tab
At certain times all items of a specific type gets discounted with a fixed
percentage
At certain times you get a second item of a certain type free if you were
to buy one item of that type
```

Generalizing the elements in the key ideas results in the following rules for specials:

```
If certain conditions are met certain items get a % discount
```

One way to formally express a grammar is by writing it in Extended Backus-Naur form (EBNF For more information on EBNF see: https://www.cs.umd.edu/class/fall2002/cmsc214/Tutorial/ebnf.html). Our restaurant example in ENBF looks like this:

```
rule: "If ", conditions, " then ", item_type, " get ", discount
conditions: condition | conditions " and " conditions | conditions " or "
conditions
condition: time_condition | item_condition | customer_condition
discount: number, "% discount" | "cheapest ", number, item_type " free"
```

```
time_condition: "today is ", day_of_week | "time is between ", time, " and ",
time | "today is a week day" | "today not a week day"
day_of_week: "Monday" | "Tuesday" | "Wednesday" | "Thursday" | "Friday" |
"Saturday" | "Sunday"
time: hours, ":", minutes
hours: hour_tens, hour_ones
hour_tens: "0" | "1"
hour_ones: digit
minutes: minute_tens, minute_ones
minute_tens: "0" | "1" | "2" | "3" | "4" | "5"
minute_ones: digit

item_condition: "item is a ", item_type | "there are ", number, " of ",
item_type
item_type: "pizza" | "burger" | "drink" | "chips"
number: {digit}
digit: "0" | "1" | "2" | "3" | "4" | "5" | "6" | "7" | "8" | "9"

customer_condition: "customer is a ", customer_type
customer_type: "member" | "non-member"
```

You have a set of terminal symbols that cannot be substituted with any pattern, as well as a set of non-terminal production rules that can be used to replace a non-terminal (a place holder symbol) with a sequence of terminals or with some recipe of other non-terminal patterns. Different ways in which a non-terminal can be substituted are separated by the pipe character "|".

When you are creating an external DSL, a package such as PyParsing can be used to translate strings written in a grammar like the one just seen to a data type that can be handled by Python code.

You have now seen an example of how you can move through the process of domain modeling by understanding the domain via conversations with domain experts, identifying key elements of the domain, codifying this understanding in some sort of domain model that can be verified by domain experts, and finally implementing the DSL as a final product of the process.

From this point on, we will be dealing with an *internal DSL*.

If we were to implement the special rules as an internal DSL, we would need to basically create one class per symbol.

We begin by creating just the stubs based on the grammar we defined earlier:

```python
class Tab(object):
    pass

class Item(object):
    pass

class Customer(object):
    pass

class Discount(object):
    pass

class Rule(object):
    pass

class CustomerType(object):
    pass

class ItemType(object):
    pass

class Conditions(object):
    pass

class Condition(object):
    pass

class TimeCondition(object):
    pass

class DayOfWeek(object):
    pass

class Time(object):
    pass

class Hours(object):
    pass

class HourTens(object):
    pass
```

```python
class HourOnes(object):
    pass

class Minutes(object):
    pass

class MinuteTens(object):
    pass

class MinuteOnes(object):
    pass

class ItemCondition(object):
    pass

class Number(object):
    pass

class Digit(object):
    pass

class CustomerCondition(object):
    pass
```

Not all of these classes will be needed in the final design, and as such you should pay attention to the YAGNI principle; basically, the idea is that you should not build things you are not going to need. In this case, I have written them all out so you can see that we took every single thing mentioned in the process of defining the grammar and created a class for each.

Before we reduce the classes and create the final internal DSL, we are going to touch on the composite pattern, which will be useful when we start building our interpreter.

Composite Pattern

When you have a container with elements that could themselves be containers, you have a good case for using the composite pattern. Look at the EBNF version of the grammar we are developing for the restaurant; an item can be a combo that contains items.

The composite pattern defines both composite (i.e., non-terminals) classes and leaf (i.e., terminals) classes that can be used to construct a composite component, such as a special rule.

```python
class Leaf(object):
  def __init__(self, *args, **kwargs):
    pass

  def component_function(self):
    print("Leaf")

class Composite(object):
  def __init__(self, *args, **kwargs):
    self.children = []

  def component_function(self):
    for child in children:
      child.component_function()

  def add(self, child):
    self.children.append(child)

  def remove(self, child):
    self.children.remove(child)
```

In less dynamic languages, you would have also had to define a super class that would be inherited by both the Composite and the Leaf classes, but since Python uses duck typing, we are once again saved from creating unnecessary boilerplate code.

Internal DSL Implementation Using the Composite Pattern

Let us consider an implementation of the first rule for discounts from the restaurant in the beginning of this chapter, as some rudimentary internal DSL.

```python
class Tab(object):
    def __init__(self, customer):
        self.items = []
        self.discounts = []
        self.customer = customer
```

```python
    def calculate_cost(self):
        return sum(x.cost for x in self.items)

    def calculate_discount(self):
        return sum(x for x in self.discounts)

class Item(object):
    def __init__(self, name, item_type, cost):
        self.name = name
        self.item_type = item_type
        self.cost = cost

class ItemType(object):
    def __init__(self, name):
        self.name = name

class Customer(object):
    def __init__(self, customer_type, name):
        self.customer_type = customer_type
        self.name = name

    def is_a(self, customer_type):
        return self.customer_type == customer_type

class Discount(object):
    def __init__(self, amount):
        self.amount = amount

class CustomerType(object):
    def __init__(self, customer_type):
        self.customer_type = customer_type

class Rule(object):
    def __init__(self, tab):
        self.tab = tab
        self.conditions = []
        self.discounts = []

    def add_condition(self, test_value):
        self.conditions.append(test_value)
```

```python
    def add_percentage_discount(self, item_type, percent):
        if item_type == "any item":
            f = lambda x: True
        else:
            f = lambda x: x.item_type == item_type

        items_to_discount = [item for item in self.tab.items if f(item)]
        for item in items_to_discount:
            discount = Discount(item.cost * (percent/100.0))
            self.discounts.append(discount)

    def apply(self):
        if all(self.conditions):
            return sum(x.amount for x in self.discounts)

        return 0

if __name__ == "__main__":
    member = CustomerType("Member")
    member_customer = Customer(member, "John")
    tab = Tab(member_customer)

    pizza = ItemType("pizza")
    burger = ItemType("Burger")
    drink = ItemType("Drink")

    tab.items.append(Item("Margarita", pizza, 15))
    tab.items.append(Item("Cheddar Melt", burger, 6))
    tab.items.append(Item("Latte", drink, 4))

    rule = Rule(tab)
    rule.add_condition(tab.customer.is_a(member))
    rule.add_percentage_discount("any item", 15)

    tab.discounts.append(
        rule.apply()
    )
```

```python
print(
    "Calculated cost: {}\nDiscount applied: {}\n{}% Discount applied".
    format(
        tab.calculate_cost(),
        tab.calculate_discount(),
        100 * tab.calculate_discount() / tab.calculate_cost()
    )
)
```

Now that we have a single rule working, using objects that result in some form of readable code, let's return to the implementation of the DSL using the composite pattern. Conditions can be a set of conjuncted conditions, a set of disjuncted conditions, or a single Boolean expression.

```python
class AndConditions(object):
    def __init__(self):
        self.conditions = []

    def evaluate(self, tab):
        return all(x.evaluate(tab) for x in self.conditions)

    def add(self, condition):
        self.conditions.append(condition)

    def remove(self, condition):
        self.conditions.remove(condition)

class OrConditions(object):
    def __init__(self):
        self.conditions = []

    def evaluate(self, tab):
        return any(x.evaluate(tab) for x in self.conditions)

    def add(self, condition):
        self.conditions.append(condition)

    def remove(self, condition):
        self.conditions.remove(condition)
```

```python
class Condition(object):
    def __init__(self, condition_function):
        self.test = condition_function

    def evaluate(self, tab):
        return self.test(tab)

class Discounts(object):
    def __init__(self):
        self.children = []

    def calculate(self, tab):
        return sum(x.calculate(tab) for x in self.children)

    def add(self, child):
        self.children.append(child)

    def remove(self, child):
        self.children.remove(child)

class Discount(object):
    def __init__(self, test_function, discount_function):
        self.test = test_function
        self.discount = discount_function

    def calculate(self, tab):
        return sum(self.discount(item) for item in tab.items if self.
        test(item))

class Rule(object):
    def __init__(self, tab):
        self.tab = tab
        self.conditions = AndConditions()
        self.discounts = Discounts()

    def add_conditions(self, conditions):
        self.conditions.add(conditions)

    def add_discount(self, test_function, discount_function):
        discount = Discount(test_function, discount_function)
        self.discounts.add(discount)
```

```
def apply(self):
    if self.conditions.evaluate(self.tab):
        return self.discounts.calculate(self.tab)

    return 0
```

Implementing the Interpreter Pattern

Two types of people use software: those who are satisfied with the offering out of the box and those who are willing to tinker and tweak to make the software fit their needs more perfectly. The interpreter pattern is interesting only to the people in this second group since they are the people who will be willing to invest the time needed to learn how to use the DSL to make the software fit their needs.

Back in the restaurant, one owner will be happy with some basic templates for specials, like a two-for-one offer, while another restaurant owner will want to tweak and expand his offers.

We can now generalize the basic implementation for the DSL we did previously to create a way of solving these problems in the future.

Every expression type gets a class (as before), and every class has an interpret method. A class and an object to store the global context will also be needed. This context is passed to the interpret function of the next object in the interpretation stream. Assume that parsing already took place.

The interpreter recursively traverses the container object until the answer to the problem is reached.

```
class NonTerminal(object):
    def __init__(self, expression):
        self.expression = expression

    def interpret(self):
        self.expression.interpret()

class Terminal(object):
    def interpret(self):
        pass
```

Finally, the interpreter pattern can be used to decide if a certain tab qualifies for any specials. First, the tab and item classes are defined, followed by the classes needed for the grammar. Then, some sentences in the grammar are implemented and tested using test tabs. Note that we hard code the types in this example so the code can be run; usually, those are the types of things you would like to store in some file or database.

```python
import datetime

class Rule(object):
    def __init__(self, conditions, discounts):
        self.conditions = conditions
        self.discounts = discounts

    def evaluate(self, tab):
        if self.conditions.evaluate(tab):
            return self.discounts.calculate(tab)

        return 0

class Conditions(object):
    def __init__(self, expression):
        self.expression = expression

    def evaluate(self, tab):
        return self.expression.evaluate(tab)

class And(object):
    def __init__(self, expression1, expression2):
        self.expression1 = expression1
        self.expression2 = expression2

    def evaluate(self, tab):
        return self.expression1.evaluate(tab) and self.expression2.
        evaluate(tab)

class Or(object):
    def __init__(self, expression1, expression2):
        self.expression1 = expression1
        self.expression2 = expression2
```

```python
    def evaluate(self, tab):
        return self.expression1.evaluate(tab) or self.expression2.
        evaluate(tab)

class PercentageDiscount(object):
    def __init__(self, item_type, percentage):
        self.item_type = item_type
        self.percentage = percentage

    def calculate(self, tab):
        return (sum([x.cost for x in tab.items if x.item_type ==
        self.item_type]) * self.percentage) / 100

class CheapestFree(object):
    def __init__(self, item_type):
        self.item_type = item_type

    def calculate(self, tab):
        try:
            return min([x.cost for x in tab.items if x.item_type ==
            self.item_type])
        except:
            return 0

class TodayIs(object):
    def __init__(self, day_of_week):
        self.day_of_week = day_of_week

    def evaluate(self, tab):
        return datetime.datetime.today().weekday() == self.day_of_week.name

class TimeIsBetween(object):
    def __init__(self, from_time, to_time):
        self.from_time = from_time
        self.to_time = to_time

    def evaluate(self, tab):
        hour_now = datetime.datetime.today().hour
        minute_now = datetime.datetime.today().minute
```

```python
        from_hour, from_minute = [int(x) for x in self.from_time.
        split(":")]
        to_hour, to_minute = [int(x) for x in self.to_time.split(":")]

        hour_in_range = from_hour <= hour_now < to_hour
        begin_edge = hour_now == from_hour and minute_now > from_minute
        end_edge = hour_now == to_hour and minute_now < to_minute

        return any(hour_in_range, begin_edge, end_edge)

class TodayIsAWeekDay(object):
    def __init__(self):
        pass

    def evaluate(self, tab):
        week_days = [
            "Monday",
            "Tuesday",
            "Wednesday",
            "Thursday",
            "Friday",
        ]
        return datetime.datetime.today().weekday() in week_days

class TodayIsAWeekedDay(object):
    def __init__(self):
        pass

    def evaluate(self, tab):
        weekend_days = [
            "Saturday",
            "Sunday",
        ]
        return datetime.datetime.today().weekday() in weekend_days

class DayOfTheWeek(object):
    def __init__(self, name):
        self.name = name
```

197

```python
class ItemIsA(object):
    def __init__(self, item_type):
        self.item_type = item_type

    def evaluate(self, item):
        return self.item_type == item.item_type

class NumberOfItemsOfType(object):
    def __init__(self, number_of_items, item_type):
        self.number = number_of_items
        self.item_type = item_type

    def evaluate(self, tab):
        return len([x for x in tab.items if x.item_type == self.item_type]) \
            == self.number

class CustomerIsA(object):
    def __init__(self, customer_type):
        self.customer_type = customer_type

    def evaluate(self, tab):
        return tab.customer.customer_type == self.customer_type

class Tab(object):
    def __init__(self, customer):
        self.items = []
        self.discounts = []
        self.customer = customer

    def calculate_cost(self):
        return sum(x.cost for x in self.items)

    def calculate_discount(self):
        return sum(x for x in self.discounts)

class Item(object):
    def __init__(self, name, item_type, cost):
        self.name = name
        self.item_type = item_type
        self.cost = cost
```

```python
class ItemType(object):
    def __init__(self, name):
        self.name = name

class Customer(object):
    def __init__(self, customer_type, name):
        self.customer_type = customer_type
        self.name = name

class CustomerType(object):
    def __init__(self, customer_type):
        self.customer_type = customer_type

member = CustomerType("Member")
pizza = ItemType("pizza")
burger = ItemType("Burger")
drink = ItemType("Drink")

monday = DayOfTheWeek("Monday")

def setup_demo_tab():
    member_customer = Customer(member, "John")
    tab = Tab(member_customer)

    tab.items.append(Item("Margarita", pizza, 15))
    tab.items.append(Item("Cheddar Melt", burger, 6))
    tab.items.append(Item("Hawaian", pizza, 12))
    tab.items.append(Item("Latte", drink, 4))
    tab.items.append(Item("Club", pizza, 17))

    return tab

if __name__ == "__main__":
    tab = setup_demo_tab()

    rules = []

    # Members always get 15% off their total tab
    rules.append(
```

```
        Rule(
            CustomerIsA(member),
            PercentageDiscount("any_item", 15)
        )
    )

    # During happy hour, which happens from 17:00 to 19:00 weekdays, all
    drinks are less 10%
    rules.append(
        Rule(
            And(TimeIsBetween("17:00", "19:00"), TodayIsAWeekDay()),
            PercentageDiscount(drink, 10)
        )
    )

    # Mondays are buy one get one free burger nights
    rules.append(
        Rule(
            And(TodayIs(monday), NumberOfItemsOfType(burger, 2)),
            CheapestFree(burger)
        )
    )

    for rule in rules:
        tab.discounts.append(rule.evaluate(tab))

    print(
        "Calculated cost: {}\nDiscount applied: {}\n".format(
            tab.calculate_cost(),
            tab.calculate_discount()
        )
    )
```

In this chapter, you saw two ways of interpreting a grammar and internal DSL. We looked at the composite pattern, then used it to interpret a rule for specials in a restaurant. Then, we built on that idea, together with the general interpreter pattern, to develop a more complete interpreter to test conditions and calculate what discounts apply. Essentially you worked through the whole process from getting business requirements to defining the problem in terms of a DSL and then implementing the DSL in code.

Parting Shots

Wherever you are on your programming journey, decide right now that you will do the hard work needed to become better. You do this by working on programming projects and doing programming challenges.

One such challenge by Jeff Bay can be found in *Thought Works Anthology*, published by The Pragmatic Programmers.

Attempt a non-trivial project (one that will require more than 1,000 lines of code to solve) by following these rules:

1. Only one level of indentation is allowed per method, thus no `if` statements in loops or nesting.

2. You're not allowed to use the keyword `else`.

3. All primitive types and strings must be wrapped in objects— specifically for the use they are put to.

4. Collections are first class, and as such require their own objects.

5. Don't abbreviate names. If names are too long, you are probably doing more than one thing in a method or class—don't do that.

6. Only one object operator allowed per line, so `object.method()` is ok, but `object.attribute.method()` is not.

7. Keep your entities small (packages < 15 objects, classes < 50 lines, methods < 5 lines).

8. No class may have more than two instance variables.

9. You are not allowed to use getters, setters, or access properties directly.

Exercises

- Follow the same thought process we used when defining a DSL for the restaurant to define a DSL that you can implement in your own to-do list application. This DSL should allow your program to pick up cues like "every Wednesday . . ." and translate them to recurring tasks. Also add awareness of date and some other indicators of time relative to some other date or time.

- Implement your DSL from the previous exercise in Python so it can interpret to-do items and extract the necessary characteristics.

- Build a basic to-do list application using one of the popular Python web frameworks and have it interpret to-do's using your DSL interpreter.

- Find some interesting improvements or expansions to make the to-do list application something you can use on a daily basis.

CHAPTER 13

Iterator Pattern

The wheels of the bus go round and round, round and round, round and round

Data structures and algorithms form an integral part of the software design and development process. Often, different data structures have different uses, and using the right data structure for a specific problem might mean a lot less work and a lot more efficiency. Choosing the correct data structure and matching it with the relevant algorithm will improve your solution.

Since data structures have different implementations, we are tempted to implement the algorithms that operate on them differently. For instance, if we were to consider a binary tree that looks something like this:

```python
class Node(object):
    def __init__(self, data):
        self.data = data
        self.left = None
        self.right = None
```

traversing the elements of the tree to make sure you visit each one might look something like this:

```python
class Node(object):
    def __init__(self, data):
        self.data = data
        self.left = None
        self.right = None

def tree_traverse(node):
    if node.left is not None:
        tree_traverse(node.left)
```

© Wessel Badenhorst 2017
W. Badenhorst, *Practical Python Design Patterns*, https://doi.org/10.1007/978-1-4842-2680-3_13

```python
    print(node.data)

    if node.right is not None:
        tree_traverse(node.right)
if __name__ == "__main__":
    root = Node("i am the root")

    root.left = Node("first left child")
    root.right = Node("first right child")

    root.left.right = Node("Right child of first left child of root")

    tree_traverse(root)
```

Contrast this to when you want to traverse a simple list:

```python
lst = [1, 2, 3, 4, 5]

for i in range(len(lst)):
    print(lst[i])
```

I know I used the for loop in a way that is not considered pythonic, but if you come from a C/C++ or Java background, this will look familiar. I do this because I want to illustrate how you could traverse a list and a binary tree and how they are distinctly different processes that produce a similar result.

Alexander Stepanov, advocate of generic programming and as the primary designer and implementer of the C++ Standard Template Library, spent a lot of time thinking about the techniques of generic programming, where the code is written in terms of algorithms that operate on data types to be defined at some future time. He married ideas from pure mathematics and algebra with computer science and concluded that most algorithms can be defined in relation to an algebraic data type called *containers*.

By decoupling the algorithm from the specific type and implementation of a container, you become free to describe the algorithm without paying any attention to the actual implementation details of the specific type of container. The result of this decoupling is more general, more reusable code.

We want to be able to traverse a collection without worrying about whether we are dealing with a list or a binary tree or some other collection.

To do this, we want to create an interface that a collection data type can inherit, which would allow it to generalize the action of traversing the contents of the collection. We do this by using the following components.

First, we define an interface that defines a function that gets the next item in the collection, and another function to alert some external function that there are no more elements left in the collection to return.

Second, we define some sort of object that can use the interface to traverse the collection. This object is called an *iterator*.

Following the traditional approach, we can implement this idea as follows:

classic_iter.py

```python
import abc

class Iterator(metaclass=abc.ABCMeta):

    @abc.abstractmethod
    def has_next(self): pass

    @abc.abstractmethod
    def next(self): pass

class Container(metaclass=abc.ABCMeta):

    @abc.abstractmethod
    def getIterator(self): pass

class MyListIterator(Iterator):
        def __init__(self, my_list):
            self.index = 0
            self.list = my_list.list

        def has_next(self):
            return self.index < len(self.list)

        def next(self):
            self.index += 1
            return self.list[self.index - 1]

class MyList(Container):
    def __init__(self, *args):
        self.list = list(args)
```

```python
    def getIterator(self):
        return MyListIterator(self)

if __name__ == "__main__":
    my_list = MyList(1, 2, 3, 4, 5, 6)
    my_iterator = my_list.getIterator()

    while my_iterator.has_next():
        print(my_iterator.next())
```

This prints out the following result:

```
1
2
3
4
5
6
```

This idea of traversing some collection is so widespread that it has a name—the iterator pattern.

Python Internal Implementation of the Iterator Pattern

As you have probably guessed by now, Python makes implementing the iterator pattern extremely simple. In fact, you have used iterators already in this book. The way for loops are implemented in Python uses the iterator pattern.

Take, for instance, this for loop:

```python
for i in range(1, 7):
  print(i)
```

This is analogous to the iterator pattern implementation we saw in the previous section.

This convenience in Python is accomplished by defining an iterator protocol that is used to create objects that are iterable and then returning some object that knows how to iterate over these iterable objects.

Python uses two specific method calls and one raised exception to provide the iterator functionality throughout the language.

The first method of an iterable is the __iter__() method, which returns an iterator object. Next, a __next__() method must be provided by the iterator object; it is used to return the next element in the iterable. Lastly, when all the elements have been iterated over, the iterator raises a StopIteration exception.

We often see the iterable collection in Python return an instance of itself, given that the class in question also implements the __next__() method and raises the StopIteration exception. An iterator similar to the classic implementation we looked at before might look something like this:

```python
class MyList(object):
    def __init__(self, *args):
        self.list = list(args)
        self.index = 0

    def __iter__(self):
        return self

    def __next__(self):
        try:
            self.index += 1
            return self.list[self.index - 1]
        except IndexError:
            raise StopIteration()

if __name__ == "__main__":
    my_list = MyList(1, 2, 3, 4, 5, 6)

    for i in my_list:
        print(i)
```

This time, you will notice that we used the Python for loop to iterate over the elements in the list, which is only possible because our MyList class has the functions required by the Python iterator protocol.

If we were to implement the binary tree we saw at the beginning of this chapter as a Python iterable, it would be implemented as follows:

bin_tree_iterator.py

```python
class Node(object):
    def __init__(self, data):
        self.data = data
        self.left = None
        self.right = None

class MyTree(object):
    def __init__(self, root):
        self.root = root

    def add_node(self, node):
        current = self.root

        while True:
            if node.data <= current.data:
                if current.left is None:
                    current.left = node
                    return
                else:
                    current = current.left
            else:
                if current.right is None:
                    current.right = node
                    return
                else:
                    current = current.right

    def __iter__(self):
        if self.root is None:
            self.stack = []
        else:
            self.stack = [self.root]
            current = self.root
```

```python
        while current.left is not None:
            current = current.left
            self.stack.append(current)

    return self

def __next__(self):
    if len(self.stack) <= 0:
        raise StopIteration

    while len(self.stack) > 0:
        current = self.stack.pop()
        data = current.data

        if current.right is not None:
            current = current.right
            self.stack.append(current)

            while current.left is not None:
                current = current.left
                self.stack.append(current)

        return data

    raise StopIteration

if __name__ == "__main__":
    tree = MyTree(Node(16))
    tree.add_node(Node(8))
    tree.add_node(Node(1))
    tree.add_node(Node(17))
    tree.add_node(Node(13))
    tree.add_node(Node(14))
    tree.add_node(Node(9))
    tree.add_node(Node(10))
    tree.add_node(Node(11))

    for i in tree:
        print(i)
```

We keep the Node class exactly as we defined it earlier, only now we have added a Container class, namely MyTree. This class implements the iterator protocol, and as such can be used in a normal Python for loop, as we have seen in the list iterator. We also included a convenience function that allows us to build a binary tree by simply calling the add_node method on the tree instance of MyTree. This allows us to forget about how exactly the tree is implemented. The process of inserting a new node into the tree simply involves looking at the current node and going left if the node to be added's data value is less than or equal to that of the current node in the tree. We keep doing this until an empty spot is found, and the new node is placed at this empty spot.

To traverse the tree, we keep a stack of nodes, then we start pushing repeatedly, moving left and pushing the current node onto the stack. This happens until there are no more left children. Then, we pop the top node from the stack and check if it has a right child. If it does, the right child gets pushed onto the stack, along with the leftmost branch of the tree from that node. We then return the value of the node popped from the stack. The stack is maintained as an instance variable of the tree object, and as such we are able to continue where we left off every time the __next__() method is called.

This results in an ordered sequence being printed, as follows:

```
1
8
9
10
11
13
14
16
17
```

We could use existing Python functions and constructs to interface with the binary tree, like for loops and max and sum functions. Just for fun, look at how easy it is to use these constructs with a completely custom data type.

You have seen that for loops work as expected; now, we will use the same code as we did in bin_tree_iterator.py, but we will add a max and sum call to the last if statement. As such, only the if statement is included in the code snippet.

```
if __name__ == "__main__":
    tree = MyTree(Node(16))
    tree.add_node(Node(8))
    tree.add_node(Node(1))
    tree.add_node(Node(17))
    tree.add_node(Node(13))
    tree.add_node(Node(14))
    tree.add_node(Node(9))
    tree.add_node(Node(10))
    tree.add_node(Node(11))

    for i in tree:
        print(i)

    print("maximum value: {}".format(max(tree)))

    print("total of values: {}".format(sum(tree)))
```

As you would expect, the results are as follows:

```
1
8
9
10
11
13
14
16
17
maximum value: 17
total of values: 99
```

The algorithms for each of these constructs were implemented completely decoupled of the data types that would later use them. Interestingly enough, you can create a list object that is iterable using a list comprehension (which is almost like a shorthand for creating iterable objects) as above, only the if statement is changed, so once again I will only include the code for the if and the code needed to transform the tree into a list.

```
if __name__ == "__main__":
    tree = MyTree(Node(16))
    tree.add_node(Node(8))
    tree.add_node(Node(1))
    tree.add_node(Node(17))
    tree.add_node(Node(13))
    tree.add_node(Node(14))
    tree.add_node(Node(9))
    tree.add_node(Node(10))
    tree.add_node(Node(11))

    print([x for x in tree])
```

Resulting in an ordered list of values

```
[1, 8, 9, 10, 11, 13, 14, 16, 17]
```

List comprehensions are fairly simple to understand. They take a function or operation and map it to an iterable. You could also add some sort of conditional statement after the iteration to exclude certain elements.

Let's alter the comprehension we just looked at to now ignore all multiples of 3.

once again a list comprehension with an if x % 6 != 0

```
if __name__ == "__main__":
    tree = MyTree(Node(16))
    tree.add_node(Node(8))
    tree.add_node(Node(1))
    tree.add_node(Node(17))
    tree.add_node(Node(13))
    tree.add_node(Node(14))
    tree.add_node(Node(9))
    tree.add_node(Node(10))
    tree.add_node(Node(11))

    print([x for x in tree if x % 3 != 0])
```

As you would hope, the 9 is not included in the final list:

```
[1, 8, 10, 11, 13, 14, 16, 17]
```

Itertools

I'm sure you are convinced of the usefulness of iterators by now. So, I will add a quick mention of the Itertools package included in the standard library. It contains a number of functions that allow you to combine and manipulate iterators in some interesting ways. These building blocks have been taken from the world of functional programming and languages like Haskell and reimagined in a pythonic way.

For an extensive list of these, do yourself a favor and read the documentation for the Itertools library. To introduce you to the library, I just want to mention three functions.

The first is `chain()`, which allows you to chain multiple iterators one after the other.

```
import itertools
```

```
print(list(itertools.chain([1, 2, 3, 4], range(5,9), "the quick and the
slow")))
```

This iterates over every value in each of the three iterables and converts them all to a single list that is printed, as follows:

```
[1, 2, 3, 4, 5, 6, 7, 8, 't', 'h', 'e', ' ', 'q', 'u', 'i', 'c', 'k', ' ',
'a', 'n', 'd', ' ', 't', 'h', 'e', ' ', 's', 'l', 'o', 'w']
```

Next, we have the infinite iterator `cycle()`, which allows you to create an iterator that will keep cycling over the elements passed to it indefinitely.

```
import itertools
```

```
cycler = itertools.cycle([1, 2, 3])
print(cycler.__next__())
print(cycler.__next__())
print(cycler.__next__())
print(cycler.__next__())
print(cycler.__next__())
print(cycler.__next__())
print(cycler.__next__())
print(cycler.__next__())
```

Every time the cycler reaches the last element, it just starts back at the beginning.

```
1
2
3
1
2
3
1
2
```

The third and final function you can look at is `zip_longest()`, which combines a set of iterables and returns their matched elements on each iteration.

zip_longest example

```python
import itertools

list1 = [1, 2, 3]
list2 = ['a', 'b', 'c']

zipped = itertools.zip_longest(list1, list2)

print(list(zipped))
```

The result is a set of pairs where the first pair contains the first elements of both lists, the second pair contains the second elements of both lists, and so on.

```python
[(1, 'a'), (2, 'b'), (3, 'c')]
```

There are many other interesting things you can do with iterators, and many of them will help you find simple solutions for tricky problems. As is probably the case with most libraries included in the Python standard library, it is worth your effort to explore and master the Itertools package.

Generator Functions

Before we begin exploring generator expressions, let's write a quick script to demonstrate what they do.

gen_func.py

```python
def gen_squares(n):
    i = 0
    while i < n:
        yield i*i
        print("next i")
        i += 1

if __name__ == "__main__":
    g = gen_squares(4)
    print(g.__next__())
    print(g.__next__())
    print(g.__next__())
    print(g.__next__())
    print(g.__next__())
```

The result you get from requesting next is the next square, as you can see here:

```
0
next i
1
next i
4
next i
9
next i
Traceback (most recent call last):
  File "gen_func.py", line 15, in <module>
    print(g.__next__())
StopIteration
```

There are a couple of interesting things you will observe from the output, the first of which is that every time you call the function the output changes. The second thing you should note is that the function starts executing from just below the yield statement and continues until it hits the yield again.

When the interpreter encounters the `yield` statement, it keeps a record of the current state of the function and returns the value that is yielded. Once the next value is requested via the __next__() method, the internal state is loaded and the function continues from where it left off.

Generators are a great way to simplify the creation of iterators since a generator is a function that produces a sequence of results and follows the interface for collections that can be iterated over as per the Python implementation of the iterator pattern. In the case of a generator function, the Python internals take care of the iterator protocol for you.

When a generator function is called, it returns a generator object but does not begin any execution until the __next__() method is called the first time. At that time, the function starts executing and runs until the yield is reached. Once the generator reaches its end, it raises the same exception as iterators do. The generator returned by the generator function is also an iterator.

Generator Expression

Much like we used list comprehensions as a shorthand to create iterators, there is a special shorthand for generators called *generator expressions*.

Look at the example generator expression that follows. It is simply an alternative for the generator function we defined earlier.

```python
g = (x*x for x in range(4))
```

Generator expressions can be used as arguments to certain functions that consume iterators, like the `max()` functions.

```python
print(max((x*x for x in range(4))))
```

This prints the number 9.

With Python, we can drop the parentheses around a generator if there is only one argument in the calling function.

```python
print(max(x*x for x in range(4)))
```

This is a little bit neater.

Parting Shots

Iterators and generators will help you do a lot of heavy lifting as you explore the world of Python, and getting comfortable using them will help you code faster. They also extend your code into the realm of functional programming, where you are more focused on defining *what* the program must do rather than *how* it must be done.

Speaking of coding faster, here are a couple of tips to improve your development speed.

- Learn to touch type. It is like being able to read and write. If you are going to do something every day, learning to do that as effectively as possible is a major force multiplier.

- Study and master your editor or IDE of choice, whether that be Vim, Emacs, Pycharm, or whatever else you use, and make sure to learn all the shortcuts.

- Eliminate distractions, as every time you need to switch context, you will take up to 30 minutes to find your groove again. Not worth it.

- Make sure your tests run fast. The slower your tests are, the greater the temptation is to skip them.

- Every moment spent searching online for an answer or example is coding and thinking time gone to waste, so learn the field, master the language, and reduce your time on forums.

- Pay down technical debt as if your life depended on it—your happiness sure does.

Exercises

- Implement a Fibonacci sequence iterable using both a generator and a regular iterator.

- Create a binary tree iterator using generator functions.

CHAPTER 14

Observer Pattern

You know, Norton, I've been watching you.

—Eddie Murphy, *Delirious*

If you did the object calisthenics exercise from chapter 12, you would have noticed how difficult it is to reduce the number of lines used in certain methods. This is especially difficult if the object is too tightly coupled with a number of other objects; i.e., one object relies too much on its knowledge of the internals of the other objects. As such, methods have too much detail that is not strictly related to the method in question.

Maybe this seems a bit vague at the moment. Allow me to clarify. Say you have a system where users are able to complete challenges, and upon completion they are awarded points, gain general experience points, and also earn skills points for the skills used to complete the task. Every task needs to be evaluated and scored where relevant. Take a moment and think about how you would implement such a system. Once you have written down the basic architecture, look at the example that follows.

What we want is some way to keep track of the user credits earned and spent, the amount of experience the user has accumulated up until this point, as well as the scores that count toward earning specific badges or achievements. You could think of this system as either some sort of habit-building challenge app or any RPG ever created.

task_completer.py

```python
class Task(object):

    def __init__(self, user, _type):
        self.user = user
        self._type = _type
```

© Wessel Badenhorst 2017
W. Badenhorst, *Practical Python Design Patterns*, https://doi.org/10.1007/978-1-4842-2680-3_14

```python
    def complete(self):
        self.user.add_experience(1)
        self.user.wallet.increase_balance(5)

        for badge in self.user.badges:
            if self._type == badge._type:
                badge.add_points(2)

class User(object):

    def __init__(self, wallet):
        self.wallet = wallet
        self.badges = []
        self.experience = 0

    def add_experience(self, amount):
        self.experience += amount

    def __str__(self):
        return "Wallet\t{}\nExperience\t{}\n+ Badges +\n{}\
        n++++++++++++++++++".format(
            self.wallet,
            self.experience,
            "\n".join([ str(x) for x in self.badges])
        )

class Wallet(object):

    def __init__(self):
        self.amount = 0

    def increase_balance(self, amount):
        self.amount += amount

    def decrease_balance(self, amount):
        self.amount -= amount

    def __str__(self):
        return str(self.amount)
```

```python
class Badge(object):

    def __init__(self, name, _type):
        self.points = 0
        self.name = name
        self._type = _type
        self.awarded = False

    def add_points(self, amount):
        self.points += amount

        if self.points > 3:
            self.awarded = True

    def __str__(self):
        if self.awarded:
            award_string = "Earned"
        else:
            award_string = "Unearned"

        return "{}: {} [{}]".format(
            self.name,
            award_string,
            self.points
        )

def main():
    wallet = Wallet()
    user = User(wallet)

    user.badges.append(Badge("Fun Badge", 1))
    user.badges.append(Badge("Bravery Badge", 2))
    user.badges.append(Badge("Missing Badge", 3))

    tasks = [Task(user, 1), Task(user, 1), Task(user, 3)]
    for task in tasks:
        task.complete()

    print(user)

if __name__ == "__main__":
    main()
```

In the output, we can see the relevant values added to the wallet, experience, and badges, with the right badge being awarded once the threshold is cleared.

```
Wallet  15
Experience      3
+ Badges +
Fun Badge: Earned [4]
Bravery Badge: Unearned [0]
Missing Badge: Unearned [2]
++++++++++++++++
```

This very basic implementation has a fairly complex set of calculations to perform whenever a task is completed. In the preceding code, we have a fairly well-implemented architecture, but the evaluation function is still clunky, and I'm sure you already get that feeling that this is code you would not like to work on once you got it working. I also think that it would not be any fun to write tests for this method. Any additions to the system would mean altering this method, forcing even more calculations and evaluations to take place.

As we stated earlier, this is a symptom of having a tightly coupled system. The Task object must know about every points object in order for it to be able to assign the correct points or credits to the correct sub-system. We want to remove the evaluation of every rule from the main part of the task complete method and place more responsibility with the sub-systems so they handle data alterations based on their own rules and not those of some foresight object.

To do this, we take the first step toward a more decoupled system, as seen here:

task_semi_decoupled.py

```python
class Task(object):

    def __init__(self, user, _type):
        self.user = user
        self._type = _type

    def complete(self):
        self.user.complete_task(self)
        self.user.wallet.complete_task(self)
        for badge in self.user.badges:
            badge.complete_task(self)
```

```python
class User(object):

    def __init__(self, wallet):
        self.wallet = wallet
        self.badges = []
        self.experience = 0

    def add_experience(self, amount):
        self.experience += amount

    def complete_task(self, task):
        self.add_experience(1)

    def __str__(self):
        return "Wallet\t{}\nExperience\t{}\n+ Badges +\n{}\
        n++++++++++++++++".format(
            self.wallet,
            self.experience,
            "\n".join([ str(x) for x in self.badges])
        )

class Wallet(object):

    def __init__(self):
        self.amount = 0

    def increase_balance(self, amount):
        self.amount += amount

    def decrease_balance(self, amount):
        self.amount -= amount

    def complete_task(self, task):
        self.increase_balance(5)

    def __str__(self):
        return str(self.amount)
```

```python
class Badge(object):

    def __init__(self, name, _type):
        self.points = 0
        self.name = name
        self._type = _type
        self.awarded = False

    def add_points(self, amount):
        self.points += amount

        if self.points > 3:
            self.awarded = True

    def complete_task(self, task):
        if task._type == self._type:
            self.add_points(2)

    def __str__(self):
        if self.awarded:
            award_string = "Earned"
        else:
            award_string = "Unearned"

        return "{}: {} [{}]".format(
            self.name,
            award_string,
            self.points
        )

def main():
    wallet = Wallet()
    user = User(wallet)

    user.badges.append(Badge("Fun Badge", 1))
    user.badges.append(Badge("Bravery Badge", 2))
    user.badges.append(Badge("Missing Badge", 3))
```

```
    tasks = [Task(user, 1), Task(user, 1), Task(user, 3)]
    for task in tasks:
        task.complete()

    print(user)

if __name__ == "__main__":
    main()
```

This results in the same output as before. This is already a much better solution. The evaluation now takes place in the objects where they are relevant, which is closer to the rules contained in the objects callisthenics exercise. I hope a little light went on for you in terms of the value of practicing these types of code callisthenics and how it serves to make you a better programmer.

It still bothers me that the Task handler is changed whenever a new type of badge or credit or alert or whatever else you can think of is added to the system. What would be ideal is if there were some sort of hooking mechanism that would not only allow you to register new sub-systems and then dynamically have their evaluations done as needed, but also free you from the requirement to make any alterations to the main task system.

The concept of callback functions is quite useful for achieving this new level of dynamics. We will add generic callback functions to a collection that will be run whenever a task is completed. Now the system is more dynamic, as these systems can be added at runtime. The objects in the system will be decoupled even more.

task_with_callbacks.py

```
class Task(object):

    def __init__(self, user, _type):
        self.user = user
        self._type = _type
        self.callbacks = [
            self.user,
            self.user.wallet,
        ]
        self.callbacks.extend(self.user.badges)

    def complete(self):
        for item in self.callbacks:
            item.complete_task(self)
```

```python
class User(object):

    def __init__(self, wallet):
        self.wallet = wallet
        self.badges = []
        self.experience = 0

    def add_experience(self, amount):
        self.experience += amount

    def complete_task(self, task):
        self.add_experience(1)

    def __str__(self):
        return "Wallet\t{}\nExperience\t{}\n+ Badges
        +\n{}\n+++++++++++++++++".format(
            self.wallet,
            self.experience,
            "\n".join([ str(x) for x in self.badges])
        )

class Wallet(object):

    def __init__(self):
        self.amount = 0

    def increase_balance(self, amount):
        self.amount += amount

    def decrease_balance(self, amount):
        self.amount -= amount

    def complete_task(self, task):
        self.increase_balance(5)

    def __str__(self):
        return str(self.amount)
```

```python
class Badge(object):

    def __init__(self, name, _type):
        self.points = 0
        self.name = name
        self._type = _type
        self.awarded = False

    def add_points(self, amount):
        self.points += amount

        if self.points > 3:
            self.awarded = True

    def complete_task(self, task):
        if task._type == self._type:
            self.add_points(2)

    def __str__(self):
        if self.awarded:
            award_string = "Earned"
        else:
            award_string = "Unearned"

        return "{}: {} [{}]".format(
            self.name,
            award_string,
            self.points
        )

def main():
    wallet = Wallet()
    user = User(wallet)

    user.badges.append(Badge("Fun Badge", 1))
    user.badges.append(Badge("Bravery Badge", 2))
    user.badges.append(Badge("Missing Badge", 3))
```

```
    tasks = [Task(user, 1), Task(user, 1), Task(user, 3)]
    for task in tasks:
        task.complete()

    print(user)

if __name__ == "__main__":
    main()
```

Now you have a list of objects to be called back when the task is completed, and the task need not know anything more about the objects in the callbacks list other than that they have a complete_task() method that takes the task that just completed as a parameter.

Whenever you want to dynamically decouple the source of a call from the called code, this is the way to go. This problem is another one of those very common problems, so common that this is another design pattern—the observer pattern. If you take a step back from the problem we are looking at and just think of the observer pattern in general terms, it will look something like this.

There are two types of objects in the pattern, an Observable class, which can be watched by other classes, and an Observer class, which will be alerted whenever an Observable object the two classes are connected to undergoes a change.

In the original *Gang of Four* book, the observer design pattern is defined as follows: *A software design pattern in which an object, called the subject, maintains a list of its dependents, called observers, and notifies them automatically of any state changes, usually by calling one of their methods. It is mainly used to implement distributed event handling systems* [Gamma, E.; Helm, R.; Johnson, R.; Vlissides, J.; *Design Patterns: Elements of Reusable Object-Oriented Software Publisher: Addison-Wesley, 1994*].

In code, it looks like this:

```
import abc

class Observer(object):
    __metaclass__ = abc.ABCMeta

    @abc.abstractmethod
    def update(self, observed): pass
```

```python
class ConcreteObserver(Observer):

    def update(self, observed):
        print("Observing: " + observed)

class Observable(object):

    def __init__(self):
        self.observers = set()

    def register(self, observer):
        self.observers.add(observer)

    def unregister(self, observer):
        self.observers.discard(observer)

    def unregister_all(self):
        self.observers = set()

    def update_all(self):
        for observer in self.observers:
            observer.update(self)
```

The use of the Abstract base class results in a Java-like interface that forces the observers to implement the update() method. As we have seen before, there is no need for the Abstract base class, because of Python's dynamic nature, and as such the preceding code can be replaced by a more pythonic version:

```python
class ConcreteObserver(object):

    def update(self, observed):
        print("Observing: " + observed)

class Observable(object):

    def __init__(self):
        self.observers = set()

    def register(self, observer):
        self.observers.add(observer)
```

```python
    def unregister(self, observer):
        self.observers.discard(observer)

    def unregister_all(self):
        self.observers = set()

    def update_all(self):
        for observer in self.observers:
            observer.update(self)
```

In the preceding code, the Observable keeps a record of all the objects observing it in a list called *observers*, and whenever relevant changes happen in the Observable, it simply runs the update() method for each observer. You will notice this every time the update() function is called with the Observable object passed as a parameter. This is the general way of doing it, but any parameters, or even no parameters, can be passed to the observers, and the code will still adhere to the observer pattern.

If we were able to send different parameters to different objects, that would be really interesting, since we would greatly increase the efficiency of the calls if we no longer needed to pass the whole object that has undergone changes. Let's use Python's dynamic nature to make our observer pattern even better. For this, we will return to our user task system.

general_observer.py

```python
class ConcreteObserver(object):

    def update(self, observed):
        print("Observing: {}".format(observed))

class Observable(object):

    def __init__(self):
        self.callbacks = set()

    def register(self, callback):
        self.callbacks.add(callback)

    def unregister(self, callback):
        self.callbacks.discard(callback)
```

```python
    def unregister_all(self):
        self.callbacks = set()

    def update_all(self):
        for callback in self.callbacks:
            callback(self)

def main():
    observed = Observable()
    observer1 = ConcreteObserver()

    observed.register(lambda x: observer1.update(x))

    observed.update_all()

if __name__ == "__main__":
    main()
```

Although there are many ways to string up the actions that can take place once the state of an Observable changes, these are two concrete examples to build on.

Sometimes, you might find that you would prefer the rest of the system be updated at a specific time and not whenever the object changes. To facilitate this requirement, we will add a changed flag in a protected variable (remember, Python does not explicitly block access to this variable; it is more a matter of convention), which can be set and unset as needed. The timed function will then only process the change and alert the observers of the Observable object at the desired time. You could use any implementation of the observer pattern combined with the flag. In the example that follows, I used the functional observer. As an exercise, implement the flag for changed on the example with the object set of observers.

```python
import time

class ConcreteObserver(object):

    def update(self, observed):
        print("Observing: {}".format(observed))
```

```python
class Observable(object):

    def __init__(self):
        self.callbacks = set()
        self.changed = False

    def register(self, callback):
        self.callbacks.add(callback)

    def unregister(self, callback):
        self.callbacks.discard(callback)

    def unregister_all(self):
        self.callbacks = set()

    def poll_for_change(self):
        if self.changed:
            self.update_all

    def update_all(self):
        for callback in self.callbacks:
            callback(self)

def main():
    observed = Observable()
    observer1 = ConcreteObserver()

    observed.register(lambda x: observer1.update(x))

    while True:
        time.sleep(3)
        observed.poll_for_change()

if __name__ == "__main__":
    main()
```

The problems that the observer pattern solves are those where a group of objects has to respond to the change of state in some other object and do so without causing more coupling inside the system. In this sense, the observer pattern is concerned with the management of events or responding to change of state in some sort of network of objects.

I mentioned coupling, so let me clarify what is meant when we talk about coupling. Generally, when we talk about the level of coupling between objects, we refer to the degree of knowledge that one object needs with regard to other objects that it interacts with. The more loosely objects are coupled, the less knowledge they have about each other, and the more flexible the object-oriented system is. Loosely coupled systems have fewer interdependencies between objects and as such are easier to update and maintain. By decreasing the coupling between objects, you further reduce the risk that changing something in one part of the code will have unintended consequences in some other part of the code. Since objects do not rely on each other, unit testing and troubleshooting become easier to do.

Other good places to use the observer pattern include the traditional Model-View-Controller design pattern, which you will encounter later in the book, as well as a textual description of data that needs to be updated whenever the underlying data changes.

As a rule, whenever you have a publish–subscribe relationship between a single object (the Observable) and a set of observers, you have a good candidate for the observer pattern. Some other examples of this type of architecture are the many different types of feeds you find online, like newsfeeds, Atom, RSS, and podcasts. With all of these, the publisher does not care who the subscribers are, and thus you have a natural separation of concern. The observer pattern will make it easy to add or remove subscribers at runtime by increasing the level of decoupling between the subscribers and the publisher.

Now, let's use the pythonic implementation of the observer pattern to implement our tracking system from the beginning of the chapter. Note how easy it is to add new classes to the code and how clean the processes of updating and changing any of the existing classes are.

```python
class Task(object):

    def __init__(self, user, _type):
        self.observers = set()
        self.user = user
        self._type = _type

    def register(self, observer):
        self.observers.add(observer)
```

```python
    def unregister(self, observer):
        self.observers.discard(observer)

    def unregister_all(self):
        self.observers = set()

    def update_all(self):
        for observer in self.observers:
            observer.update(self)

class User(object):

    def __init__(self, wallet):
        self.wallet = wallet
        self.badges = []
        self.experience = 0

    def add_experience(self, amount):
        self.experience += amount

    def update(self, observed):
        self.add_experience(1)

    def __str__(self):
        return "Wallet\t{}\nExperience\t{}\n+ Badges
        +\n{}\n+++++++++++++++++".format(
            self.wallet,
            self.experience,
            "\n".join([ str(x) for x in self.badges])
        )

class Wallet(object):

    def __init__(self):
        self.amount = 0

    def increase_balance(self, amount):
        self.amount += amount
```

```python
    def decrease_balance(self, amount):
        self.amount -= amount

    def update(self, observed):
        self.increase_balance(5)

    def __str__(self):
        return str(self.amount)

class Badge(object):

    def __init__(self, name, _type):
        self.points = 0
        self.name = name
        self._type = _type
        self.awarded = False

    def add_points(self, amount):
        self.points += amount

        if self.points > 3:
            self.awarded = True

    def update(self, observed):
        if observed._type == self._type:
            self.add_points(2)

    def __str__(self):
        if self.awarded:
            award_string = "Earned"
        else:
            award_string = "Unearned"

        return "{}: {} [{}]".format(
            self.name,
            award_string,
            self.points
        )
```

```python
def main():
    wallet = Wallet()
    user = User(wallet)

    badges = [
        Badge("Fun Badge", 1),
        Badge("Bravery Badge", 2),
        Badge("Missing Badge", 3)
    ]

    user.badges.extend(badges)

    tasks = [Task(user, 1), Task(user, 1), Task(user, 3)]

    for task in tasks:
        task.register(wallet)
        task.register(user)
        for badge in badges:
            task.register(badge)

    for task in tasks:
        task.update_all()

    print(user)

if __name__ == "__main__":
    main()
```

Parting Shots

You should have a clear understanding of the observer pattern by now, and also have a feeling for how implementing this pattern in the real world allows you to build systems that are more robust, easier to maintain, and a joy to extend.

Exercises

- Use the observer pattern to model a system where your observers can subscribe to stocks in a stock market and make buy/sell decisions based on changes in the stock price.

- Implement the flag for changed on an example with the object set of observers.

CHAPTER 15

State Pattern

Under pressure.

—Queen, "Under Pressure"

A very useful tool for thinking through software problems is the state diagram. In a state diagram, you construct a graph, where nodes represent the state of the system and edges are transitions between one node in the system and another. State diagrams are useful because they let you think visually about the state of your system given certain inputs. You are also guided to consider the ways in which your system transitions from one state to the next.

Since we mentioned creating games earlier in this book, we can model the player character as a state machine. The player might start out in the standing state. Pressing the left or right arrow keys might change the state to moving left or moving right. The up arrow can then take the character from whatever state they're in into the jumping state, and, similarly, the down button will take the character into the crouching state. Even though this is an incomplete example, you should begin to understand how we might use a state diagram. It also becomes clear that when the up arrow key is pressed, the character will jump up and then come back down; if the key has not been released, the character will jump again. Releasing any key will take the character from whatever state it was in back to the standing state.

Another example from a more formal sphere would be looking at an ATM machine. A simplified state machine for an ATM machine might include the following states:

- waiting

- accepting card

- accepting PIN input

- validating PIN

© Wessel Badenhorst 2017
W. Badenhorst, *Practical Python Design Patterns*, https://doi.org/10.1007/978-1-4842-2680-3_15

- rejecting PIN

- Getting transaction selection

- A set of states for every part of every transaction

- finalizing transaction

- returning card

- printing slip

- dispensing slip

Specific system and user actions will cause the ATM to move from one state to the next. Inserting a card into the machine will cause the machine to transition from the `waiting` state to the `accepting_card` state, and so on.

Once you have drawn up a complete state diagram for a system, you will have a fairly complete picture of what the system should be doing every step of the way. You will also have clarity on how your system should be moving from one step to another. All that remains is to translate your state diagram into code.

A naive way to translate the diagram into runnable code is to create an object that represents the state machine. The object will have an attribute for its state, which will determine how it reacts to input. If we were to code up the first example of the game character, it would look something like this.

Window systems have issues with curses, but that can be fixed by installing Cygwin, which gives you a Linux-like terminal that works well with the curses library curses. To download Cygwin, head to the main website at `https://www.cygwin.com/` and download the current DLL version that matches your machine. If you find you have to set up Python again, just follow the steps under the Linux section of the installation guide from the beginning of this book.

```python
import time

import curses

def main():
    win = curses.initscr()
    curses.noecho()

    win.addstr(0, 0, "press the keys w a s d to initiate actions")
    win.addstr(1, 0, "press x to exit")
```

```
    win.addstr(2, 0, "> ")
    win.move(2, 2)

    while True:
        ch = win.getch()
        if ch is not None:
            win.move(2, 0)
            win.deleteln()
            win.addstr(2, 0, "> ")
            if ch == 120:
                break
            elif ch == 97:    # a
                print("Running Left")
            elif ch == 100:   # d
                print("Running Right")
            elif ch == 119:   # w
                print("Jumping")
            elif ch == 115:   # a
                print("Crouching")
            else:
                print("Standing")
        time.sleep(0.05)

if __name__ == "__main__":
    main()
```

As an exercise, you can expand upon this code using the pygame module from chapter 4 to create a character that can run and jump on the screen instead of just printing out the action the character is currently taking. It might be useful to look at the pygame documentation to see how to load a sprite image from a file (sprite sheet) instead of just drawing a simple block on the screen.

By this time, you know that the if statement we use to determine what to do with the input is a problem. It smells bad to your code sense. Since state diagrams are such useful representations of object-oriented systems, and the resulting state machines are widespread, you can be sure that there is a design pattern to clean up this code smell. The design pattern you are looking for is the state pattern.

State Pattern

On an abstract level, all object-oriented systems concern themselves with the actors in a system and how the actions of each impact the other actors and the system as a whole. This is why a state machine is so helpful in modeling the state of an object and the things that cause said object to react.

In object-oriented systems, the state pattern is used to encapsulate behavior variations based on the internal state of an object. This encapsulation solves the monolithic conditional statement we saw in our previous example.

This sounds great, but how would this be accomplished?

What you need is some sort of representation for the state itself. Sometimes, you may even want all the states to share some generic functionality, which will be coded into the State base class. Then, you have to create a concrete State class for every discrete state in your state machine. Each of these can have some sort of handler function to deal with input and cause a transition of state, as well as a function to complete the action required of that state.

In the following code snippet, we define an empty base class that the concrete State classes will be inherited from. Note that, as in previous chapters, Python's duck-typing system allows you to drop the State class in this most basic implementation. I include the base class State in the snippet for clarity only. The concrete states also lack action methods, as this implementation takes no action, and as such these methods would be empty.

```python
class State(object):
    pass

class ConcreteState1(State):

    def __init__(self, state_machine):
        self.state_machine = state_machine

    def switch_state(self):
        self.state_machine.state = self.state_machine.state2

class ConcreteState2(State):

    def __init__(self, state_machine):
        self.state_machine = state_machine
```

```python
    def switch_state(self):
        self.state_machine.state = self.state_machine.state1

class StateMachine(object):

    def __init__(self):
        self.state1 = ConcreteState1(self)
        self.state2 = ConcreteState2(self)
        self.state = self.state1

    def switch(self):
        self.state.switch_state()

    def __str__(self):
        return str(self.state)

def main():
    state_machine = StateMachine()
    print(state_machine)

    state_machine.switch()
    print(state_machine)

if __name__ == "__main__":
    main()
```

From the result, you can see where the switch happens from ConcreteState1 to ConcreteState2. The StateMachine class represents the context of execution and provides a single interface to the outside world.

```
<__main__.ConcreteState1 object at 0x7f184f7a7198>
<__main__.ConcreteState2 object at 0x7f184f7a71d0>
```

As you progress down the path to becoming a better programmer, you will find yourself spending more and more time thinking about how you can test certain code constructs. State machines are no different. So, what can we test about a state machine?

1.   That the state machine initializes correctly

2.   That the action method for each concrete State class does what it should do, like return the correct value

3. That, for a given input, the machine transitions to the correct subsequent state

4. Python includes a very solid unit-testing framework, not surprisingly called *unittest*.

To test our generic state machine, we could use the following code:

```python
import unittest

class GenericStatePatternTest(unittest.TestCase):
    def setUp(self):
        self.state_machine = StateMachine()

    def tearDown(self):
        pass

    def test_state_machine_initializes_correctly(self):
        self.assertIsInstance(self.state_machine.state, ConcreteState1)

    def test_switch_from_state_1_to_state_2(self):
        self.state_machine.switch()

        self.assertIsInstance(self.state_machine.state, ConcreteState2)

    def test_switch_from_state2_to_state1(self):
        self.state_machine.switch()
        self.state_machine.switch()

        self.assertIsInstance(self.state_machine.state, ConcreteState1)

if __name__ == '__main__':
    unittest.main()
```

Play around with the options for asserts and see what other interesting tests you can come up with.

We will now return to the problem of the player character either running or walking, as we discussed in the beginning of this chapter. We will implement the same functionality from before, but this time we will use the state pattern.

```python
import curses
import time
class State(object):
    def __init__(self, state_machine):
        self.state_machine = state_machine

    def switch(self, in_key):
        if in_key in self.state_machine.mapping:
            self.state_machine.state = self.state_machine.mapping[in_key]
        else:
            self.state_machine.state = self.state_machine.
            mapping["default"]

class Standing(State):
    def __str__(self):
        return "Standing"

class RunningLeft(State):
    def __str__(self):
        return "Running Left"

class RunningRight(State):
    def __str__(self):
        return "Running Right"

class Jumping(State):
    def __str__(self):
        return "Jumping"

class Crouching(State):
    def __str__(self):
        return "Crouching"

class StateMachine(object):

    def __init__(self):
        self.standing = Standing(self)
        self.running_left = RunningLeft(self)
        self.running_right = RunningRight(self)
```

```
        self.jumping = Jumping(self)
        self.crouching = Crouching(self)

        self.mapping = {
            "a": self.running_left,
            "d": self.running_right,
            "s": self.crouching,
            "w": self.jumping,
            "default": self.standing,
        }

        self.state = self.standing

    def action(self, in_key):
        self.state.switch(in_key)

    def __str__(self):
        return str(self.state)

def main():
    player1 = StateMachine()
    win = curses.initscr()
    curses.noecho()

    win.addstr(0, 0, "press the keys w a s d to initiate actions")
    win.addstr(1, 0, "press x to exit")
    win.addstr(2, 0, "> ")
    win.move(2, 2)

    while True:
        ch = win.getch()
        if ch is not None:
            win.move(2, 0)
            win.deleteln()
            win.addstr(2, 0, "> ")
            if ch == 120:
                break
```

```
        player1.action(chr(ch))
        print(player1.state)
    time.sleep(0.05)

if __name__ == "__main__":
    main()
```

How do you feel about the altered code? What do you like about it? What have you learned? What do you think can be improved?

I want to encourage you to begin looking at code online and asking yourself these questions. You will often find you learn more from reading other people's code than from all the tutorials you could ever find online. That is also the point where you take another big step forward in your learning, when you begin to think critically about the code you find online rather than just copying it into your project and hoping for the best.

Parting Shots

In this chapter, we discovered how closely we could link actual code in Python to an abstract tool for solving multiple types of problems, namely the state machine.

All state machines are composed of states and the transitions taking the machine from one state to another based on certain inputs. Usually, the state machine will also execute some actions while in a state before transitioning to another state.

We also looked at the actual code you could use to build your very own state machine in Python.

Here are some quick and simple ideas for constructing your own state machine-based solutions.

1. Identify the states your machine can be in, such as `running` or `walking` or, in the case of a traffic light, `red`, `yellow`, and `green`.

2. Identify the different inputs you expect for each state.

3. Draw a transition from the current state to the next state based on the input. Note the input on the transition line.

4. Define the actions taken by the machine in each state.

5. Abstract the shared actions into the base `State` class.

6. Implement concrete classes for each state you identified.

7. Implement a set of transition methods to deal with the expected inputs for every state.

8. Implement the actions that need to be taken by the machine in every state. Remember, these actions live in the concrete State class as well as in the base State class.

There you have it—a fully implemented state machine that has a one-to-one relation to the abstract diagram solving the problem.

Exercises

- Expand on the simple state machine for the player character by using pygame to create a visual version. Load a sprite for the player and then model some basic physics for the jump action.

- Explore the different types of assert statements available to you as part of the Python unittest library.

CHAPTER 16

Strategy Pattern

Move in silence, only speak when it's time to say Checkmate.

—Unknown

From time to time, you might find yourself in a position where you want to switch between different ways of solving a problem. You essentially want to be able to pick a strategy at runtime and then run with it. Each strategy might have its own set of strengths and weaknesses. Suppose you want to reduce two values to a single value. Assuming these values are numeric values, you have a couple of options for reducing them.

As an example, consider using simple addition and subtraction as strategies for reducing the two numbers. Let's call them `arg1` and `arg2`. A simple solution would be something like this:

```python
def reducer(arg1, arg2, strategy=None):
    if strategy == "addition":
        print(arg1 + arg2)
    elif strategy == "subtraction":
        print(arg1 - arg2)
    else:
        print("Strategy not implemented...")

def main():
    reducer(4, 6)
    reducer(4, 6, "addition")
    reducer(4, 6, "subtraction")

if __name__ == "__main__":
    main()
```

© Wessel Badenhorst 2017
W. Badenhorst, *Practical Python Design Patterns*, https://doi.org/10.1007/978-1-4842-2680-3_16

This solution results in the following:

```
Strategy not implemented...
10
-2
```

This is what we want. Sadly, we suffer from the same problem we encountered in previous chapters, namely that whenever we want to add another strategy to the reducer, we have to add another `elif` statement to the function together with another block of code to handle that strategy. This is a surefire way to grow a sprawling `if` statement. We would much prefer a more modular solution that would allow us to pass in new strategies on the fly without our having to alter the code that uses or executes the strategy.

As you have come to expect by now, we have a design pattern for that.

This design pattern is aptly named the strategy pattern because it allows us to write code that uses some strategy, to be selected at runtime, without knowing anything about the strategy other than that it follows some execution signature.

Once again, we turn to an object to help us solve this problem. We will also reach for the fact that Python treats functions as first-class citizens, which will make the implementation of this pattern much cleaner than the original implementation.

We will start with the traditional implementation of the strategy pattern.

```python
class StrategyExecutor(object):
    def __init__(self, strategy=None):
        self.strategy = strategy

    def execute(self, arg1, arg2):
        if self.strategy is None:
            print("Strategy not implemented...")
        else:
            self.strategy.execute(arg1, arg2)

class AdditionStrategy(object):
    def execute(self, arg1, arg2):
        print(arg1 + arg2)

class SubtractionStrategy(object):
    def execute(self, arg1, arg2):
        print(arg1 - arg2)
```

```python
def main():
    no_strategy = StrategyExecutor()
    addition_strategy = StrategyExecutor(AdditionStrategy())
    subtraction_strategy = StrategyExecutor(SubtractionStrategy())

    no_strategy.execute(4, 6)
    addition_strategy.execute(4, 6)
    subtraction_strategy.execute(4, 6)

if __name__ == "__main__":
    main()
```

This again results in the required output:

```
Strategy not implemented...
10
-2
```

At least we dealt with the sprawling if statement as well as the need to update the executor function every time we add another strategy. This is a good step in the right direction. Our system is a little more decoupled, and each part of the program only deals with the part of the execution it is concerned with without its worrying about the other elements in the system.

In the traditional implementation, we made use of duck typing, as we have done many times in this book. Now, we will use another powerful Python tool for writing clean code—using functions as if they were any other value. This means we can pass a function to the Executor class without first wrapping the function in a class of its own. This will not only greatly reduce the amount of code we have to write in the long run, but it will also make our code easier to read and easier to test since we can pass arguments to the functions and assert that they return the value we expect.

```python
class StrategyExecutor(object):

    def __init__(self, func=None):
        if func is not None:
            self.execute = func

    def execute(self, *args):
        print("Strategy not implemented...")
```

```python
def strategy_addition(arg1, arg2):
    print(arg1 + arg2)

def strategy_subtraction(arg1, arg2):
    print(arg1 - arg2)

def main():
    no_strategy = StrategyExecutor()
    addition_strategy = StrategyExecutor(strategy_addition)
    subtraction_strategy = StrategyExecutor(strategy_subtraction)

    no_strategy.execute(4, 6)
    addition_strategy.execute(4, 6)
    subtraction_strategy.execute(4, 6)

if __name__ == "__main__":
    main()
```

Again, we get the required result:

```
Strategy not implemented...
10
-2
```

Since we are already passing around functions, we might as well take advantage of having first-class functions and abandon the Executor object in our implementation, leaving us with a very elegant solution to the dynamic-strategy problem.

```python
def executor(arg1, arg2, func=None):
    if func is None:
        print("Strategy not implemented...")
    else:
        func(arg1, arg2)

def strategy_addition(arg1, arg2):
    print(arg1 + arg2)

def strategy_subtraction(arg1, arg2):
    print(arg1 - arg2)
```

```
def main():
    executor(4, 6)
    executor(4, 6, strategy_addition)
    executor(4, 6, strategy_subtraction)

if __name__ == "__main__":
    main()
```

As before, you can see that the output matches the requirement:

```
Strategy not implemented...
10
-2
```

We created a function that could take a pair of arguments and a strategy to reduce them at runtime. A multiplication or division strategy, or any binary operation to reduce the two values to a single value, can be defined as a function and passed to the reducer. We do not run the risk of a sprawling `if` growing in our executor and causing code rot to appear.

One thing that is a bit bothersome about the preceding code snippet is the `else` statement in the executor. We know that we will usually not be printing text in the terminal as the result of something happening inside our program. It is way more likely that the code will return some value. Since the print statements are used to demonstrate the concepts we are dealing with in the strategy pattern in a tangible manner, I will implement the strategy pattern, using a print statement in the main function to simply print out the result of the executor. This will allow us to use an early return to get rid of the dangling `else`, and thus clean up our code even more.

The cleaned-up version of our code now looks something like this:

```
def executor(arg1, arg2, func=None):
    if func is None:
        return "Strategy not implemented..."

    return func(arg1, arg2)

def strategy_addition(arg1, arg2):
    return arg1 + arg2
```

```
def strategy_subtraction(arg1, arg2):
    return arg1 - arg2

def main():
    print(executor(4, 6))
    print(executor(4, 6, strategy_addition))
    print(executor(4, 6, strategy_subtraction))

if __name__ == "__main__":
    main()
```

Once again, we test that the code results in the output we saw throughout this chapter:

```
Strategy not implemented...
10
-2
```

Indeed it does. Now we have a clean, clear, and simple way to implement different strategies in the same context. The executor function now also uses an early return to discard invalid states, which makes the function read more easily in terms of the actual execution of the optimal case happening on a single level.

In the real world, you might look at using different strategies for evaluating the stock market and making purchasing decisions; alternatively, you might look at different pathfinding techniques and switch strategies there.

Parting Shots

The broken windows theory works just as well in code as in real life. Never tolerate broken windows in your code. Broken windows, in case you were wondering, are those pieces of code that you know are not right and will not be easy to maintain or extend. It is the type of code you really feel like slapping a *TODO* comment on, that you know you need to come back and fix but never will. To become a better coder, you need to take responsibility for the state of the codebase. After you have had it in your care, it should be better, cleaner, and more maintainable than before. Next time you feel the temptation to leave a to-do as a booby trap for the poor developer who passes this way after you, roll up your sleeves and knock out that fix you had in mind. The next poor coder who has to work on this code might just be you, and then you will thank the coder who came before and cleaned things up a little.

Exercises

- See if you can implement a maze generator that will print a maze using "#" and " " to represent walls and paths, respectively. Before generating the maze, have the user pick one of three strategies. Use the strategy pattern to have the generator strategy passed to the maze generator. Then use that strategy to generate the maze.

CHAPTER 17

Template Method Pattern

Success without duplication is merely future failure in disguise.

—Randy Gage in How to build a multi-level
money machine: the science of network marketing

In life, as in coding, there are patterns, snippets of actions that you can repeat step by step and get the expected result. In more complex situations, the details of the unique steps may vary, but the overall structure remains the same. In life, you get to write standard operating procedures or devise rules of thumb (or mental models, if that is how you roll). When we write code, we turn to code reuse.

Code reuse is the promised land that ushered in the almost ubiquitous obsession with object-oriented programming. The dream is that you would follow the DRY principle not only within a specific project, but also across multiple projects, building up a set of tools as you went along. Every project would not only make you a better programmer, but would also result in another set of tools in your ever-growing arsenal. Some would argue that the content of this very book is a violation of the DRY principle since the existence of a set of patterns that come up enough times to be codified and solved means that such problems should not need solving again.

Complete code reuse has yet to be achieved, as any programmer with more than a couple of years' worth of experience can testify. The proliferation and constant reimagining of programming languages indicate that this is far from a solved problem.

I do not want to demoralize, but you need to be aware that we as developers need to be pragmatic, and often we need to make decisions that do not fit the way the world should be. Being irritated with these decisions and desiring a better solution is not a problem unless it keeps you from doing the actual work. That said, using patterns like the strategy pattern allows us to improve the way we do things without needing to rewrite the whole program. Separation of concern, as we have been talking about throughout this book, is yet another way of enabling less work to be done whenever things change—and things always change.

© Wessel Badenhorst 2017
W. Badenhorst, *Practical Python Design Patterns*, https://doi.org/10.1007/978-1-4842-2680-3_17

What are we to do when we identify a solid pattern of actions that need to be taken in a variety of contexts, each with its own nuances?

Functions are one form of a recipe. Consider the pattern for calculating n!, where n! = n * n -1 * ... * 1 where n > 2 else n! is 1. Solving this for the case where n = 4, we could simply write:

```
fact_5 = 5 * 4 * 3 * 2 * 1
```

That is fine if the only factorial you are ever going to be interested in is that of five, but it is way more helpful to have a general solution to the problem, such as this:

```python
def fact(n):
    if n < 2:
        return 1

    return n * fact(n-1)

def main():
    print(fact(0))
    print(fact(1))
    print(fact(5))

if __name__ == "__main__":
    main()
```

What we see here is an illustration where a specific set of steps leads to a predictable result. Functions are really great at capturing this idea of an algorithm or set of steps leading to an expected result for some set of input values. It does become more difficult when we begin to think about situations that might be more complicated than simply following a predefined set of instructions. Another consideration is what you would do should you want to use the same steps in a different way, or implement the steps using a more efficient algorithm. It might not be clear from the trivial case of the factorial function, so let's look at a more involved example.

Your point of sales system suddenly became popular, and now customers want to have all kinds of funny things. The chief of these requests is to interface with some third-party system they have been using forever to keep track of stock levels and pricing changes. They are not interested in replacing the existing system, because there are customers who are already using it, so you have to do the integration.

You sit down and identify the steps needed to integrate with the remote system.

- Sync stock items between the point of sale and the third-party system.

- Send transactions to the third party.

This is a simplified set of steps, but it will serve us well enough.

In the world of simple functions we had before, we could write code for each step in the process and place each step's code in separate functions, each of which could be called at the appropriate time. See here:

```python
def sync_stock_items():
    print("running stock sync between local and remote system")
    print("retrieving remote stock items")
    print("updating local items")
    print("sending updates to third party")

def send_transaction(transaction):
    print("send transaction: {0!r}".format(transaction))

def main():
    sync_stock_items()

    send_transaction(
        {
            "id": 1,
            "items": [
                {
                    "item_id": 1,
                    "amount_purchased": 3,
                    "value": 238
                }
            ],
        }
    )

if __name__ == "__main__":
    main()
```

The result looks something like this:

```
running stock sync between local and remote system
retrieving remote stock items
updating local items
sending updates to third party
send transaction: {'items': [{'amount_purchased': 3, 'item_id': 1,
                  'value': 238}], 'id': 1}
```

Next, we will evaluate the code in terms of what happens in the real world. If there is one third-party system you need to integrate with, there will be others. What if you are handed not one but two other third-party applications to integrate with?

You could do the easy thing and create a couple of sprawling if statements to direct traffic inside of the function to each of the three systems you need to cater to, resulting in something like the incomplete code snippet that follows, which is included only to demonstrate the effect of the sprawling if on the neatness of the code.

```
def sync_stock_items(system):
    if system == "system1":
        print("running stock sync between local and remote system1")
        print("retrieving remote stock items from system1")
        print("updating local items")
        print("sending updates to third party system1")
    elif system == "system2":
        print("running stock sync between local and remote system2")
        print("retrieving remote stock items from system2")
        print("updating local items")
        print("sending updates to third party system2")
    elif system == "system3":
        print("running stock sync between local and remote system3")
        print("retrieving remote stock items from system3")
        print("updating local items")
        print("sending updates to third party system3")
    else:
        print("no valid system")
```

```
def send_transaction(transaction, system):
    if system == "system1":
        print("send transaction to system1: {0!r}".format(transaction))
    elif system == "system2":
        print("send transaction to system2: {0!r}".format(transaction))
    elif system == "system3":
        print("send transaction to system3: {0!r}".format(transaction))
    else:
        print("no valid system")
```

The test cases we included in the main function result in output similar to the one that follows. Just be aware that since dictionaries are not ordered in terms of their keys, the order of the items in the dictionary that is printed may vary from machine to machine. What is important is that the overall structure remains the same, as do the values of the keys.

```
==========
running stock sync between local and remote system1
retrieving remote stock items from system1
updating local items
sending updates to third party system1
send transaction to system1: ({'items': [{'item_id': 1, 'value':
                              238, 'amount_purchased': 3}], 'id': 1},)
==========
running stock sync between local and remote system2
retrieving remote stock items from system2
updating local items
sending updates to third party system2
send transaction to system2: ({'items': [{'item_id': 1, 'value':
                              238, 'amount_purchased': 3}], 'id': 1},)
==========
running stock sync between local and remote system3
retrieving remote stock items from system3
updating local items
sending updates to third party system3
send transaction to system3: ({'items': [{'item_id': 1, 'value':
                              238, 'amount_purchased': 3}], 'id': 1},)
```

261

Not only do you have to pass in the arguments needed to execute the specific functionality, but also you have to pass around the name of the service relevant to the current user of the system. It is also obvious from our previous discussions that this way of building a system of any non-trivial scale will be a disaster in the long run. What options are left? Since this is a book on design patterns, we want to come up with a solution that uses design patterns to solve the problem in question—a solution that is easy to maintain, update, and extend. We want to be able to add new third-party providers without any alterations to the existing code. We could try to implement the strategy pattern for each of the three functions, as follows:

```python
def sync_stock_items(strategy_func):
    strategy_func()

def send_transaction(transaction, strategy_func):
    strategy_func(transaction)

def stock_sync_strategy_system1():
    print("running stock sync between local and remote system1")
    print("retrieving remote stock items from system1")
    print("updating local items")
    print("sending updates to third party system1")

def stock_sync_strategy_system2():
    print("running stock sync between local and remote system2")
    print("retrieving remote stock items from system2")
    print("updating local items")
    print("sending updates to third party system2")

def stock_sync_strategy_system3():
    print("running stock sync between local and remote system3")
    print("retrieving remote stock items from system3")
    print("updating local items")
    print("sending updates to third party system3")

def send_transaction_strategy_system1(transaction):
    print("send transaction to system1: {0!r}".format(transaction))

def send_transaction_strategy_system2(transaction):
    print("send transaction to system2: {0!r}".format(transaction))
```

```python
def send_transaction_strategy_system3(transaction):
    print("send transaction to system3: {0!r}".format(transaction))

def main():
    transaction = {
            "id": 1,
            "items": [
                {
                    "item_id": 1,
                    "amount_purchased": 3,
                    "value": 238
                }
            ],
        },

    print("="*10)
    sync_stock_items(stock_sync_strategy_system1)
    send_transaction(
        transaction,
        send_transaction_strategy_system1
    )
    print("="*10)
    sync_stock_items(stock_sync_strategy_system2)
    send_transaction(
        transaction,
        send_transaction_strategy_system2
    )
    print("="*10)
    sync_stock_items(stock_sync_strategy_system3)
    send_transaction(
        transaction,
        send_transaction_strategy_system1
    )

if __name__ == "__main__":
    main()
```

We have the same results with the test cases included in the main function as we had for the version using multiple if statements.

```
==========
running stock sync between local and remote system1
retrieving remote stock items from system1
updating local items
sending updates to third party system1
send transaction to system1: ({'items': [{'item_id': 1, 'amount_purchased':
                              3, 'value': 238}], 'id': 1},)
==========
running stock sync between local and remote system2
retrieving remote stock items from system2
updating local items
sending updates to third party system2
send transaction to system2: ({'items': [{'item_id': 1, 'amount_purchased':
                              3, 'value': 238}], 'id': 1},)
==========
running stock sync between local and remote system3
retrieving remote stock items from system3
updating local items
sending updates to third party system3
send transaction to system1: ({'items': [{'item_id': 1, 'amount_purchased':
                              3, 'value': 238}], 'id': 1},)
```

Two things bother me about this implementation. The first is that the functions we are following are clearly steps in the same process, and, as such, they should live in a single entity instead of being scattered. We also don't want to pass in a strategy based on the system that is being targeted for every step of the way, as this is another violation of the DRY principle. Instead, what we need to do is implement another design pattern called the template method pattern.

The template method does exactly what it says on the box. It provides a method template that can be followed to implement a specific process step by step, and then that template can be used in many different scenarios by simply changing a couple of details.

In the most general sense, the template method pattern will look something like this when implemented:

```python
import abc

class TemplateAbstractBaseClass(metaclass=abc.ABCMeta):

    def template_method(self):
        self._step_1()
        self._step_2()
        self._step_n()

    @abc.abstractmethod
    def _step_1(self): pass

    @abc.abstractmethod
    def _step_2(self): pass

    @abc.abstractmethod
    def _step_3(self): pass

class ConcreteImplementationClass(TemplateAbstractBaseClass):

    def _step_1(self): pass

    def _step_2(self): pass

    def _step_3(self): pass
```

This is the first instance where the use of Python's Abstract base class library is truly useful. Up until now, we got away with ignoring the base classes that are so often used by other, less dynamic languages because we could rely on the duck-typing system. With the template method, things are a little different. The method used to execute the process is included in the Abstract base class (ABC), and all classes that inherit from this class are forced to implement the methods for each step in their own way, but all child classes will have the same execution method (unless it is overridden for some reason).

Now, let's use this idea to implement our third-party integrations using the template method pattern.

```python
import abc

class ThirdPartyInteractionTemplate(metaclass=abc.ABCMeta):
    def sync_stock_items(self):
        self._sync_stock_items_step_1()
        self._sync_stock_items_step_2()
        self._sync_stock_items_step_3()
        self._sync_stock_items_step_4()

    def send_transaction(self, transaction):
        self._send_transaction(transaction)

    @abc.abstractmethod
    def _sync_stock_items_step_1(self): pass

    @abc.abstractmethod
    def _sync_stock_items_step_2(self): pass

    @abc.abstractmethod
    def _sync_stock_items_step_3(self): pass

    @abc.abstractmethod
    def _sync_stock_items_step_4(self): pass

    @abc.abstractmethod
    def _send_transaction(self, transaction): pass

class System1(ThirdPartyInteractionTemplate):
    def _sync_stock_items_step_1(self):
        print("running stock sync between local and remote system1")

    def _sync_stock_items_step_2(self):
        print("retrieving remote stock items from system1")

    def _sync_stock_items_step_3(self):
        print("updating local items")
```

```python
    def _sync_stock_items_step_4(self):
        print("sending updates to third party system1")

    def _send_transaction(self, transaction):
        print("send transaction to system1: {0!r}".format(transaction))

class System2(ThirdPartyInteractionTemplate):
    def _sync_stock_items_step_1(self):
        print("running stock sync between local and remote system2")

    def _sync_stock_items_step_2(self):
        print("retrieving remote stock items from system2")

    def _sync_stock_items_step_3(self):
        print("updating local items")

    def _sync_stock_items_step_4(self):
        print("sending updates to third party system2")

    def _send_transaction(self, transaction):
        print("send transaction to system2: {0!r}".format(transaction))

class System3(ThirdPartyInteractionTemplate):
    def _sync_stock_items_step_1(self):
        print("running stock sync between local and remote system3")

    def _sync_stock_items_step_2(self):
        print("retrieving remote stock items from system3")

    def _sync_stock_items_step_3(self):
        print("updating local items")

    def _sync_stock_items_step_4(self):
        print("sending updates to third party system3")

    def _send_transaction(self, transaction):
        print("send transaction to system3: {0!r}".format(transaction))
```

```
def main():
    transaction = {
            "id": 1,
            "items": [
                {
                    "item_id": 1,
                    "amount_purchased": 3,
                    "value": 238
                }
            ],
        },

    for C in [System1, System2, System3]:
        print("="*10)
        system = C()
        system.sync_stock_items()
        system.send_transaction(transaction)

if __name__ == "__main__":
    main()
```

Once again, our test code results in the output we would hope for. As in the previous section, the order of the key value pairs in the dictionaries returned by your implementation might be different, but the structure and values will remain consistent.

```
==========
running stock sync between local and remote system1
retrieving remote stock items from system1
updating local items
sending updates to third party system1
send transaction to system1: ({'items': [{'amount_purchased': 3, 'value':
                        238, 'item_id': 1}], 'id': 1},)
==========
running stock sync between local and remote system2
retrieving remote stock items from system2
updating local items
sending updates to third party system2
```

```
send transaction to system2: ({'items': [{'amount_purchased': 3, 'value':
                            238, 'item_id': 1}], 'id': 1},)
==========
running stock sync between local and remote system3
retrieving remote stock items from system3
updating local items
sending updates to third party system3
send transaction to system3: ({'items': [{'amount_purchased': 3, 'value':
                            238, 'item_id': 1}], 'id': 1},)
```

Parting Shots

Knowing which pattern to use where, and where to not rely on any of the patterns in this or any other book, is a form of intuition. As is the case with martial arts, it is helpful to practice implementing these patterns wherever you find the opportunity. When you implement them, be aware of what is working and what is not. Where are the patterns helping you, and where are they hampering your progress? Your goal is to develop a feeling for the kinds of problems that a specific pattern would solve using a clear and known implementation, and where the pattern would just get in the way.

Since I just mentioned knowledge and the need for experimentation, I suggest you look at the documentation of your favorite editor and find out if it has some sort of snippet function that you could use to handle some of the boilerplate code you find yourself writing repeatedly. This might include the preamble you use to start coding in a new file, or the structure around the `main()` function. This harkens back to the idea that if you are going to use a tool every day, you really need to master that tool. Being comfortable using snippets, and especially creating your own, is a good place to gain an extra bit of leverage over your tools and remove some wasteful keystrokes.

Exercises

- Implement a fourth system, and this time see what happens when you leave out one of the steps.

- Explore the challenges associated with trying to keep two systems in sync without being able to stop the whole world and tie everything together nicely; you will need to look at race conditions, among other things.

- Think of some other systems where you know what steps you need to take, but the specifics of what gets done in each of these steps differ from case to case.

- Implement a basic template pattern–based system to model the situation you thought of in the previous exercise.

CHAPTER 18

Visitor Pattern

I want to believe.

—X-Files

Since Python can be found in many places, you might one day want to do a little bit of home automation. Get a couple of single-board and micro computers and connect them to some hardware sensors and actuators, and soon you have a network of devices, all controlled by you. Each of these items in the network has its own functionality, and each performs different interactions like metering the light levels in the home, or checking the temperature. You could encapsulate the functionality of each device as an object in a virtual network that matches the physical wired network, then treat the whole system like you would any other network of objects. This chapter will focus on that side of the implementation, assuming all the elements have already been wired up and are modeled as objects in the system.

The network in our simulation will have the following components:

- Thermostat
- Temperature regulator
- Front door lock
- Coffee machine
- Bedroom lights
- Kitchen lights
- Clock

Suppose each object class has the functionality to check the status of the device it is connected to. These return different values. Lights might return 1 for "the lights are on" and 0 for "the lights are off," and an error message, -1, when the lights controller

© Wessel Badenhorst 2017
W. Badenhorst, *Practical Python Design Patterns*, https://doi.org/10.1007/978-1-4842-2680-3_18

cannot be reached. The thermostat might return the actual temperature it is reading and None if it is offline. The front door lock is similar to the lights, with 1 being locked, 0 unlocked, and -1 error. The coffee machine has states for error, off, on, brewing, waiting, and heating using integers from -1 to 4, respectively. The temperature regulator has states for heating, cooling, on, off, and error. The clock either returns None if the device is disconnected or the time as a Python time value.

The classes involved with concrete instances will look something like this:

```python
import random

class Light(object):
    def __init__(self):
        pass

    def get_status(self):
        return random.choice(range(-1,2))

class Thermostat(object):
    def __init__(self):
        pass

    def get_status(self):
        temp_range = [x for x in range(-10, 31)]
        temp_range.append(None)
        return random.choice(temp_range)

class TemperatureRegulator(object):
    def __init__(self):
        pass

    def get_status(self):
        return random.choice(['heating', 'cooling', 'on', 'off', 'error'])

class DoorLock(object):
    def __init__(self):
        pass

    def get_status(self):
        return random.choice(range(-1,2))
```

```python
class CoffeeMachine(object):
    def _init_(self):
        pass

    def get_status(self):
        return random.choice(range(-1,5))

class Clock(object):
    def __init__(self):
        pass

    def get_status(self):
        return "{}:{}".format(random.randrange(24), random.randrange(60))

def main():
    device_network = [
        Thermostat(),
        TemperatureRegulator(),
        DoorLock(),
        CoffeeMachine(),
        Light(),
        Light(),
        Clock(),
    ]

    for device in device_network:
        print(device.get_status())

if __name__ == "__main__":
    main()
```

The output is somewhat messy and looks like this:

```
0
off
-1
2
0
-1
9:26
```

This is a lot cleaner than the types of output you will encounter in the real world, but this is a good representation of the messy nature of real-world devices. We now have a simulation of a network of devices. We can move on to the parts we are really interested in, namely doing something with these devices.

The first thing we are interested in is checking the status of the device attached to the object to determine if the device is online or not. Let's create a flat collection containing the nodes in the network and then implement an `is_online` method to tell us if the device is online or not. Then, we can look at each device in turn and ask if it is online or not. We also added a `name` parameter to each constructor so we can easily see what device we are currently dealing with.

```python
import random

class Light(object):
    def __init__(self, name):
        self.name = name

    def get_status(self):
        return random.choice(range(-1,2))

    def is_online(self):
        return self.get_status() != -1

class Thermostat(object):
    def __init__(self, name):
        self.name = name

    def get_status(self):
        temp_range = [x for x in range(-10, 31)]
        temp_range.append(None)
        return random.choice(temp_range)

    def is_online(self):
        return self.get_status() is not None

class TemperatureRegulator(object):
    def __init__(self, name):
        self.name = name
```

```python
    def get_status(self):
        return random.choice(['heating', 'cooling', 'on', 'off', 'error'])

    def is_online(self):
        return self.get_status() != 'error'

class DoorLock(object):
    def __init__(self, name):
        self.name = name

    def get_status(self):
        return random.choice(range(-1,2))

    def is_online(self):
        return self.get_status() != -1

class CoffeeMachine(object):
    def __init__(self, name):
        self.name = name

    def get_status(self):
        return random.choice(range(-1,5))

    def is_online(self):
        return self.get_status() != -1

class Clock(object):
    def __init__(self, name):
        self.name = name

    def get_status(self):
        return "{}:{}".format(random.randrange(24), random.randrange(60))

    def is_online(self):
        return True
```

```
def main():
    device_network = [
        Thermostat("General Thermostat"),
        TemperatureRegulator("Thermal Regulator"),
        DoorLock("Front Door Lock"),
        CoffeeMachine("Coffee Machine"),
        Light("Bedroom Light"),
        Light("Kitchen Light"),
        Clock("System Clock"),
    ]

    for device in device_network:
        print("{} is online: \t{}".format(device.name, device.is_online()))

if __name__ == "__main__":
    main()
```

Since the simulated response is randomly generated, you should not expect your output to be an exact match of the one given here, but the general shape of the output should hold.

```
General Thermostat is online:    True
Thermal Regulator is online:     True
Front Door Lock is online:       True
Coffee Machine is online:        False
Bedroom Light is online:         False
Kitchen Light is online:         True
System Clock is online:          True
```

We now want to add a boot sequence to turn on all the devices and get them into their initial state, like setting the clock to 00:00, starting the coffee machine, turning off all the lights, and turning on but not setting any settings on the temperature system. We will leave the front door in the state that it is in.

Since we are now becoming interested in the actual state of the system, we will remove the get_status method and instead set a status attribute to a random value in the __init__() method.

One other thing that you should note is that we now import the TestCase class from the unittest library, which allows us to write tests to make sure that, after applying the boot sequence to a device, that device is indeed in the state we expect it to be. This is not an in-depth tutorial on unit testing, but will be good for you to see so you gain a deeper level of comfort with the testing tools available in Python.

```python
import random
import unittest

class Light(object):
    def __init__(self, name):
        self.name = name
        self.status = self.get_status()

    def get_status(self):
        return random.choice(range(-1,2))

    def is_online(self):
        return self.status != -1

    def boot_up(self):
        self.status = 0

class Thermostat(object):
    def __init__(self, name):
        self.name = name
        self.status = self.get_status()

    def get_status(self):
        temp_range = [x for x in range(-10, 31)]
        temp_range.append(None)
        return random.choice(temp_range)

    def is_online(self):
        return self.status is not None

    def boot_up(self):
        pass
```

```python
class TemperatureRegulator(object):
    def __init__(self, name):
        self.name = name
        self.status = self.get_status()

    def get_status(self):s
        return random.choice(['heating', 'cooling', 'on', 'off', 'error'])

    def is_online(self):
        return self.status != 'error'

    def boot_up(self):
        self.status = 'on'

class DoorLock(object):
    def __init__(self, name):
        self.name = name
        self.status = self.get_status()

    def get_status(self):
        return random.choice(range(-1,2))

    def is_online(self):
        return self.status != -1

    def boot_up(self):
        pass

class CoffeeMachine(object):
    def __init__(self, name):
        self.name = name
        self.status = self.get_status()

    def get_status(self):
        return random.choice(range(-1,5))

    def is_online(self):
        return self.status != -1

    def boot_up(self):
        self.status = 1
```

```python
class Clock(object):
    def __init__(self, name):
        self.name = name
        self.status = self.get_status()

    def get_status(self):
        return "{}:{}".format(random.randrange(24), random.randrange(60))

    def is_online(self):
        return True

    def boot_up(self):
        self.status = "00:00"

class HomeAutomationBootTests(unittest.TestCase):
    def setUp(self):
        self.thermostat = Thermostat("General Thermostat")
        self.thermal_regulator = TemperatureRegulator("Thermal Regulator")
        self.front_door_lock = DoorLock("Front Door Lock")
        self.coffee_machine = CoffeeMachine("Coffee Machine")
        self.bedroom_light = Light("Bedroom Light")
        self.system_clock = Clock("System Clock")

    def test_boot_thermostat_does_nothing_to_state(self):
        state_before = self.thermostat.status
        self.thermostat.boot_up()
        self.assertEqual(state_before, self.thermostat.status)

    def test_boot_thermal_regulator_turns_it_on(self):
        self.thermal_regulator.boot_up()
        self.assertEqual(self.thermal_regulator.status, 'on')

    def test_boot_front_door_lock_does_nothing_to_state(self):
        state_before = self.front_door_lock.status
        self.front_door_lock.boot_up()
        self.assertEqual(state_before, self.front_door_lock.status)

    def test_boot_coffee_machine_turns_it_on(self):
        self.coffee_machine.boot_up()
        self.assertEqual(self.coffee_machine.status, 1)
```

```
    def test_boot_light_turns_it_off(self):
        self.bedroom_light.boot_up()
        self.assertEqual(self.bedroom_light.status, 0)

    def test_boot_system_clock_zeros_it(self):
        self.system_clock.boot_up()
        self.assertEqual(self.system_clock.status, "00:00")

if __name__ == "__main__":
    unittest.main()
```

Setting the execution function for when the program is run from the command line to unittest.main() tells Python to look for instances of the unittest.TestCase class and then to run the tests in that class. We set up six tests, and the status after running the tests looks something like this:

```
. . . . . .
--------------------------------------------------------------------
Ran 6 tests in 0.001s

OK
```

Each of these had us implement functions we would expect of each function, but how would the system look if we wanted to implement different profiles? Say person1 and person2 share the house, and they have different preferences, such as time to get up, time to go to bed, and what should happen in the morning or evening. They also have different temperatures that they feel most comfortable with. Since they are friendly people, they have agreed on a middle ground for when both of them are home, but when one or the other is home they would like to have the system settings set to their perfect configuration.

A simple extension of the system we saw up to now would see an implementation like this:

```
import random
import unittest

class Light(object):
    def __init__(self, name):
        self.name = name
        self.status = self.get_status()
```

```python
    def get_status(self):
        return random.choice(range(-1,2))

    def is_online(self):
        return self.status != -1

    def boot_up(self):
        self.status = 0

    def update_status(self, person_1_home, person_2_home):
        if person_1_home:
            if person_2_home:
                self.status = 1
            else:
                self.status = 0
        elif person_2_home:
            self.status = 1
        else:
            self.status = 0

class Thermostat(object):
    def __init__(self, name):
        self.name = name
        self.status = self.get_status()

    def get_status(self):
        temp_range = [x for x in range(-10, 31)]
        temp_range.append(None)
        return random.choice(temp_range)

    def is_online(self):
        return self.status is not None

    def boot_up(self):
        pass

    def update_status(self, person_1_home, person_2_home):
        pass
```

```python
class TemperatureRegulator(object):
    def __init__(self, name):
        self.name = name
        self.status = self.get_status()

    def get_status(self):
        return random.choice(['heating', 'cooling', 'on', 'off', 'error'])

    def is_online(self):
        return self.status != 'error'

    def boot_up(self):
        self.status = 'on'

    def update_status(self, person_1_home, person_2_home):
        if person_1_home:
            if person_2_home:
                self.status = 'on'
            else:
                self.status = 'heating'
        elif person_2_home:
            self.status = 'cooling'
        else:
            self.status = 'off'

class DoorLock(object):
    def __init__(self, name):
        self.name = name
        self.status = self.get_status()

    def get_status(self):
        return random.choice(range(-1,2))

    def is_online(self):
        return self.status != -1

    def boot_up(self):
        pass
```

```python
    def update_status(self, person_1_home, person_2_home):
        if person_1_home:
            self.status = 0
        elif person_2_home:
            self.status = 1
        else:
            self.status = 1

class CoffeeMachine(object):
    def __init__(self, name):
        self.name = name
        self.status = self.get_status()

    def get_status(self):
        return random.choice(range(-1,5))

    def is_online(self):
        return self.status != -1

    def boot_up(self):
        self.status = 1

    def update_status(self, person_1_home, person_2_home):
        if person_1_home:
            if person_2_home:
                self.status = 2
            else:
                self.status = 3
        elif person_2_home:
            self.status = 4
        else:
            self.status = 0

class Clock(object):
    def __init__(self, name):
        self.name = name
        self.status = self.get_status()
```

```python
    def get_status(self):
        return "{}:{}".format(random.randrange(24), random.randrange(60))

    def is_online(self):
        return True

    def boot_up(self):
        self.status = "00:00"

    def update_status(self, person_1_home, person_2_home):
        if person_1_home:
            if person_2_home:
                pass
            else:
                "00:01"
        elif person_2_home:
            "20:22"
        else:
            pass
```

As an exercise, write tests for these states where person1 and person2 are either there or not. Make sure you cover all the possible options in these tests.

This is an already messy implementation, and you know we are going to do some cleanup. We could implement the system using a state machine, but implementing a state machine for each device for each state of the inhabitancy of the house just seems wrong; it is also a lot of work without a lot of value. There has to be a better way.

To get us there, let's consider what we want to do.

The Visitor Pattern

Once again, we are going to tease apart a complex piece of functionality into more discrete parts, then abstract these parts in such a way that the one does not need to be intimately familiar with the other. This pattern of separation and isolation is one you will see over and over again as you spend time optimizing, extending, and cleaning up existing systems.

It is necessary to mention Martin Fowler's take on developing micro service–based architectures. Fowler posits that one first has to develop the monolith because at the outset you do not know which elements will coalesce to form good micro services and which can be kept separate. As you work on and grow a system, a single object becomes a network of objects. When these networks become too complex, you refactor, separate, and clean up the code in ways that would not make any sense at a smaller scale.

This is another high-level instance of the You Ain't Gonna Need It principle (YAGNI), which simply implores the developer to not build functionality or structures that will not be used. This is much like the young developer who upon creating a new object immediately proceeds to add Create, Read, Update, and Delete functionality even though the object can never be updated (or whatever business rule applies). Immediately abstracting any function or idea into some sort of meta class will leave a lot of dead code in your system, code that needs to be maintained, reasoned about, debugged, and tested, but never actually used. New team members will need to slog through this code only to realize after the whole system is analyzed that it was a waste of time and effort. If this type of code proliferates the system, the push for a complete rewrite will become stronger, and more time will be wasted. If dead code is again implemented, the new developers will head straight into the same problem. In short, do not write code you are not going to use.

A good rule of thumb is to wait until you have to do the same thing (or very similar thing) the third time before you abstract it. The flip side of this rule is that as soon as you come across the same requirement or problem in your project the third time, you should not proceed without abstracting the solution, so that whenever you next come across this situation, you will have a solution ready to go. You have now found a balance.

With this in mind, imagine that you have needed to alter objects twice to allow some function to be performed over the entire collection of objects, and now you have a third algorithm you want to implement specific to the structure. Clearly, you want to abstract the algorithms being implemented in terms of the data structure. Ideally, you want to be able to dynamically add new algorithms and have them be executed relative to the same data structure without any alterations needing to be made to the classes that make up the elements of said data structure.

Look at the generic implementation of the visitor pattern and get a feel for the code. We will dig into the details after this code snippet.

```python
import abc

class Visitable(object):
    def accept(self, visitor):
        visitor.visit(self)

class CompositeVisitable(Visitable):
    def __init__(self, iterable):
      self.iterable = iterable

    def accept(self, visitor):
      for element in self.iterable:
        element.accept(visitor)

      visitor.visit(self)

class AbstractVisitor(object):
    __metaclass__ = abc.ABCMeta

    @abc.abstractmethod
    def visit(self, element):
        raise NotImplementedError("A visitor needs to define a visit method")

class ConcreteVisitable(Visitable):
    def __init__(self):
        pass

class ConcreteVisitor(AbstractVisitor):
    def visit(self, element):
      pass
```

We can now return to the example of our friends who are sharing a house. Let's abstract the setting up of the system for each of them using the visitor pattern. We will do this by creating a visitor for each of the three potential configurations of people inside the house, and then we check who is home before visiting each device and setting it accordingly.

```python
import abc
import random
import unittest

class Visitable(object):
    def accept(self, visitor):
        visitor.visit(self)

class CompositeVisitable(Visitable):
    def __init__(self, iterable):
      self.iterable = iterable

    def accept(self, visitor):
      for element in self.iterable:
        element.accept(visitor)

      visitor.visit(self)

class AbstractVisitor(object):
    __metaclass__ = abc.ABCMeta

    @abc.abstractmethod
    def visit(self, element):
        raise NotImplementedError("A visitor need to define a visit method")

class Light(Visitable):
    def __init__(self, name):
        self.name = name
        self.status = self.get_status()

    def get_status(self):
        return random.choice(range(-1,2))

    def is_online(self):
        return self.status != -1

    def boot_up(self):
        self.status = 0
```

```python
class LightStatusUpdateVisitor(AbstractVisitor):
    def __init__(self, person_1_home, person_2_home):
        self.person_1_home = person_1_home
        self.person_2_home = person_2_home

    def visit(self, element):
        if self.person_1_home:
            if self.person_2_home:
                element.status = 1
            else:
                element.status = 0
        elif self.person_2_home:
            element.status = 1
        else:
            element.status = 0

class Thermostat(Visitable):
    def __init__(self, name):
        self.name = name
        self.status = self.get_status()

    def get_status(self):
        temp_range = [x for x in range(-10, 31)]
        temp_range.append(None)
        return random.choice(temp_range)

    def is_online(self):
        return self.status is not None

    def boot_up(self):
        pass

class ThermostatStatusUpdateVisitor(AbstractVisitor):
    def __init__(self, person_1_home, person_2_home):
        self.person_1_home = person_1_home
        self.person_2_home = person_2_home

    def visit(self, element):
        pass
```

```python
class TemperatureRegulator(Visitable):
    def __init__(self, name):
        self.name = name
        self.status = self.get_status()

    def get_status(self):
        return random.choice(['heating', 'cooling', 'on', 'off', 'error'])

    def is_online(self):
        return self.status != 'error'

    def boot_up(self):
        self.status = 'on'

class TemperatureRegulatorStatusUpdateVisitor(AbstractVisitor):
    def __init__(self, person_1_home, person_2_home):
        self.person_1_home = person_1_home
        self.person_2_home = person_2_home

    def visit(self, element):
        if self.person_1_home:
            if self.person_2_home:
                element.status = 'on'
            else:
                element.status = 'heating'
        elif self.person_2_home:
            element.status = 'cooling'
        else:
            element.status = 'off'

class DoorLock(Visitable):
    def __init__(self, name):
        self.name = name
        self.status = self.get_status()

    def get_status(self):
        return random.choice(range(-1,2))
```

```python
    def is_online(self):
        return self.status != -1

    def boot_up(self):
        pass

class DoorLockStatusUpdateVisitor(AbstractVisitor):
    def __init__(self, person_1_home, person_2_home):
        self.person_1_home = person_1_home
        self.person_2_home = person_2_home

    def visit(self, element):
        if self.person_1_home:
            element.status = 0
        elif self.person_2_home:
            element.status = 1
        else:
            element.status = 1

class CoffeeMachine(Visitable):
    def __init__(self, name):
        self.name = name
        self.status = self.get_status()

    def get_status(self):
        return random.choice(range(-1,5))

    def is_online(self):
        return self.status != -1

    def boot_up(self):
        self.status = 1

class CoffeeMachineStatusUpdateVisitor(AbstractVisitor):
    def __init__(self, person_1_home, person_2_home):
        self.person_1_home = person_1_home
        self.person_2_home = person_2_home
```

```python
    def visit(self, element):
        if self.person_1_home:
            if self.person_2_home:
                element.status = 2
            else:
                element.status = 3
        elif self.person_2_home:
            element.status = 4
        else:
            element.status = 0

class Clock(Visitable):
    def __init__(self, name):
        self.name = name
        self.status = self.get_status()

    def get_status(self):
        return "{}:{}".format(random.randrange(24), random.randrange(60))

    def is_online(self):
        return True

    def boot_up(self):
        self.status = "00:00"

class ClockStatusUpdateVisitor(AbstractVisitor):
    def __init__(self, person_1_home, person_2_home):
        self.person_1_home = person_1_home
        self.person_2_home = person_2_home

    def visit(self, element):
        if self.person_1_home:
            if self.person_2_home:
                pass
            else:
```

```python
                element.status = "00:01"
        elif self.person_2_home:
            element.status = "20:22"
        else:
            pass

class CompositeVisitor(AbstractVisitor):
    def __init__(self, person_1_home, person_2_home):
        self.person_1_home = person_1_home
        self.person_2_home = person_2_home

    def visit(self, element):
        try:
            c = eval("{}StatusUpdateVisitor".format
                (element.__class__.__name__))
        except:
            print("Visitor for {} not found".format
                (element.__class__.__name__))
        else:
            visitor = c(self.person_1_home, self.person_2_home)
            visitor.visit(element)

class MyHomeSystem(CompositeVisitable):
    pass

class MyHomeSystemStatusUpdateVisitor(AbstractVisitor):
    def __init__(self, person_1_home, person_2_home):
        self.person_1_home = person_1_home
        self.person_2_home = person_2_home

    def visit(self, element):
        pass

class HomeAutomationBootTests(unittest.TestCase):
    def setUp(self):
        self.my_home_system = MyHomeSystem([
            Thermostat("General Thermostat"),
            TemperatureRegulator("Thermal Regulator"),
```

```python
            DoorLock("Front Door Lock"),
            CoffeeMachine("Coffee Machine"),
            Light("Bedroom Light"),
            Clock("System Clock"),
        ])

    def test_person_1_not_home_person_2_not_home(self):
        expected_state = map(
            str,
            [
                self.my_home_system.iterable[0].status,
                'off',
                1,
                0,
                0,
                self.my_home_system.iterable[5].status
            ]
        )
        self.visitor = CompositeVisitor(False, False)
        self.my_home_system.accept(self.visitor)
        retrieved_state = sorted([str(x.status) for x in
                        self.my_home_system.iterable])
        self.assertEqual(retrieved_state, sorted(expected_state))

    def test_person_1_home_person_2_not(self):
        expected_state = map(
            str,
            [
                self.my_home_system.iterable[0].status,
                'heating',
                0,
                3,
                0,
                "00:01"
            ]
        )
```

```python
        self.visitor = CompositeVisitor(True, False)
        self.my_home_system.accept(self.visitor)
        retrieved_state = sorted([str(x.status) for x in
                            self.my_home_system.iterable])
        self.assertEqual(retrieved_state, sorted(expected_state))

    def test_person_1_not_home_person_2_home(self):
        expected_state = map(
            str,
            [
                self.my_home_system.iterable[0].status,
                'cooling',
                1,
                4,
                1,
                "20:22"
            ]
        )
        self.visitor = CompositeVisitor(False, True)
        self.my_home_system.accept(self.visitor)
        retrieved_state = sorted([str(x.status) for x in
                            self.my_home_system.iterable])
        self.assertEqual(retrieved_state, sorted(expected_state))

    def test_person_1_home_person_2_home(self):
        expected_state = map(
            str,
            [
                self.my_home_system.iterable[0].status,
                'on',
                0,
                2,
                1,
                self.my_home_system.iterable[5].status
            ]
        )
```

```
        self.visitor = CompositeVisitor(True, True)
        self.my_home_system.accept(self.visitor)
        retrieved_state = sorted([str(x.status) for x in
                        self.my_home_system.iterable])
        self.assertEqual(retrieved_state, sorted(expected_state))
if __name__ == "__main__":
    unittest.main()
```

I have just a couple of notes on the preceding code. First, if you are taking input from a user, never, ever use the eval function, as Python blindly executes whatever is in the string passed to eval. Second, we are choosing to balance the general nature of eval by using the name of the class to be visited, which is not the best way in Python, as now you rely on naming conventions and magic, which is not explicit. Still, you could implement the pattern.

If you were thinking a state machine might help the situation, you are not wrong. This brings us to something that would seem obvious once you read it, but might not be so obvious from the get-go, and that is the fact that you can use more than one design pattern in a single implementation. In this case, it should be clear that the state of the house resembles a state machine. We have four states:

- Person1 is not home, Person2 is not home

- Person1 is not home, Person2 is home

- Person1 is home, Person2 is not home

- Person1 is home, Person2 is home

Whenever a person either leaves or arrives at home the state of the system changes. So, implementing a state machine for the visitor seems like a good idea.

Try implementing the state pattern on the previous code snippet as an exercise.

When you separate the data structures in the system from the algorithms that operate on them, you gain an added benefit. You can adhere to the open-closed principle much more easily. This principle sees you write code where your objects are open to extension (using inheritance) but closed to alteration (by setting or changing values in an object or altering the methods on an object). Like the DRY and YAGNI principles, the open-closed principle serves as a guiding light as you plan and develop a system. Violations of these principles also serve as an early-warning system that you are writing unmaintainable code that will come back and hurt you down the line.

Parting Shots

Sometimes you just need to write code, so type out the example line by line to get a feel for the idea expressed. Whenever I find descriptions of an algorithm or idea that I do not quite understand from the way it is described, I reach for this tool. There is something different that happens when you get down and write out the code rather than just reading it. Often, nuances that were not clear before get exposed when working your way through the code.

With design patterns that you find complicated or high-level algorithms, I suggest typing out the generic version, then typing out some specific implementation, and finally altering some details to fit your own example beyond those in the text you are looking at. Finally, implement the pattern or algorithm from scratch for a specific instance.

This type of work is usually not the fun part of programming, but it is the deliberate practice that you need to do in order to become a better programmer.

There is a whole world of ideas to explore once you get past the simple elements of syntax and the more general outline of writing idiomatic Python. That world is where you move from being able to write words in the language, or being able to string sentences together, to expressing ideas in code. In the long run, that is what you want to get better at—the process of expressing your thoughts and reasoning in Python, our language of choice for this book. As with all forms of expression, you will get better the more you do it, but only if you challenge yourself.

You can even use this process to explore new libraries where the documentation is lacking or opaque. You could begin by exploring what tests are included in the repository, and, failing to make enough headway through that, you could type your way through some of the key methods and classes in the library. Not only will you get a better idea of what is going on and how the library should be used, but you might also pick up a couple of interesting ideas that you could explore further.

In the end, as with all ideas, try them on and see where they work and where they let you down. Keep what fits your brain and discard what trips you up, as long as you only discard an idea after you have gained clarity, and not while you still find it hard.

Exercises

- Use the process from the "Parting Shots" section and code your way to a deeper understanding of the visitor pattern, if you have not been doing so throughout the book.

- Find an interesting Python package in the standard library and code through that, seeing how these developers do things differently from you.

- Write the tests for these states where person1 and person2 are either there or not. Make sure you cover all the possible options in these tests.

- Extend the code in each instance to accommodate friends coming over for a social gathering.

- Think about the other design patterns in this book; are there other ones that would make the code better? If so, implement the solution using this design pattern.

- In order to crystallize the reason why the visitor pattern makes adhering to the open-closed principle easier, you are going to add another device to our system—a streaming media entertainment center. This device comes with Python bindings, but we do not have access to the inner workings of the device for some reason. Add this object to our network and define a dummy interface to mimic the interface provided. Then, add custom settings for each of the states in the home.

- Add the state pattern to the final piece of code in this chapter to allow you to handle the four scenarios we discussed. How do you need to think differently about the code we wrote in the chapter? Then, decide if implementing the state pattern, in this case, makes the solution better or worse. Think specifically about maintenance and the principles we talked about thus far.

CHAPTER 19

Model-View-Controller Pattern

Always, worlds within worlds.

—Clive Barker, *Weaveworld*

Not far along in your journey as a programmer, you begin to see some other patterns emerge—more like patterns of patterns. Like this one. Most if not all programs consist of some sort of external action that initiates the program. The initiating action may or may not have data, but if it does, the program consumes that data, sometimes persisting it, sometimes not. Finally, your program has an effect on the world. That's it, basically; all programs you will ever encounter will have this pattern.

Let me give you a simple example and then one that you might not see from the start.

The first example is that of a visitor signing up to receive email updates from a website. It does not matter how the user enters the information, as from the system's perspective everything begins with a POST request hitting the program. The request contains a *name* and *email address*. Now the program is initiated as in the preceding example, and we have some extra data. The program goes through the process of checking if the email is already in the database. If not, it is persisted together with the name of the visitor. If it is, then no further action is taken. Finally, the system returns a status code alerting the calling program that everything went as expected. Note that there are two places where the program changes the world outside of the execution of the program itself, namely the database and the response to the calling system.

We could also look at a game, where you have the game in some state and the player interacts with the game via the keyboard and mouse. These peripheral actions are translated into commands by the game engine, the commands are processed, and the game state updates, which is relayed back to the player in terms of visual, audio, and possible tactile feedback. The process remains the same: input, process, output.

W. Badenhorst, *Practical Python Design Patterns*, https://doi.org/10.1007/978-1-4842-2680-3_19

Seeing programs in this way helps, since you become better at asking questions about what happens at each step in the process. Sadly, this view is too general and leaves too much out, and thus it is not completely helpful when it comes to the actual nuts and bolts development work. Still, it is a useful tool to have.

This book is called *Practical Python Design Patterns*, and not *Abstract Programming Models*, so let's get practical.

Without completely discarding the idea of the three parts of a program, different types of programs take different perspectives on the idea. Games execute a game loop, while web applications take user input and use that input together with some form of stored data to produce an output to be displayed in the user's browser window.

For the sake of this chapter, we are going to use a command-line dummy program to demonstrate the ideas I want you to internalize. Once you have a clear grasp of the basic ideas, we will implement them, using a couple of Python libraries to build a basic web application that can serve web pages from your local machine.

Our first program will simply take a name as an argument. If the name is already stored, it will welcome the visitor back; otherwise, it will tell the visitor that it is nice to meet them.

```python
import sys

def main(name):
    try:
        with open('names.dat', 'r') as data_file:
            names = [x for x in data_file.readlines()]

    except FileNotFoundError as e:
        with open('names.dat', 'w') as data_file:
            data_file.write(name)

        names = []

    if name in names:
        print("Welcome back {}!".format(name))
    else:
        print("Hi {}, it is good to meet you".format(name))
        with open('names.dat', 'a') as data_file:
            data_file.write(name)
```

```
if __name__ == "__main__":
    main(sys.argv[1])
```

The program uses the sys package in the standard library to expose the arguments passed to the program. The first argument is the name of the script being executed. In our example program, the first additional argument that is expected is the name of a person. We have some checks included, ensuring that some string was in fact passed to the program. Next, we check if the program encountered the name previously, and it displays the relevant text.

Now, for all the reasons discussed throughout the book, we know that this is not good. The script is doing too much in the main function, so we proceed to decompose it into different functions.

```
import sys
import os

def get_append_write(filename):
    if os.path.exists(filename):
        return 'a'

    return 'w'

def name_in_file(filename, name):
    if not os.path.exists(filename):
        return False

    return name in read_names(filename)

def read_names(filename):
    with open(filename, 'r') as data_file:
        names = data_file.read().split('\n')

    return names

def write_name(filename, name):
    with open(filename, get_append_write(filename)) as data_file:
            data_file.write("{}\n".format(name))

def get_message(name):
    if name_in_file('names.dat', name):
        return "Welcome back {}!".format(name)
```

```
        write_name('names.dat', name)
        return "Hi {}, it is good to meet you".format(name)

def main(name):
    print(get_message(name))

if __name__ == "__main__":
    main(sys.argv[1])
```

I'm sure you suspect that there is more to come in terms of cleaning up this code, so why go through this process again? The reason for following these steps is that I want you to get a feel for when you need to deconstruct a function or method. If all programs stayed the way they were planned in the beginning of the project, this sense of when and how to break things into smaller parts would not be needed. Following the same logic, the process is incremental. You might start out like we did, breaking the program into functions. After a while, the program grows significantly, and now the single file becomes a burden, a good sign that you need to break the one file program into separate files. But how will you do that? We will see as we grow our initial program.

They say always be you, unless you can be a lion, in which case always be a lion.

So, in that spirit, we will now extend the program to display a special message for certain arguments, specifically *lion*.

```
import sys
import os

def get_append_write(filename):
    if os.path.exists(filename):
        return 'a'

    return 'w'

def name_in_file(filename, name):
    if not os.path.exists(filename):
        return False

    return name in read_names(filename)

def read_names(filename):
    with open(filename, 'r') as data_file:
        names = data_file.read().split('\n')
```

```python
        return names

def write_name(filename, name):
    with open(filename, get_append_write(filename)) as data_file:
            data_file.write("{}\n".format(name))

def get_message(name):
    if name == "lion":
        return "RRRrrrrroar!"

    if name_in_file('names.dat', name):
        return "Welcome back {}!".format(name)

    write_name('names.dat', name)
    return "Hi {}, it is good to meet you".format(name)

def main(name):
    print(get_message(name))

if __name__ == "__main__":
    main(sys.argv[1])
```

Now, we finally begin to see another pattern appear. What we have here are three distinct types of functions, which are the result of separating the concerns as much as we can. We end up with code that deals with getting the greeting to return, code writing the greeting to the console, and some code to handle the flow of the program, sending the relevant requests to the data-retrieval code, getting the greeting, and sending that to the code that ultimately displays it on the console.

Model-View-Controller Skeleton

In general terms, we want to capture the pattern discussed in the previous paragraph in a reusable pattern. We also want to bake the open-closed principle into the code, and, to that end, we want to encapsulate key parts of the program in objects.

Before anything can happen, our program must receive some form of a request. This request must be interpreted and then kick off the relevant actions. All of this happens inside an object that exists solely for controlling the flow of the program. This object handles actions like requesting data, receiving data, and dispatching responses to the command line. The object in question is all about control, and, unsurprisingly, objects of this class are called *controllers*. They are the glue that holds the system together, and usually the place where the most action takes place.

Here are the control functions from our previous program.

controller_functions.py

```python
def name_in_file(filename, name):
    if not os.path.exists(filename):
        return False

    return name in read_names(filename)

def get_message(name):
    if name_in_file('names.dat', name):
        return "Welcome back {}!".format(name)

    write_name('names.dat', name)
    return "Hi {}, it is good to meet you".format(name)

if __name__ == "__main__":
    main(sys.argv[1])
```

These are not yet encapsulated in an object, but at least they are in one place. Now, let's proceed with the next part of the system, grouping functions as we go before we return to them and clean up the parts.

Once a request is received and the controller decides what must happen to the request, some data from the system is needed. Since we are dealing with the grouping together of code that shares functionality, we will now grab all the functions that have anything to do with the retrieval of data and place them into a function file. Often, the structural representation of data is referred to as a data model, and so the part of the program that deals with the data is called the *model*.

Here are the model functions from our previous program.

model_functions.py

```python
def get_append_write(filename):
    if os.path.exists(filename):
        return 'a'
```

```
    return 'w'

def read_names(filename):
    with open(filename, 'r') as data_file:
        names = data_file.read().split('\n')

    return names

def write_name(filename, name):
    with open(filename, get_append_write(filename)) as data_file:
            data_file.write("{}\n".format(name))
```

Once the code is encapsulated into an object, you will find that as a program grows different types of data are required, and each of these gets placed into its own model object. Usually, model objects each end up in their own file.

What remains is the code that is focused on delivering some sort of information back to the user. In our case, this is done via the standard output port to the console. This, as you have guessed by now, is called the *view* code.

Here are the remaining view functions from our previous program.

view_functions.py

```
def main(name):
    print(get_message(name))
```

As I am certain you noticed, the grouping of functions is not as clear-cut as we would like it to be. Ideally, you should be able to change anything in either one of the groups of functions (without changing their interfaces), and this should not have any effect on the other modules.

Before we make a clean split and encapsulate the three classes of functions into separate classes, let's look at the elements that go into the pattern.

Controllers

The controller is the heart of the pattern, the part that marshalls all the other classes. Users interact with the controller, and through it the whole system. The controller takes the user input, handles all the business logic, gets data from the model, and sends the data to the view to be transformed into the representation to be returned to the user.

```python
class GenericController(object):

    def __init__(self):
        self.model = GenericModel()
        self.view = GenericView()

    def handle(self, request):
        data = self.model.get_data(request)
        self.view.generate_response(data)
```

Models

Models deal with data: getting data, setting data, updating data, and deleting data. That's it. You will often see models doing more than that, which is a mistake. Your models should be a program-side interface to your data that abstracts away the need to directly interact with the data store, allowing you to switch from a file-based store to some key-value store or a full-on relational database system.

Often, a model will contain the fields used as attributes on the object, allowing you to interact with the database as with any other object, with some sort of save method to persist the data to the data store.

Our GenericModel class contains only a simple method to return some form of data.

```python
class GenericModel(object):

    def __init__(self):
        pass

    def get_data(self, request):
        return {'request': request}
```

Views

As with models, you do not want any business logic in your views. Views should only deal with the output or rendering of data passed to it into some sort of format to be returned to the user, be that print statements to the console or a 3D render to the player of a game. The format of the output does not make a major difference in what the view does. You will also be tempted to add logic to the view; this is a slippery slope and not a path you should head down.

The following is a simple `GenericView` class that you can use as a base for building your own views, be they for returning JSON to an HTTP call or plotting graphs for data analysis.

```python
class GenericView(object):
    def __init__(self):
        pass

    def generate_response(self, data):
        print(data)
```

Bringing It All Together

Finally, here is a full program using the model, view, and controller to give you an idea of how these elements interact.

```python
import sys

class GenericController(object):

    def __init__(self):
        self.model = GenericModel()
        self.view = GenericView()

    def handle(self, request):
        data = self.model.get_data(request)
        self.view.generate_response(data)

class GenericModel(object):

    def __init__(self):
        pass

    def get_data(self, request):
        return {'request': request}

class GenericView(object):
    def __init__(self):
        pass
```

```python
    def generate_response(self, data):
        print(data)

def main(name):
    request_handler = GenericController()
    request_handler.handle(name)

if __name__ == "__main__":
    main(sys.argv[1])
```

Now that we have a clear picture of what each of the object classes should look like, let's proceed to implement the code in our example for this chapter in terms of these object classes.

As we have done thus far, we will lead with the Controller object.

controller.py

```python
import sys
from model import NameModel
from view import GreetingView

class GreetingController(object):

    def __init__(self):
        self.model = NameModel()
        self.view = GreetingView()

    def handle(self, request):
        if request in self.model.get_name_list():
            self.view.generate_greeting(name=request, known=True)
        else:
            self.model.save_name(request)
            self.view.generate_greeting(name=request, known=False)

def main(main):
    request_handler = GreetingController()
    Request_handler.handle(name)

if __name__ == "__main__":
    main(sys.argv[1])
```

Next, we create the Model object that retrieves a greeting from file or returns the standard greeting.

model.py

```python
import os

class NameModel(object):

    def __init__(self):
        self.filename = 'names.dat'

    def _get_append_write(self):
        if os.path.exists(self.filename):
            return 'a'
        return 'w'

    def get_name_list(self):
        if not os.path.exists(self.filename):
            return False

        with open(self.filename, 'r') as data_file:
            names = data_file.read().split('\n')

        return names

    def save_name(self, name):
        with open(self.filename, self._get_append_write()) as data_file:
            data_file.write("{}\n".format(name))
```

Lastly, we create a View object to display the greeting to the user.

view.py

```python
class GreetingView(object):
    def __init__(self):
        pass

    def generate_greeting(self, name, known):
        if name == "lion":
            print("RRRrrrrroar!")
            return
```

```
    if known:
        print("Welcome back {}!".format(name))
    else:
        print("Hi {}, it is good to meet you".format(name))
```

Great! If you want to make a request, start the program like this:

```
$ python controller.py YOUR_NAME
```

The first time you run this script, the response, as expected, looks like this:

```
Hi YOUR_NAME, it is good to meet you
```

Before we go on, I want you to see why this is such a great idea. Let's say we grow our program, and at some time we decide to include different types of greetings that depend on the time of day. To do this, we can add a time model to the system, which would then retrieve the system time and decide if it is morning, afternoon, or evening based on the time. This information is sent along with the name data to the view to generate the relevant greeting.

controller.py

```
class GreetingController(object):

    def __init__(self):
        self.name_model = NameModel()
        self.time_model = TimeModel()
        self.view = GreetingView()

    def handle(self, request):
        if request in self.name_model.get_name_list():
            self.view.generate_greeting(
                name=request,
                time_of_day=self.time_model.get_time_of_day(),
                known=True
                )
        else:
            self.name_model.save_name(request)
            self.view.generate_greeting(
                name=request,
```

```
            time_of_day=self.time_model.get_time_of_day(),
            known=False
            )
```

view.py

```python
class GreetingView(object):
    def __init__(self):
        pass

    def generate_greeting(self, name, time_of_day, known):
        if name == "lion":
            print("RRRrrrrroar!")
            return

        if known:
            print("Good {} welcome back {}!".format(time_of_day, name))
        else:
            print("Good {} {}, it is good to meet you".format(time_of_day,
            name))
```

models.py

```python
class NameModel(object):

    def __init__(self):
        self.filename = 'names.dat'

    def _get_append_write(self):
        if os.path.exists(self.filename):
            return 'a'

        return 'w'

    def get_name_list(self):
        if not os.path.exists(self.filename):
            return False

        with open(self.filename, 'r') as data_file:
            names = data_file.read().split('\n')

        return names
```

311

```python
    def save_name(self, name):
        with open(self.filename, self._get_append_write()) as data_file:
            data_file.write("{}\n".format(name))

class TimeModel(object):
    def __init__(self):
        pass

    def get_time_of_day(self):
        time = datetime.datetime.now()
        if time.hour < 12:
            return "morning"
        if 12 <= time.hour < 18:
            return "afternoon"
        if time.hour >= 18:
            return "evening"
```

Alternatively, we could use a database to store the greetings instead of saving them in different files. The beauty of it all is that it does not matter to the rest of the system what we do in terms of storage. Just to illustrate this fact, we will alter our model to store the greeting in a JSON file rather than in plain text.

Implementing this functionality will require the `json` package in the standard library.

The hardest part of adapting this approach to programming is that you have to decide what goes where. How much do you place in the model, or what level of processing goes into the view? Here, I like the concept of fat controllers and skinny models and views. We want models to just deal with the creation, retrieval, updating, and deletion of data. Views should only concern themselves with displaying data. Everything else should sit in the controller. Sometimes, you might implement helper classes for the controller, and that is good, but do not let yourself get tempted into doing more than you should in a model or view.

A classic example of a model doing too much is having one model that requires another model, like having a `UserProfile` class that requires a `User` class so you know which user the profile belongs to. The temptation is there to send all the information to the `UserProfile` model's constructor and have it create the `User` instance on the fly; it is all data after all.

That would be a mistake, as you would have the model controlling some of the flow of the program, which should rest on the controller and its helper classes. A much better solution would be to have the controller create the User instance and then force it to pass the User object to the constructor of the UserProfile model class.

The same problems could arise on the view side of the picture. The key thing to remember is that every object should have one responsibility and one responsibility only. If it is displaying information to the user, it should not do calculations on the information; if it is handling data, it should not concern itself with creating missing pieces on the fly; and if it is controlling the flow, it should not pay any attention to how data is stored or retrieved or how the data is formatted or displayed.

Parting Shots

The more cleanly you separate the concerns in your objects, and the better you isolate their purpose, the easier it will be to maintain your code, update it, or find and fix bugs.

One of the most important concepts you should take with you on your journey toward programming mastery is the paradox of the *Ship of Theseus*. The paradox is stated as such: Imagine you have a ship, and on the ship they have enough lumber to completely rebuild the ship. The ship sets out, and along the way, each piece of lumber built into the ship is replaced by some of the stock carried on the ship. The replaced piece is discarded. By the time the ship reaches its destination, not a single plank from the original ship remains. The question is, at what point do you have a new ship? When does the ship cease being the ship you set out with?

What does this have to do with programming?

You should build your programs in such a way that you can constantly swap out bits of the program without changing any other part of the code. Every period—depending on the size and scope of your project, this might mean a year or five years or six months—you want to have cycled out all the old code and replaced it with better, more elegant, and more efficient code.

Keep asking yourself how much of a pain it will be to replace the part of the code you are currently working on with something completely different. If the answer is that you hope such a replacement is not needed before you have moved on, rip up the code and start over.

Exercises

- Swap out the view from the last implementation of the greeting program to display its output in a graphical pop-up; you could look at pygame or pyqt for this, or any other graphics package available to you.

- Alter the model to read and write from and to a JSON file rather than a flat text file

- Install SQLAlchemy and SQLite on your local system and swap out the model object so it uses the database instead of the file system.

CHAPTER 20

Publish–Subscribe Pattern

Yelling is a form of publishing.

—Margaret Atwood

If you think back to the observer pattern we looked at in Chapter 14, you will remember that we had an Observable class and some Observer classes. Whenever the Observable object changed its state and was polled for a change, it alerted all the observers registered with it that they needed to activate a callback.

There is no need to jump back to that chapter, as the code we are talking about is in this snippet:

```python
class ConcreteObserver(object):

    def update(self, observed):
        print("Observing: {}".format(observed))

class Observable(object):

    def __init__(self):
        self.callbacks = set()
        self.changed = False

    def register(self, callback):
        self.callbacks.add(callback)
```

© Wessel Badenhorst 2017
W. Badenhorst, *Practical Python Design Patterns*, https://doi.org/10.1007/978-1-4842-2680-3_20

```python
    def unregister(self, callback):
        self.callbacks.discard(callback)

    def unregister_all(self):
        self.callbacks = set()

    def poll_for_change(self):
        if self.changed:
            self.update_all

    def update_all(self):
        for callback in self.callbacks:
            callback(self)
```

Although the observer pattern allows us to decouple the objects that are observed from knowing anything about the objects observing them, the observer objects still need to know which objects they need to observe. So, we still have more coupling than we saw in the previous chapter, where we were able to change the view code without needing to change the controller or model code, and the same goes for the model code. Even the controller, which sits between the models and the views, is fairly decoupled from both. When we changed the view, we had no need to also update the controller, and vice versa.

The observer pattern we dealt with previously works well when a number of potential observable classes that an observer needs to register with is limited. As with many things in programming, we are often faced with challenges that do not comply with the ideal case, and so we need to adapt.

What we are going in search of in this chapter is a way to decouple the observer from the observable even more. We want neither the observer nor the observable to know anything about each other. Each class and its instances should be able to change without any changes being needed on the other side of the equation. New observers and observables should not require alterations in the code of the other classes in the system, as this would cause our code to be less flexible. In an attempt to reach this ideal, we will be looking at ways to extend the one-to-many methodologies of the observer pattern to a many-to-many relationship between observables and observers, such that one class of objects does not need to know much about the other.

These blind observables will be called *publishers*, and the disconnected observers will be named *subscribers*.

The first step might seem trivial, but you will soon realize how simple it is to change the way you think about things by just changing what you call them.

```python
class Subscriber(object):

    def update(self, observed):
        print("Observing: {}".format(observed))

class Publisher(object):

    def __init__(self):
        self.callbacks = set()
        self.changed = False

    def register(self, callback):
        self.callbacks.add(callback)

    def unregister(self, callback):
        self.callbacks.discard(callback)

    def unregister_all(self):
        self.callbacks = set()

    def poll_for_change(self):
        if self.changed:
            self.update_all

    def update_all(self):
        for callback in self.callbacks:
            callback(self)
```

Like I said, this makes no difference in what the program can actually do, but what it does do is help us see things differently. We could now take another step forward and rename the methods in both these classes to reflect the publisher-subscriber model more closely.

```python
class Subscriber(object):

    def process(self, observed):
        print("Observing: {}".format(observed))

class Publisher(object):

    def __init__(self):
        self.subscribers = set()

    def subscribe(self, subscriber):
        self.subscribers.add(subscriber)

    def unsubscribe(self, subscriber):
        self.subscribers.discard(subscriber)

    def unsubscribe_all(self):
        self.subscribers = set()

    def publish(self):
        for subscriber in self.subscribers:
            subscriber.process(self)
```

Now it is clear that we are dealing with two classes, one that deals with publishing and another focused completely on processing something. In the code snippet, it is not yet clear what should be published and what should be processed. We proceed in our attempt to clear up any uncertainty in our model definition by adding a Message class that could be published and processed.

```python
class Message(object):

    def __init__(self):
        self.payload = None

class Subscriber(object):

    def process(self, message):
        print("Message: {}".format(message.payload))
```

```python
class Publisher(object):

    def __init__(self):
        self.subscribers = set()

    def subscribe(self, subscriber):
        self.subscribers.add(subscriber)

    def unsubscribe(self, subscriber):
        self.subscribers.discard(subscriber)

    def unsubscribe_all(self):
        self.subscribers = set()

    def publish(self, message):
        for subscriber in self.subscribers:
            subscriber.process(message)
```

Next, we remove the final link between the publisher and the subscriber by adding a single *dispatcher class* through which all messages will pass. The aim is to have a single location to which publishers send messages. The same location keeps an index of all the subscribers. The result is that the number of publishers and subscribers can vary without having any impact on the rest of the system. This gives us a very clean and decoupled architecture to work with.

```python
class Message(object):
    def __init__(self):
        self.payload = None

class Subscriber(object):
    def __init__(self, dispatcher):
        dispatcher.subscribe(self)

    def process(self, message):
        print("Message: {}".format(message.payload))

class Publisher(object):
    def __init__(self, dispatcher):
        self.dispatcher = dispatcher
```

```python
    def publish(self, message):
        self.dispatcher.send(message)

class Dispatcher(object):
    def __init__(self):
        self.subscribers = set()

    def subscribe(self, subscriber):
        self.subscribers.add(subscriber)

    def unsubscribe(self, subscriber):
        self.subscribers.discard(subscriber)

    def unsubscribe_all(self):
        self.subscribers = set()

    def send(self, message):
        for subscriber in self.subscribers:
            subscriber.process(message)
```

Not all subscribers are interested in all the messages from all publishers. Since the point of this whole exercise was to decouple subscribers from publishers, we do not want to couple them together in any way. The solution we are looking for should allow the dispatcher to send categories of messages to specific subscribers. We are going to add a topic to the messages. Publishers will now add a topic to the messages they publish, and subscribers can then subscribe to specific topics.

```python
class Message(object):
    def __init__(self):
        self.payload = None
        self.topic = "all"

class Subscriber(object):
    def __init__(self, dispatcher, topic):
        dispatcher.subscribe(self, topic)

    def process(self, message):
        print("Message: {}".format(message.payload))
```

```python
class Publisher(object):
    def __init__(self, dispatcher):
        self.dispatcher = dispatcher

    def publish(self, message):
        self.dispatcher.send(message)

class Dispatcher(object):
    def __init__(self):
        self.topic_subscribers = dict()

    def subscribe(self, subscriber, topic):
        self.topic_subscribers.setdefault(topic, set()).add(subscriber)

    def unsubscribe(self, subscriber, topic):
        self.topic_subscribers.setdefault(topic, set()).discard(subscriber)

    def unsubscribe_all(self, topic):
        self.subscribers = self.topic_subscribers[topic] = set()

    def send(self, message):
        for subscriber in self.topic_subscribers[message.topic]:
            subscriber.process(message)

def main():
    dispatcher = Dispatcher()

    publisher_1 = Publisher(dispatcher)
    subscriber_1 = Subscriber(dispatcher, 'topic1')

    message = Message()
    message.payload = "My Payload"
    message.topic = 'topic1'

    publisher_1.publish(message)

if __name__ == "__main__":
    main()
```

Now we see the code resulting in the message (shown below) printed by the subscriber.

```
Message: My Payload
```

Distributed Message Sender

Sending messages from many machines. Now that we have arrived at a clean implementation of the PubSub pattern, let's use the ideas we have developed so far to build our own simple message sender. For this, we are going to use the socket package from the Python standard library. We use XML-RPC to handle the remote connections; it lets us make calls to remote procedures as if they were part of the local system. In order to make our dispatcher work with messages, we need to send dictionaries as parameters rather than as Python objects, which we do. The code below illustrates how we do that.

dispatcher.py

```python
from xmlrpc.client import ServerProxy
from xmlrpc.server import SimpleXMLRPCServer

class Dispatcher(SimpleXMLRPCServer):
    def __init__(self):
        self.topic_subscribers = dict()
        super(Dispatcher, self).__init__(("localhost", 9000))
        print("Listening on port 9000...")

        self.register_function(self.subscribe, "subscribe")
        self.register_function(self.unsubscribe, "unsubscribe")
        self.register_function(self.unsubscribe_all, "unsubscribe_all")

        self.register_function(self.send, "send")

    def subscribe(self, subscriber, topic):
        print('Subscribing {} to {}'.format(subscriber, topic))
        self.topic_subscribers.setdefault(topic, set()).add(subscriber)
        return "OK"

    def unsubscribe(self, subscriber, topic):
        print('Unsubscribing {} from {}'.format(subscriber, topic))
        self.topic_subscribers.setdefault(topic, set()).discard(subscriber)
        return "OK"

    def unsubscribe_all(self, topic):
        print('unsubscribing all from {}'.format(topic))
```

```python
        self.subscribers = self.topic_subscribers[topic] = set()
        return "OK"

    def send(self, message):
        print("Sending Message:\nTopic: {}\nPayload: {}".
        format(message["topic"], message["payload"]))
        for subscriber in self.topic_subscribers
        [message.get("topic", "all")]:
            with ServerProxy(subscriber) as subscriber_proxy:
                subscriber_proxy.process(message)

        return "OK"

def main():
    dispatch_server = Dispatcher()
    dispatch_server.serve_forever()

if __name__ == "__main__":
    main()
```

publisher.py

```python
from xmlrpc.client import ServerProxy

class Publisher(object):
    def __init__(self, dispatcher):
        self.dispatcher = dispatcher

    def publish(self, message):
        with ServerProxy(self.dispatcher) as dispatch:
            dispatch.send(message)

def main():
    message = {"topic": "MessageTopic", "payload":
            "This is an awesome payload"}
    publisher = Publisher("http://localhost:9000")
    publisher.publish(message)

if __name__ == "__main__":
    main()
```

subscriber.py

```python
from xmlrpc.client import ServerProxy
from xmlrpc.server import SimpleXMLRPCServer

class Subscriber(SimpleXMLRPCServer):
    def __init__(self, dispatcher, topic):
        super(Subscriber, self).__init__(("localhost", 9001))
        print("Listening on port 9001...")
        self.register_function(self.process, "process")

        self.subscribe(dispatcher, topic)

    def subscribe(self, dispatcher, topic):
        with ServerProxy(dispatcher) as dispatch:
            dispatch.subscribe("http://localhost:9001", topic)

    def process(self, message):
        print("Message: {}".format(message.get("payload",
        "Default message")))
        return "OK"

def main():
    subscriber_server = Subscriber("http://localhost:9000", "MessageTopic")
    subscriber_server.serve_forever()

if __name__ == "__main__":
    main()
```

To run the program and see its true effects, you have to open three terminal windows and activate the virtual environment for your code in each of the windows. We will run each part of the application in its own window to simulate the interaction between independent systems. Each command that follows assumes that the virtualenv is already activated.

window 1: dispatcher

```
$ python dispatcher.py
```

window 2: subscriber

```
$ python subscriber.py
```

window 3: publisher

```
$ python publisher.py
```

With each of the windows running its process, let's enter a message into the publisher window and see what happens.

We see the dispatcher received the message and sent it to the subscriber.

```
Listening on port 9000...
Subscribing http://localhost:9001 to MessageTopic
127.0.0.1 - - [16/Aug/2017 20:59:06] "POST /RPC2 HTTP/1.1" 200 -
Sending Message:
Topic: MessageTopic
Payload: This is an awesome payload
127.0.0.1 - - [16/Aug/2017 20:59:09] "POST /RPC2 HTTP/1.1" 200 -
```

The subscriber receives the message and prints the message.

```
Listening on port 9001...
Message: This is an awesome payload
127.0.0.1 - - [16/Aug/2017 20:59:09] "POST /RPC2 HTTP/1.1" 200 -
```

Parting Shots

The PubSub pattern has many uses, especially as systems expand and grow into the cloud. This process of growing, expanding, and evolving is one of the reasons I chose to start with the simple implementation of the observer pattern we saw in Chapter 14 and then move through the steps of improved design to the final full PubSub implementation. This is the same pattern of growth that you will repeat in your own projects. A simple project grows a little bit, and with every bit of functionality that you add, you should be asking yourself what ideas from this book, or elsewhere, will make this project easier to maintain in the future. Once you hit upon such an idea, do not hesitate—improve the code. You will quickly come to realize that a bit of time spent at the tail end of a project will make your development time significantly shorter in future phases of the project.

As Jocko Willink (Navy SEAL Commander - Task Unit Bruser) likes to say, discipline equals freedom. The discipline you apply to your coding practice will lead to freedom from the pain of maintaining cumbersome systems. You will also avoid the inevitable dump and rewrite that most software products head for from the moment the first line of code is written.

Exercises

- See if you can find information about proto buffers and how they could be used to send data to remote procedure calls.

- Read up on queueing software like ZeroMQ and RabbitMQ, together with packages like Celery. Implement the simple chat application using one of these instead of the Python implementation from this chapter.

- Write a proposal for how you would use the publish–subscribe pattern to enable the addition of gamification to an existing Software as a service - SaaS application.

Design Pattern Quick Reference

Quick Checks for the Code

1. Singleton Pattern

2. Prototype Pattern

3. Factory Pattern

4. Builder Pattern

5. Adapter Pattern

6. Decorator Pattern

7. Facade Pattern

8. Proxy Pattern

9. Chain of Responsibility Pattern

10. Composite

11. Command Pattern

12. Interpreter Pattern

13. Iterator Pattern

14. Observer Pattern

15. State Pattern

16. Strategy Pattern

© Wessel Badenhorst 2017
W. Badenhorst, *Practical Python Design Patterns*, https://doi.org/10.1007/978-1-4842-2680-3

Singleton

singleton.py

```python
class SingletonObject(object):
  class __SingletonObject():
    def __init__(self):
      self.val = None

    def __str__(self):
      return "{0!r} {1}".format(self, self.val)

    # the rest of the class definition will follow here, as per the
    previous logging script

  instance = None

  def __new__(cls):
    if not SingletonObject.instance:
      SingletonObject.instance = SingletonObject.__SingletonObject()

    return SingletonObject.instance

  def __getattr__(self, name):
    return getattr(self.instance, name)

  def __setattr__(self, name):
    return setattr(self.instance, name)
```

Prototype

prototype_1.py

```python
from abc import ABCMeta, abstractmethod

class Prototype(metaclass=ABCMeta):
  @abstractmethod
  def clone(self):
    pass
```

concrete.py

```python
from prototype_1 import Prototype
from copy import deepcopy

class Concrete(Prototype):
  def clone(self):
    return deepcopy(self)
```

Factory

factory.py

```python
import abc

class AbstractFactory(object):
  __metaclass__ = abc.ABCMeta

  @abc.abstractmethod
  def make_object(self):
    return

class ConcreteFactory(AbstractFactory):
  def make_object(self):
    # do something
    return ConcreteClass()
```

Builder

form_builder.py

```python
from abc import ABCMeta, abstractmethod

class Director(object, metaclass=ABCMeta):

    def __init__(self):
        self._builder = None

    @abstractmethod
    def construct(self):
        pass

    def get_constructed_object(self):
        return self._builder.constructed_object

class Builder(object, metaclass=ABCMeta):

    def __init__(self, constructed_object):
        self.constructed_object = constructed_object

class Product(object):
  def __init__(self):
    pass

  def __repr__(self):
    pass

class ConcreteBuilder(Builder):
  pass

class ConcreteDirector(Director):
  pass
```

Adapter

third_party.py

```python
class WhatIHave(object):
  def provided_function_1(self): pass
  def provided_function_2(self): pass

class WhatIWant(object):
  def required_function(): pass
```

adapter.py

```python
from third_party import WhatIHave

class ObjectAdapter(object):
  def __init__(self, what_i_have):
    self.what_i_have = what_i_have

  def required_function(self):
    return self.what_i_have.provided_function_1()

  def __getattr__(self, attr):
    # Everything else is handled by the wrapped object
    return getattr(self.what_i_have, attr)
```

Decorator

decorator.py

```python
from functools import wraps

def dummy_decorator(f):

    @wraps(f)
    def wrap_f():
        print("Function to be decorated: ", f.__name__)
        print("Nested wrapping function: ", wrap_f.__name__)
        return f()

    return wrap_f
```

```python
@dummy_decorator
def do_nothing():
    print("Inside do_nothing")
if __name__ == "__main__":
    print("Wrapped function: ",do_nothing.__name__)
    do_nothing()
```

Facade

simple_facade.py

```python
class Invoice:
  def __init__(self, customer): pass
class Customer:
  Altered customer class to try to fetch a customer on init or creates a
  new one
  def __init__(self, customer_id): pass
class Item:
  # Altered item class to try to fetch an item on init or creates a new one
  def __init__(self, item_barcode): pass

class Facade:
  @staticmethod
  def make_invoice(customer): return Invoice(customer)

  @staticmethod
  def make_customer(customer_id): return Customer(customer_id)

  @staticmethod
  def make_item(item_barcode): return Item(item_barcode)
  # ...
```

Proxy

proxy.py

```python
import time

class RawClass(object):

    def func(self, n):
        return f(n)

def memoize(fn):
    __cache = {}

    def memoized(*args):
        key = (fn.__name__, args)
        if key in __cache:
            return __cache[key]

        __cache[key] = fn(*args)
        return __cache[key]

    return memoized

class ClassProxy(object):

    def __init__(self, target):
        self.target = target

        func = getattr(self.target, 'func')
        setattr(self.target, 'func', memoize(func))

    def __getattr__(self, name):
        return getattr(self.target, name)
```

Chain of Responsibility

chain_of_responsibility.py

```python
class EndHandler(object):
    def __init__(self):
        pass

    def handle_request(self, request):
        pass

class Handler1(object):
    def __init__(self):
        self.next_handler = EndHandler()

    def handle_request(self, request):

        self.next_handler.handle_request(request)

def main(request):
    concrete_handler = Handler1()

    concrete_handler.handle_request(request)

if __name__ == "__main__":
    # from the command line we can define some request
    main(request)
```

Alternative

chain_of_responsibility_alt.py

```python
class Dispatcher(object):

  def __init__(self, handlers=[]):
    self.handlers = handlers

    def handle_request(self, request):
      for handler in self.handlers:
        request = handler(request)

      return request
```

Command

command.py

```python
class Command:
    def __init__(self, receiver, text):
        self.receiver = receiver
        self.text = text

    def execute(self):
        self.receiver.print_message(self.text)

class Receiver(object):
    def print_message(self, text):
      print("Message received: {}".format(text))

class Invoker(object):
    def __init__(self):
        self.commands = []

    def add_command(self, command):
        self.commands.append(command)

    def run(self):
        for command in self.commands:
            command.execute()
if __name__ == "__main__":
    receiver = Receiver()

    command1 = Command(receiver, "Execute Command 1")
    command2 = Command(receiver, "Execute Command 2")

    invoker = Invoker()
    invoker.add_command(command1)
    invoker.add_command(command2)
    invoker.run()
```

Composite

composite.py

```python
class Leaf(object):
  def __init__(self, *args, **kwargs):
    pass

  def component_function(self):
    print("Leaf")

class Composite(object):
  def __init__(self, *args, **kwargs):
    self.children = []

  def component_function(self):
    for child in children:
      child.component_function()

  def add(self, child):
    self.children.append(child)

  def remove(self, child):
    self.children.remove(child)
```

Interpreter

interpreter.py

```python
class NonTerminal(object):
    def __init__(self, expression):
        self.expression = expression

    def interpret(self):
        self.expression.interpret()

class Terminal(object):
    def interpret(self):
        pass
```

Iterator

classic_iterator.py

```python
import abc

class Iterator(metaclass=abc.ABCMeta):

    @abc.abstractmethod
    def has_next(self): pass

    @abc.abstractmethod
    def next(self): pass

class Container(metaclass=abc.ABCMeta):

    @abc.abstractmethod
    def getIterator(self): pass

class MyListIterator(Iterator):
        def __init__(self, my_list):
            self.index = 0
            self.list = my_list.list

        def has_next(self):
            return self.index < len(self.list)

        def next(self):
            self.index += 1
            return self.list[self.index - 1]

class MyList(Container):
    def __init__(self, *args):
        self.list = list(args)

    def getIterator(self):
        return MyListIterator(self)
```

```python
if __name__ == "__main__":
    my_list = MyList(1, 2, 3, 4, 5, 6)
    my_iterator = my_list.getIterator()

    while my_iterator.has_next():
        print(my_iterator.next())
```

Alternative

iterator_alt.py

```python
for element in collection:
    do_something(element)
```

Observer

observer.py

```python
class ConcreteObserver(object):

    def update(self, observed):
        print("Observing: {}".format(observed))

class Observable(object):

    def __init__(self):
        self.callbacks = set()
        self.changed = False

    def register(self, callback):
        self.callbacks.add(callback)

    def unregister(self, callback):
        self.callbacks.discard(callback)

    def unregister_all(self):
        self.callbacks = set()
```

```python
    def poll_for_change(self):
        if self.changed:
            self.update_all

    def update_all(self):
        for callback in self.callbacks:
            callback(self)
```

State

state.py

```python
class State(object):
    pass

class ConcreteState1(State):

    def __init__(self, state_machine):
        self.state_machine = state_machine

    def switch_state(self):
        self.state_machine.state = self.state_machine.state2

class ConcreteState2(State):
    def __init__(self, state_machine):
        self.state_machine = state_machine

    def switch_state(self):
        self.state_machine.state = self.state_machine.state1

class StateMachine(object):

    def __init__(self):
        self.state1 = ConcreteState1(self)
        self.state2 = ConcreteState2(self)
        self.state = self.state1

    def switch(self):
        self.state.switch_state()
```

```python
    def __str__(self):
        return str(self.state)

def main():
    state_machine = StateMachine()
    print(state_machine)

    state_machine.switch()
    print(state_machine)

if __name__ == "__main__":
    main()
```

Strategy

strategy.py

```python
def executor(arg1, arg2, func=None):
    if func is None:
        return "Strategy not implemented..."

    return func(arg1, arg2)

def strategy_1(arg1, arg2):
    return f_1(arg1, arg2)

def strategy_2(arg1, arg2):
    return f_2(arg1, arg2)
```

Template Method

template_method.py

```python
import abc

class TemplateAbstractBaseClass(metaclass=abc.ABCMeta):

    def template_method(self):
        self._step_1()
        self._step_2()
        self._step_n()
```

```python
    @abc.abstractmethod
    def _step_1(self): pass

    @abc.abstractmethod
    def _step_2(self): pass

    @abc.abstractmethod
    def _step_3(self): pass

class ConcreteImplementationClass(TemplateAbstractBaseClass):

    def _step_1(self): pass

    def _step_2(self): pass

    def _step_3(self): pass
```

Visitor

visitor.py

```python
import abc

class Visitable(object):
    def accept(self, visitor):
        visitor.visit(self)

class CompositeVisitable(Visitable):
    def __init__(self, iterable):
        self.iterable = iterable

    def accept(self, visitor):
        for element in self.iterable:
            element.accept(visitor)

        visitor.visit(self)
```

```python
class AbstractVisitor(object):
    __metaclass__ = abc.ABCMeta

    @abc.abstractmethod
    def visit(self, element):
        raise NotImplementedError("A visitor need to define a visit method")

class ConcreteVisitable(Visitable):
    def __init__(self):
        pass

class ConcreteVisitor(AbstractVisitor):
    def visit(self, element):
        pass
```

Model–View–Controller

mvc.py

```python
import sys

class GenericController(object):

    def __init__(self):
        self.model = GenericModel()
        self.view = GenericView()

    def handle(self, request):
        data = self.model.get_data(request)
        self.view.generate_response(data)

class GenericModel(object):

    def __init__(self):
        pass

    def get_data(self, request):
        return {'request': request}
```

```python
class GenericView(object):
    def __init__(self):
        pass

    def generate_response(self, data):
        print(data)

def main(name):
    request_handler = GenericController()
    request_handler.handle(name)

if __name__ == "__main__":
    main(sys.argv[1])
```

Publisher–Subscriber

publish_subscribe.py

```python
class Message(object):
    def __init__(self):
        self.payload = None
        self.topic = "all"

class Subscriber(object):
    def __init__(self, dispatcher, topic):
        dispatcher.subscribe(self, topic)

    def process(self, message):
        print("Message: {}".format(message.payload))

class Publisher(object):
    def __init__(self, dispatcher):
        self.dispatcher = dispatcher

    def publish(self, message):
        self.dispatcher.send(message)
```

```python
class Dispatcher(object):

    def __init__(self):
        self.topic_subscribers = dict()

    def subscribe(self, subscriber, topic):
        self.topic_subscribers.setdefault(topic, set()).add(subscriber)

    def unsubscribe(self, subscriber, topic):
        self.topic_subscribers.setdefault(topic, set()).discard(subscriber)

    def unsubscribe_all(self, topic):
        self.subscribers = self.topic_subscribers[topic] = set()

    def send(self, message):
        for subscriber in self.topic_subscribers[message.topic]:
            subscriber.process(message)
```

Final Words

Well done! You have learned many useful patterns. I hope that you will continue to practice and become a better programmer every day.

Thank you for going on this journey with me. Goodbye and good luck.

Index

A

Abstract base class (ABC), 265
Adapter pattern
    class adapter, 97
    don't repeat yourself, 93
    duck typing, 99
    implementation, 100
    mail_sender.py, 92
    object, 98
    parting shots, 102
    problem, 96
    send_email.py, 91
    separation of concern, 94
    users.csv file, 92

B

Barracks, 38
Builder pattern
    abstraction, 89
    anti-patterns, 84
    basic_form_generator.py, 76
    cleaned_html_dictionary_form_
        generator.py, 80
    course correct, 8
    deliberate practice, 4
    focus, 5
    giants, 7
    graphical library/machine-learning
        setup, 6
    html_dictionary_form_generator.py, 78
    html_form_generator.py, 76–77

oop_html_form_generator.py, 82
rapid feedback loop, 5
Vinci, Leonardo da, 7
widgets and interfaces, 75

C

Chain of Responsibility pattern, 165
    authentication headers, 146
    response object, 144
    functions, 151–153
    implementation, 154
    middleware, 143
    print function, 153–154
    Python (*see* Pythonic implementation)
    single responsibility principle, 151
    WSGI server, 145
clone() method, 51
Closures, 113
Command pattern
    commands, 169, 171
    execute() method, 174
    function definition, 176
    implementation, 170
    invoker, 170
    macros, 171
    multi-level undo stack, 171
    multiplication, 171
    receiver, 170
    relevant parameters, 175
    turtle, 167
Composite pattern, 188

W. Badenhorst, *Practical Python Design Patterns*, https://doi.org/10.1007/978-1-4842-2680-3

D

E

Get the eBook for only $5!

Why limit yourself?

With most of our titles available in both PDF and ePUB format, you can access your content wherever and however you wish—on your PC, phone, tablet, or reader.

Since you've purchased this print book, we are happy to offer you the eBook for just $5.

To learn more, go to http://www.apress.com/companion or contact support@apress.com.

Apress®

Printed in the United States
By Bookmasters